ONE SIGNAL
PUBLISHERS

ATRIA

THE
RESILIENCE
MYTH

New Thinking on Grit, Strength,
and Growth After Trauma

SORAYA CHEMALY

ONE SIGNAL
PUBLISHERS

ATRIA

NEW YORK   LONDON   TORONTO   SYDNEY   NEW DELHI

ONE SIGNAL
PUBLISHERS

ATRIA

An Imprint of Simon & Schuster, LLC
1230 Avenue of the Americas
New York, NY 10020

Copyright © 2024 by Soraya Chemaly

First One Signal Publishers/Atria Books hardcover edition May 2024

ONE SIGNAL PUBLISHERS / ATRIA BOOKS and colophon are trademarks of Simon & Schuster, LLC

Simon & Schuster: Celebrating 100 Years of Publishing in 2024

For information about special discounts for bulk purchases, please contact Simon & Schuster Special Sales at 1-866-506-1949 or business@simonandschuster.com.

The Simon & Schuster Speakers Bureau can bring authors to your live event. For more information or to book an event, contact the Simon & Schuster Speakers Bureau at 1-866-248-3049 or visit our website at www.simonspeakers.com.

Interior design by Kyoko Watanabe

Manufactured in the United States of America

1 3 5 7 9 10 8 6 4 2

Library of Congress Cataloging-in-Publication Data has been applied for.

ISBN 978-1-9821-7076-9
ISBN 978-1-9821-7078-3 (ebook)

What *are* you?
I am here.
With you.
Where borders fade
And we shrug:
Nou se lanmè.
Nou la, ansanm.
Feel the vibrant thrill of it.

CONTENTS

PREFACE

Chances are you, like me, are curious about why some individuals adapt positively in the face of stress, adversity, and loss while others struggle. Most of us want to know how to best adjust and help our loved ones do the same under challenging circumstances or after traumatic events. Life is full of setbacks, and weathering them in healthy ways is essential.

Our culture's solution to this problem is to teach us to "be resilient." But I must warn you that this book dismantles the very heart of our prevailing notions of individual resilience. Instead of talking about how you can optimize yourself, we will reimagine the world so that coping, recovery, and survival rely not solely on individual attributes such as self-sufficiency, mental toughness, and strength, but on our mutual dependence and interconnectedness with . . . everything. We'll explore the ideas behind what makes us who we are and why we are inseparable from one another. We will discover the many ways healthy resilience emerges from nurturing our relationships with people, spaces, stories, history, and time itself.

To answer our questions about how we positively adapt to traumas, losses, and adversity, we have to deeply consider how we think about the idea of resilience itself; what effects this goal—of being strong and overcoming, of being optimistic and growing from our pain—has on us. What does having to "be resilient" *do to* us as individuals and a society?

———

Trauma and resilience are recurring themes in my work as an activist. Being part of social justice movements means navigating complex histories, political obstacles, and personal tragedies. I have witnessed and continue to write about people's incredible capacity to find joy, community, friendship, and support in the most trying circumstances and after tragic events. This ability to survive and thrive despite challenges and losses rarely follows a set path but instead attests to people's infinite capacity for creating themselves and their relationships anew.

My interest in human adaptability also isn't solely professional. In the past few years, my family experienced a series of unsettling crises. In December 2016, my husband received a diagnosis of potentially life-threatening cancer. Fortunately, his treatment, while grueling and unpredictable, was effective. However, his diagnosis was a shock that had cascading effects and altered the course of our lives. During the same period, my father, living in another country, was sliding into dementia, requiring constant care and medical attention. Amid these changes, Hurricane Dorian, one of the most powerful storms ever to make landfall in the Atlantic basin, completely devastated several communities in The Bahamas, my country of origin.

All of this occurred between the 2016 presidential election and the onset of the COVID-19 pandemic. With three adolescent children, aging parents, a recuperating spouse, a demanding work life, and a native home at risk, I constantly felt overwhelmed. No matter where I turned, there was heightened uncertainty and, with it, powerful pressure to be, always, resilient. At the time, I primarily thought of resilience as a matter of individual effort and attributes. In other words, I had absorbed the many messages we get about being strong, cultivating grit, embracing optimism, and finding purpose. Control what you can; don't let the rest bring you down! Learn to meditate and take care of yourself!

I remember one particular moment of quietness and reflection during this tumultuous time. It was a summer morning in 2019, and my husband and father had both entered surgeries simultaneously, five hundred miles and an ocean apart. Tired, emotionally spent, and feeling helpless, I sat in my car, unsure of what to do while waiting. I felt too tired, even, to talk to anyone. So, I decided to take a walk. I soon came to a bench near a city pond filled with hundreds of yellow plastic ducks. The frivolous scene felt at odds with the weight of what I was feeling in the moment, but it also made me think about how it was possible, even as my anxiety mounted, to feel a fleeting pleasure that introduced a moment of lightness into the day. The ducks, silly to be sure, had the unexpected effect of focusing my attention on externalities; it made me appreciate the small kindnesses of strangers and the complex assortment of circumstances and advantages that had brought me to this place.

Was the ability to feel this glimmer of joy a kind of resilience?

I had no idea.

I had yet to think explicitly about what resilience meant or required. An enormous gap existed, I realized, between dominant resilience norms and what I knew about how people best manage stress, cope, and adapt. The former is singularly focused on cultivating resilience from within, when, in reality, resilience draws its power from mutually nurturing relationships in supportive environments, serendipitous experiences, sharing resources, and creating tolerant, compassionate communities. Unlike trauma, which both stems from and results in separation and disconnection, resilience comes from connection and reintegration with others and place.

A few months after that afternoon by the pond, resilience became a global priority for all of us. Like everyone else, my family felt the shock of the pandemic as it wreaked its chaos. We experienced unexpected separations, struggled with anxieties and fears, and had periods of both grievous loneliness and crowded togetherness. Because of uncertainty over my husband's immunity, like millions of other families we had to manage heightened protective protocols. And still, the cultural message, loud and strong, was that the best way to handle these struggles was to smile and embrace resilience.

How can one word—*resilience*—apply to the infinite diversity of people and crises? Where did the ideals of personal resilience—as a trait, an attitude, a behavior, a discipline, and a virtue—come from, and why have they run roughshod over us all during the past two decades?

───────

Resilience is the leitmotif of our accelerated and chaotic times, a magical incantation in the Age of Adversity. However, our current use of the word would have bewildered the average person living 150 years ago.

Derived from the Latin verb *resilire*, meaning "to rebound or bounce," *resilience* entered English in the early 1500s when it appeared in the state papers of King Henry VIII to mean "returning to a former position." It referred to his desire to have his marriage to Catherine of Aragon annulled. *Resilience* next made a meaningful appearance in the 1600s when Sir Francis Bacon used it to mean the same thing but in a scientific and mechanical context. The word retained this general meaning for the next several centuries, until the mid-1950s, when psychologists and experts in child development began applying it to children's capacity to thrive despite difficult childhoods.

In the early 1970s, however, a new understanding of the concept emerged. Canadian ecologist Professor Crawford "Buzz" Holling used the term to describe the ability of systems to absorb change while maintaining stability. This use not only firmly embedded *resilience* into the realm of systems and the ecological sciences, but more firmly into the study of complex human responses to poverty, stress, war, and grief.

Within a scant few years, *resilience* was being used by sociologists, psychologists, economists, military experts, bankers, coaches, educators, and more. By the mid-1990s, the concept was prominent as a component of positive psychology—an emerging field focused on human flourishing. Alongside learning to be optimistic, developing a mindset that embraced challenges, and cultivating the power of grit, resilience became part of the burgeoning self-help industry's "personal tool kit" for success.

Perhaps nothing, however, pressed the concept of resilience into the national cultural consciousness as much as the events of September 11, 2001. Overnight, resilience became a mandate and a necessity, a patriotic virtue synonymous with strength, power, and our ability to bounce back.

In the weeks, months, and years following 9/11, developing and demonstrating resilience became one of the most vital symbols of American strength and power. The idea clearly took hold of our imaginations.

"More than education, more than experience, more than training," the *Harvard Business Review* announced a scant eight months after September 11, 2001, "a person's level of resilience will determine who succeeds and who fails. That's true in the cancer ward, it's true in the Olympics, and it's true in the boardroom."[1]

In 2002, the American Psychological Association (APA) launched "The Road to Resilience," a public education campaign that armed psychologists with materials that they could use to educate their local communities. The APA even produced a documentary, *Aftermath: The Road to Resilience*, which used the events of September 11 to demonstrate the power of resilience in response to obstacles and hardships ranging from terrorist threats to job loss. By 2013, "the journey toward resilience," wrote Andrew Zolli and Ann Marie Healy, authors of a 2013 *New York Times* bestseller on the topic, had become "the great moral quest of our age."[2]

Reflecting moral character, national competitiveness, and the ability to overcome and win, resilience infused every aspect of life, from educating kindergarteners and athletes to training CEOs and astronauts. Name your sector—ecology, psychology, child development, trauma studies, social science, education, economics, health, medicine, computer science, neurology, disaster relief, security, climate science, and AI development—and it has its bespoke flavor of resilience.

"Building resilience" is now a ubiquitous catchphrase, fodder for corporate websites, international conference pamphlets, school newsletters, the agendas of military academies, disaster-relief programs, and community resources worldwide. Countless articles with titles such as "10 Ways to Build Resilience," "How to Be a Resilient Leader," and "Six Ways to Raise a Resilient Child" promise comforting formulas. Bestselling books and podcasts package resilience and perseverance as self-optimization tools that carry us into better futures.

Yet, despite this ubiquity, defining resilience with any consistency remains elusive. Resilience is a sprawling, amorphous concept. As an idea, resilience continues to defy a standard definition, begging more questions than providing answers.

Ask ten people what resilience is, and you will get ten different answers. The word might describe a trait, an outcome, a process, a system, a plan, a policy, a program, a critical-analysis framework, or all the above. It describes individual characteristics, genetic dispositions, ecological systems, the tensile quality of matter, corporate cultures, political agendas, and organizational goals. What we are mainly left with is a vague and oversimplified cultural script that looks like this:

A person's life is "normal," then a terrible event happens, causing that person sadness, grief, and pain. After a period of shock, however, the person adopts a positive outlook, overcomes fear, is grateful for whatever good fortune they enjoy. They persist. This person is usually depicted as gritty and optimistic, willing to turn obstacles into challenges. The person doesn't complain while doing the hard work necessary to roll with the punches, stay busy and productive, and get back to normal as quickly as possible. The script provides role models who overcame tragedy to be happy and prosperous, often portrayed as exceptional or a celebrity. Think Oprah, Bill Gates, Lady Gaga, Nelson Mandela, Malala Yousafzai, or Michael Jordon.

In these stories, resilience is presented in wildly different contexts, ranging from how one well-known person managed years of professional rejection before achieving success, to how another survived a terrifying assault or catastrophic flood. When social support is mentioned, it is characterized as "nice to have" rather than essential. The support of friends and family is acknowledged, but what really matters—what unites these jarringly different stories—is the protagonist's individual strength and mind-over-matter determination. As televangelist Joel Osteen tells his hundreds of millions of followers, nothing in life happens to you but *for you*.

This script, with its arc of trauma to resilience to personal growth, is a mainstay of media coverage, the self-help industry, military biographies, athletic programs, viral TikToks, and corporate agendas alike. As a story, it's compelling because it helps us make sense of crisis by featuring people who reassert control and agency after temporarily losing their self-determination. The script also restores faith in the world's general benevolence and belief in an ever-improving future. At its core is a familiar promise: with the right attitude and hard work, anyone can overcome trauma, experience transformative change, and be happy and successful in the end.

In sum, this script is a parable of good old-fashioned bootstrapping as the socially, culturally, and politically preferred response to hardship. It's a good tale, but it's a myth that has far more to do with perpetuating status quo norms than modeling how people can improve their ability to face challenges and crises. In this script, resilience is a Trojan horse that enshrines cultural beliefs, protects political hierarchies, and reflects powerful philosophical ideals. According to this model, resilience makes no demands on anyone, erases social context, and absolves us of the responsibility to care for one another.

In spectacular arrogance, our mainstream vision of resilience encourages us to ignore, minimize, and even punish the desire for our greatest resilience assets: interdependence, collective versatility, and shared care. Instead of revealing our relationships to one another, our environments, and the systems we live in, this vision highlights and glorifies self-sufficiency, limitless positivity, and individual strength against all odds.

It makes us less resilient, not more.

Every expert I spoke to for this book bemoans the enduring, oversized, and misleading portrayal of resilience primarily as an individual strength or a skill a person can acquire and hone through hard work and power of mind.

"I'm still amazed by how quickly people slip towards the individual," explained Michael Ungar, founder and director of the Resilience Research Centre at Dalhousie University in Canada, when we spoke in early 2022. "They'll give a head nod to resilience being about systems all around us, but then will give a definition of resilience as the individual ability to cope." A family therapist and professor of social work, Ungar's understanding that the pursuit of individual resilience must be "activated or facilitated by the environments around us" is on target but elusive in our popular understanding. As we will see, his conclusions resonate with a pluriverse of countercultural histories, movements, and philosophies.

I'm not asking you to renounce resilience as an idea but as an ideology that clings perilously to some of our most damaging cultural ideals. To be sure, we should make choices and change habits and behaviors to improve our capacity to cope and adapt, but our resilience over time ultimately depends on looking outward and toward others: in the connections—intimate, familial, political, and societal—that we forge. We take turns being resilient for one another during, over, and beyond our lifetimes.

———

A growing knowledge of the gap between what we need to achieve resilient outcomes and what we are culturally *told* we need compelled me to delve deeply into this topic. What does resilience look like to different people? How has our understanding evolved over time? What do we miss, and what do we lose when we turn resilience ideals inward, inward, inward, and turn away from one another?

Countless research papers and studies informed my understanding of the scope of resilience creep. I read extensively about how our understanding of trauma evolved and about resilience's rise in the modern imagination. I talked to activists about their stamina and fatigue. I interviewed experts in child development, social work, psychology, and the science of performance and productivity.

I recognize it is a great luxury to contemplate these themes. When we lose a loved one, grieve a warming Earth, consider how precarious the lives of tens of millions of people are, or contemplate the ravages of war, it's hard to think philosophically about norms, stories, or history as paths to recovery. When we struggle with work, poverty, health scares, or the stark realities of oppression, we want better futures, not a focus on difficult pasts. Nonetheless, whether we seek them out or not, history, culture, and power—the pith of our worldviews—weave their way into our self-conceptions, decisions, and relationships.

Even as we hurtle into the future, we are affected by historical forces and the ideas that shaped us. The risks we face, from rising authoritarianism, climate recklessness, and unfettered technologies, to the legacies of genocide, slavery, and colonialism, are complex, global, and mutually reinforcing. All of these crises share a quality: they define us as separate and depend on keeping us disconnected from one another and the world. The self-sufficiency, strength, mental toughness, and positivity making up our mainstream resilience do the same: they are ultimately based on the belief that you cannot trust or rely on anyone else, certainly not your society, to nurture and care for you.

No one is resilient alone at all times and in all contexts, and none should feel they must be. Yet disconnection, hierarchy, and alienation from one another and the world are the premises of our conventional resilience. Our cultural script for resilience, therefore, is part of the same systems and worldviews that require us to be so resilient to begin with.

But resilience is ours to define, and we have to reimagine adapting in ways that don't blindly reproduce the corrosive powers, beliefs, and ideals that have brought us to the brink of today's numerous and incipient catastrophes. We have to rethink resilience so that our focus, at every level of our understanding, isn't on individuals and disconnection but on relationships and mutual care. My aim is to leave you exhilarated, comforted, and better prepared for this paradigm shift.

I've thought deeply about resilience in the hopes of leading a more compassionate and purposeful life. In these pages, I share what I have learned. We will imagine a world where all people—not just certain people—can be resilient in ways that confirm our joint humanity and where our many alternatives for understanding resilience are valued instead of disdained.

I hope you see this book as an invitation to be resilient for one another.

1

THE MISGUIDED GOAL OF STRENGTH AND SELF-SUFFICIENCY

> To live past the end of your myth is a perilous thing.
>
> **—Anne Carson**

It's frequently the case that when we want to support people going through a terrible hardship, we tell them they are strong. This is equated with resilience, but what does it entail? Is it mental toughness? Grit and a distorted sense of stoicism? Why does this particular quality, however it's defined, persist as essential to navigating adversity?

These questions loomed large for me in the fall of 2019. That August, my father's already weakened health took a turn for the worse. At eighty-one and suffering from dementia, he'd tripped and broken his hip. Both age and frailty complicated the surgery he needed, but there was no other option. Luckily, his operation went well, and after a brief stay in the hospital, he returned home, where my mother, along with home-aid workers, made him as comfortable as possible.

His movements were limited, and he required round-the-clock care, but it was a relief that he was stable, and our family was heartened. Just over a month later, as often happens in such cases, though, he was back in the hospital. In a terrible presaging of COVID, he developed pneumonia, had to be intubated under duress, and was put on a ventilator. He was then, only days later, quarantined in an ICU with a superbug. Exhausted and wizened, he fought off the half dozen medical staff intubating him and administering intravenous medicine and food. We couldn't see him or touch him as he struggled.

My father's suffering was difficult to watch. He would have hated his dependence and helplessness. Tall, energetic, and fit for most of his life, he stood at six foot two and always hovered around 185 pounds. It was sad to know that he was in pain, scared, and confused, and, almost surely, he felt physically violated by medical procedures that, though they saved his life, he couldn't understand. Again, though, he rebounded, returning home, where he sat up in a wheelchair, demanding a hair comb to keep in his shirt pocket.

Throughout his life, my father had been self-sufficient, mentally tough, productive, optimistic, and goal oriented. The Haitian son of Lebanese immigrants, he was a Catholic man's man: faithful, caring, stubborn, authoritarian, fiercely protective of his family, and rigid in his gender-role beliefs. At twenty-seven, he and my mother uprooted themselves from Haiti, and he became the third generation of our family to migrate in sixty years. In this case, they moved to her family's country of origin, The Bahamas, where, speaking in a new language, he started a business.

As a father, he was always affectionate and prone to easy laughter, especially when he slipped into his native Creole. He fanatically followed American baseball, was an accomplished dancer, learned to play tennis, and was a great lover of music. He left the care and disciplining of his children to my mother and dedicated his waking hours to work. You would generally have considered him resilient and strong in the conventional sense.

Like many men, however, his way of adapting to the stress and uncertainties of migration was to double down on the traditional mores of manhood, which provided a much-needed sense of competence.

His idea of masculinity was wrapped up in his assessment of risks and rewards and could be unflinchingly sexist, racist, and homophobic.

When I chastised him for loudly teasing a friend, a young man, for wearing an earring, my father explained that boys were bullied for far less in Haiti. When I suggested that he, my father, was artistic because he loved music and the feel of certain fabrics, was highly selective about color, and loved arranging flowers, he said art was for girls and women. He cooked, but mainly meat and only outside. As my mother gave birth to my younger brother, my father disappeared, as was expected at the time, only to reappear, having won a car in a poker game. Bodies, children, and their care were women's work.

The kind of patriarchal masculinity my father embodied is a universal translator, understood across cultures. It defines relationships that allow men to exercise authority and control where possible, regardless of status, citizenship, race, or geography. It promotes self-sufficiency, virility, strength, and power—all masculine qualities that underlie the idea of resilient strength.

The conventions of this traditional masculinity undoubtedly buffered my father, mediating stress and confirming his identity as he adapted to a new country where he had no cultural knowledge, political capital, or social resources. These conventions enabled him to stand on his own two feet, work hard, enjoy financial rewards, and support our family.

But there were steep costs.

His ways of coping as a man made it all but impossible for him to be mentally and physically healthy over time and isolated him socially. He relied on stubbornness, alcohol, and my mother's generous caretaking to self-soothe.

The same attributes that made him resilient also had harmful effects on our family. My mother he treated as an extension of himself. His standards for his sons could be emotionally limiting and harshly demanding. Always protective and caring, he could not understand daughters who defied his gender expectations and were often more like him than their mother. I spent my life circling him, knowing he somehow loved us unconditionally yet contingently. So, like all of us, he was flawed.

While he gave every appearance of positive adaptability, his strength and resilience were unsustainable. They took a tremendous toll on his body. They wore on him and our family.

Being Human Means Being "Needy"

It is rarely our conscious intent, but we do three things simultaneously when we talk about resilience as strength and mental toughness. First, we implicitly confirm belief in a mind/body split. Second, with that split, we inscribe the hierarchy of mind over body. Third, we tacitly institutionalize this ordering of ideas, in our thinking and doing, in damaging gender stereotypes.

Our imaginations are permeated with a chain of understanding: resilience = strength = mental toughness = self-sufficiency and physical power. This makes need—for comfort, help, or resources—a weakness. In this estimation, the mind isn't simply more important than the body, but its prioritization winnows the body's meaning, capacities, and value.

Mind-over-matter resilience is replete with scorn for "unfit" bodies, quickly making ableism foundational. This framework creates a fundamental structural problem for resilience: systematized cultural disdain for bodies, their needs, and the people who care for them. This makes it easier to subject bodies to brutalization and to minimize our material needs: food, water, care, and time to heal.

Take mental toughness. A play on resilient strength, *mental toughness* conveys both strength of mind and, slyly and consequentially, a disdain for physical weakness. The linguistic inverse of mental toughness is *physical frailty*. An essential element of any mental toughness program is learning to ignore physical pain and emotional distress. People who don't, won't, or can't do this are somehow inferior.

It's worth pointing out how deeply gendered all of this thinking is. Need, bodies, and their vulnerabilities are seen as feminine qualities juxtaposed with masculine strength and rationality. Demeaning and making people feel vulnerable is tantamount to putting them in a feminine box: dependent, needy, and physically vulnerable. Even if a woman is mentally tough, qualities associated with manhood define her resilience. In contrast, qualities associated with femininity— emotions, needs, irrationality, physical weakness, dependence— undermine her power in the eyes of others. By these standards, can you be resilient and still have human needs? Can you be soft, sensitive, feminine?

Is Endurance Strength?

Despite a preponderance of emotionally resonant stories featuring people demonstrating exceptional character or disciplined effort to overcome hardship, resilience is *unexceptional*.

"A resilience trajectory," explains Dr. George Bonanno, who has spent decades studying people's responses to loss and stress, "is not only most common, it's the majority." In a comprehensive meta-analysis, Bonanno and his research associates examined individuals' well-being following experiences such as combat, the loss of a loved one, or life-altering injuries. After a time of sadness, grief, or anxiety, most of us return to a sense of calm and stability after a few hours, days, or weeks, even after major shocks. The majority of people in New York City who lived through the attacks of 9/11, for example, did not suffer prolonged psychological distress.[1]

We evolved to positively adapt to traumas and threats collectively. So why do we emphasize concepts, language, and stereotypes that prioritize strength and self-sufficiency as core components of resilience?

Because the value we place on a narrowly circumscribed "strength" justifies a specific type of gendered power.

In 2017, Jasmin Paris, a thirty-four-year-old veterinarian and long-distance runner, participated in the Montane Spine Race—an incredibly demanding 268-mile track along England's hilly Pennine Way. Despite running on less than three hours of sleep and needing to breastfeed her baby at various stops throughout the race, Paris emerged victorious. She shattered the world record by over twelve hours, while the fastest man finished fifteen hours later. By then, Paris was back home in Edinburgh. "It took a long time to recover, mentally and physically," she modestly explained.[2]

Women often win contests such as the Spine, but only sometimes are endurance sports followed by the public or extensively highlighted in the media. I suspect that if Paris had not been expressing milk for an infant when she won the race, her victory would likely not have been as globally publicized. Paris's accomplishment challenged her competitors and the notion of men's superior athleticism, competitive drive, strength, and mental toughness.

It is universally acknowledged that men, compared to women, have superior strength, right? While men exhibit greater physical strength and aerobic capacity on average, women often excel in ultra-endurance sports due to their muscles' resistance to exhaustion. During a standard marathon, for example, men might gain speed and lose speed more quickly than women. As distances become more extreme, however, women frequently outrace them. A 2020 study of more than 15,400 ultramarathons (longer than a standard marathon of 26.2 miles) revealed that women, better at timing and pacing themselves, were faster than men in more than 99 percent of hundred-mile races. Men's muscle mass strength, as well as their overconfidence, noted researchers, while ideal for bursts of energy, are disadvantages in these races.[3]

The valorization of brute strength over other types of human capacities is deeply embedded in how we organize our world. The myth of Man the Hunter and Woman the Gatherer was an influential building block of how most of us were taught to think about human evolution and survival. For decades, this theory—which posited that men hunted for the meat that human tribes needed to survive while women tended to babies, stayed close to home, and gathered plants—has dominated not only anthropology but our cultural imagination broadly. This one theory endlessly fuels silly and sexist norms and standards, including, today, entire TikTok trends shaming "beta men" who "used to hunt" for being reduced to doing things like "asking for oat milk in their coffee" or being "simps," men who are nice to women without the expectation of a sexual reward (a meat-for-sex proxy).[4]

The problem with this theory is that it is simply not true.[5] One of the most important new findings in this field of study is that women, not men, were and still are physiologically better suited to long-distance endurance running, the type needed for the hunting that our ancestors participated in.[6]

Man the Hunter was based on both biased anthropological and biased medical research.[7]

The belief in men's superiority, endurance, and resilience in the face of physical hardships trumped evidence of women's capacities and counter-stereotypical roles. What we now know is that male bodies tend to be physically larger and more muscular, which results in their generally being better at intense but intermittent activities. Female bodies contain more fat and estrogen, a hormone whose role in high-performance athletic ability is only now being appreciated, and are built for sustained stress and endurance.

A long-range study of more than 250 years of disasters, wars, and crises found that women survive disasters at higher rates than men, despite greater social and political vulnerabilities and rates of injury. They adapt more effectively to climate crises, epidemics, war, starvation, and enslavement, surviving in consistently higher numbers than men. Women's roles, emotional and social skills, and physical abilities appear to yield more positive outcomes and generate more resilient responses to hardship. Researchers concluded that although socialization and culture matter to these outcomes, "the survival advantage of women has fundamental biological underpinnings."[8] Even baby girls, for example, have higher survival rates than baby boys.

So why don't we think of or talk about men as inherently weaker than women? Why aren't endurance and survival popularly admired resilience standards?

The idea that women are frail and weak is a stubborn and harmful societal choice.

Traditional Masculine Strength Requires Women to Be Vulnerable

A widespread belief that women are weak is often used to justify male strength and the violence accompanying it. Traditional concepts of masculinity revolve around men's roles as protectors and providers, with women as the beneficiaries of their sacrifice. Men learn to think of resilience in terms of how well they can fulfill these roles. All hell breaks loose when this masculinity and these roles are called into question or rejected.

The #MeToo movement, for instance, detonated these core aspects of men's identities and continues to highlight multiple ways in which the truth of women's lives is an affront to prevailing masculine ideals. For a woman to assert that she wants to compete fairly in the workplace and provide for herself means she doesn't need or want a man to do it for her. For her to describe that she is subject to male sexual predation everywhere and anywhere—at work, school, during sports, in houses of faith, and at home—means that the men in her life cannot ever be adequate protectors.

In the light of #MeToo revelations, what did most men do? To protect their identities and justify a system that insists men are strong and effective protectors, millions of men, and for similar systems-justifying reasons, women, denied and diminished what women with #MeToo stories said. They failed to be resilient in the face of the brutal realities of women's lives because these realities challenged their sense of what it means to be "good men."

In terms of *men's resilience* to "#MeToo," it pays to consider: What is the real nature of the threat attributed to #MeToo "excesses"? That a few women might lie or the vast majority are telling the truth?

To make matters worse, men were also coming forward with #MeToo stories to describe widespread sexual male predation of younger, less powerful boys and men. Even though boys and men are sexually harassed and assaulted and are as physically vulnerable to penetration as girls and women, the latter are considered "naturally" more vulnerable. A social fantasy of masculine inviolability endangers boys to buttress the notion of superior strength. The men who came forward with #MeToo stories, however, openly discussed men's vulnerability to sexual assault and its humiliating and feminizing degradations.

The reason I have focused on #MeToo here is because sexual violence goes to the heart of much of how we are taught to think of strength and vulnerability because the operative lever in sexual violence is penetrability and its harms. Vulnerability, at its most basic level, is a fear of being polluted and of having your borders violated. Of being denied "self" and "control."

Both resisting *and wielding* this vulnerability—the threat of penetration and degradation—are key components of a resilience based in myths of strength and self-sufficiency.

How Our Skin Factors In

Mainstream resilience ideals are grounded in the idea of a contained individual selfhood. We experience apartness from one another and learn to think in terms of being in isolation from one another. From this perspective, the most crucial organ in our bodies isn't our brain or mind. It's our skin. Skin is what enables our separateness, our individuality, and our selfhood. Physically and metaphorically, it contains and protects us. Historically speaking, the more influential the ideas of selfhood, personhood, individuality, and the rights of man became in Western thought, the more significant skin became as a marker of status and power.

As these concepts evolved, different skins became fixed to different types of selfhood, organized in a series of binaries: Male and Female, Europeans and Others, Thinking and Feeling, White and Black, "Man" and Nature (a category into which many people were conveniently sorted). In this schema, the skin of Europeans, particularly of European men, "contained" the most rational and potentially transcendent minds. These minds, in turn, define a person capable and worthy of freedom, control, autonomy, and self-governance. Together, these qualities—and the skin that made them possible—rationalized superiority, strength, and the right to rule others.

The less rational, less worthy, less mind-full—those with less personhood—were contained in feminized black and brown skins and assigned levels of baseness and brutishness. Further, black skin became a container for what Europeans and their intellectual descendants found frightening and undesirable: death, disease, pollution, pain, disgust, and terror.[9] At the very heart of this entire rank system is, again, unrelenting ableism, since, compared to the acme of human existence—an able-bodied, rational, pale male—everyone else suffers from degrading disabilities and, so, is assigned varying degrees of worth and of woundedness. The word for when our skin fails us, *wound*, is the root of the word *trauma*. Specifically, to be wounded is to be penetrated.

Skin as a both a metaphorical and literal protector deepens this thinking. As a personal border, skin shields each of us against violations, invasion, infection, impurities, and impregnations of all sorts.

It repels pollutants—variously understood as germs, bacteria, viruses, vaccines. Its penetration, via sex, leads to the possibility of "bad blood," a stigmatizing proxy for all kinds of purported inferiorities.

In the United States, for instance, white men protecting white women from the danger of penetration and racial pollution of all sorts has been a pillar of white power. From this angle, the belief that women are vulnerable and weak reveals a different formulation: *that women are a vulnerability and weakness.*

Because women bear children, their freedom to pick whom to love, have sex with, or have children with is always a risk to assertions of racial superiority. Penetrability, therefore, is what defines being weak and vulnerable. As a result, being able to penetrate others, in effect feminizing them, becomes both a strength and a weapon of domination. Consider, for instance, that Black women, as property, were considered legally incapable of being raped but were instead freely accessible sexually and reproductively to their owners, and that Black men have historically been policed, deprived of guns, and incarcerated en masse, making them penetrable to surveillance, bullets, and sexual violation in ways that white men have structurally imposed and institutionally protected themselves from.

Narrowly defining resilience as strength and mental toughness without accepting that it sits on these types of foundations is, to put it mildly, misguided and troubling. The sexualized white fright we are subjected to politically today—in xenophobic violence and the overturning of *Roe v. Wade*, for instance—is infused with powerful cultural defenses of protective masculinity, strength, and superiority. These same ideals elide resilience with impenetrability—to other men and to sperm, to be sure, but also to weapons, to viruses, and, writ large in the body politic, to "dirty foreigners."

Which inexorably brings us to vampires and Mike Pence.

It Isn't Resilience If It Makes You Sick and Diminishes Care

Have you ever read Bram Stoker's 1897 novel *Dracula*? Or Stephenie Meyer's 2005 *Twilight* series?

Stoker's Gothic tale oozes traumatic shocks and their aftereffects. His monster looks human but is an ugly foreigner who strips his victims of rationality in highly sexualized acts of blood-tainting penetration. In entering them, he ravages their minds and leaves them at the mercy of their insatiable and uncontrollable bodies. He degrades men by luring them with emasculating sexual fluidity and, worse still, empowers women by transferring the ability to penetrate anyone they choose and to act on overwhelming strength and desire.

The story is variously interpreted as being about Freudian repression, reverse colonization, anxieties about progress, the power of new technologies, theories of pathogenic spread, fear of Jews and Muslims, dread of homosexuality, and panic over women's increasing freedoms. It is filled with descriptions of disgust and bodily functions: rank odors, rotting teeth and flesh, and diseased yellowed eyes make characters recoil in horror. It isn't only that Dracula's attacks are traumatizing, but that he is modern trauma personified—temporal disruptions, unnatural speeds, psychic distress, the possibility of unmoored and fluid identity—all are woven into the protagonist and his victims' transformations.

The vampire's seductive and perverse allure was specifically depicted, however, as a threat to the purity of the English Rose.[10] This threat was inseparable from his challenge to White European culture and masculinity. In the end, the strengths of Anglo culture and manhood defeat Dracula's base atavism. Using mind-over-matter determination and advanced science, thinking men triumph over a dark, bodily invasive, blood-tainting menace. They use rationality, technological prowess, progressive beliefs, and, importantly, an understanding of time—which Dracula's irrational and unnatural life seemed to defy—itself.

British imperialism was cresting during the period that Stoker wrote his masterpiece. As the nineteenth century wound down and the British Empire fractured, fears were growing that colonized people would infiltrate—and degrade—England. At the same time, the country was grappling with industrialization's harmful effects, one of which was that dense urban concentrations of people had, for decades, been causing widespread and deadly diseases.

Stoker was an Irish "home ruler" living in England. In the 1830s, his mother had famously survived a deadly cholera epidemic, called the Asiatic flu, and her childhood stories influenced his work. The author's brothers and uncle were prominent doctors, actively treating infectious diseases. Unfaithful to his wife, Stoker himself contracted and eventually died from syphilis.

Small wonder that this horror novel ends with the birth of a hybrid-blooded baby whose existence blurs the lines between aggressor and victim, colonizer and colonized.[11]

At the turn of the nineteenth century, germs, foreign menaces, and invasive threats filled the air and threatened established powers. Then, as is the case now, a desire to avoid pathogens animated human fear and moral outrage, motivating the kind of violence, racism, xenophobia, and sexual disgust propelling authoritarian populist movements worldwide.

Almost one hundred years after Stoker published *Dracula*, Meyer's vampire series *Twilight* took off like wildfire in a political environment of similar fears. The first volume was published in 2005, in the aftermath of the 9/11 attacks, in which brown-skinned Islamic extremists used airplanes—which, it must be said, are classically phallic projectiles—to penetrate U.S. airspace and destroy equally phallic symbols of U.S. power. Leaders and the media framed the attacks in the language of disease and infection, of dangerous pathogens and the threat of a horribly infected nation.[12]

Meyer cleverly inverted the racial dynamics of *Dracula*. Her heroic and immortal vampires, capable of superhuman strength, are irresistibly rich, beautiful creatures with blindingly white, adamantine skin. In defense of their survival and beliefs, they fight armies of weaker, foreign, and—in the films—louche, darker-skinned, sexually rapacious parasites held in the thrall of deranged, old-world bloodlust.

The vampires we are supposed to identify with and cheer on use mental discipline and superior physical prowess to sublimate animalistic bodily needs, abstaining from killing humans and, in the case of the male protagonist, resisting having sex with a weak woman who is eventually "converted," after much hardship, to their superior way of being. This disaffected teenage girl, an unintentionally funny White Feminist™, appears not to care if her powerful vampire lover kills for sport, food, power, or sex as long as she can eventually exercise similar control. Her post-traumatic growth frees her from her body's frailties and turns her into a bloodsucking *Überfrau*.

Twilight's success, driven by young women and a queering culture, elicited moral panic and homophobic backlash, but it suited the zeitgeist of an alien and fearful post-9/11 world reasserting Western power and dominance. It was the same world consumed with expressing resilience in a frenzy of individualized strength, militarism, hypermasculine posturing, retrograde purity culture, and the crushing resurgence of near-cultish motherhood ideals.

If each of us, we were told in so many ways, did our part as individuals and were resilient through our optimism, grit, mental toughness, and strength, then, adding us all up, the country would be, too.

———

Twenty years later, when the pandemic struck, many of the resilience lessons we learned then were applied wholesale and inappropriately to the COVID crisis. Each of us had to think about how to assess risk, overcome anxieties, and live through the potential traumas of COVID, but we had to adapt to an *actual* virus, not a symbolic one.

On the afternoon of April 28, 2020, in the first months of the COVID crisis, then–vice president Mike Pence walked into the Mayo Clinic, a renowned medical facility already strained by unprecedented care demands. Despite public and private requests by hospital administrators that anyone entering the hospital wear a mask, Pence refused to don one. Undoubtedly, he meant to convey that he was mentally tough (no one would tell him what to do) and physically fit (he was healthy, strong, and didn't fear illness), but Pence's refusal to wear a mask also put everyone around him at risk in ways they hadn't consented to.

Pence was hardly the only prominent public figure scoffing at mask mandates and, soon after, vaccines.[13] In the desire to look strong, rational, and firm in a crisis, leaders frequently portrayed mask wearing as a sign of feminized weakness and fear.

"If you're healthy, you and your family, it's a great time to go out and go to a local restaurant," said Devin Nunes, a California GOP representative at the time. Like George Bush during the weeks after 9/11, Nunes encouraged people to go shopping, get on with life, and not show "the enemy" that you were scared. He did it on the day that Dr. Anthony Fauci, an experienced and knowledgeable public health adviser, asked people to isolate. One conservative pundit joked that former vice president Joe Biden, who encouraged mask wearing, "might as well carry a purse with that mask." Senator Kelly Loeffler, a Republican from Georgia, shared a video in which Trump physically pinned the coronavirus to the ground.

When COVID struck, millions of people embraced a static resilience calibrated to 9/11. "Don't show fear, don't hide in your home, go out, live as normally as possible" worked in response to a terrorist attack but was spectacularly ill-suited to the threat posed by a viral pandemic.[14] The result was higher rates of avoidable deaths, eroded social trust, and the denial of medical expertise and community care.

Pence's status and identity did, in fact, mean that his individual risk of contracting COVID was relatively low. But, while personally accurate, his decision was medically unsound and politically craven. By the spring of 2020, Indigenous, Black, and Pacific Islander Americans, followed closely by Hispanic Americans, were experiencing the highest death rates from COVID-19, which highlighted the impacts of systemic inequality on the health of communities.[15]

As these communities were able to mask and adopt vaccines, the harm shifted to those that continued to resist. From September 2020 on, white Americans, especially older white men, began dying COVID-related deaths at higher rates than any other demographic groups. By 2023, because of a combination of demographics, distorted risk assessment, denialism, and disinformation, having voted for Donald Trump was statistically a risk factor for COVID death. In Florida and Ohio, for instance, excess death rates among people identifying as Republicans were 43 percent higher than for Democrats.[16]

Refusing masks and vaccines is a prime example of how maladaptive a resilience of strength, impenetrability, and self-sufficiency can be. For years, researchers have known that men are far less likely than women to get vaccines—for virtually any purpose—and are far more likely to refuse to wear masks than women. Throughout the pandemic, men were far less likely to wear masks, wash their hands, or get vaccinated, all behaviors that display a belief in impenetrability.[17] Men, however, *aren't* impenetrable and have also been more likely to contract and die of COVID-19.[18] There are many reasons why this might be the case, but masculinity—appearing strong, self-sufficient, and inviolable—appears to be the primary driver of the difference.[19] Rigid adherence to masculine ideals and cognitive inflexibility increased risk-taking behaviors, all while actively putting other people at risk.

Viral illnesses don't respect individuality, gender identity, or personal belief. Our health and the health of the people around us are intertwined, an understanding that is central to resilient adaptation. In fact, *viruses* evolved to leverage our interconnectedness to powerful effect even as we continue to minimize the same.

At the exact time that Pence was walking through the Mayo

Clinic, I was watching Dr. Joyce Dorado talk about stress, COVID-19, trauma, and resilience. Dorado is the cofounder and director of a program that helps traumatized children. "This pandemic is showing how connected we are," she was explaining. "When I am wearing a mask, it is not really about keeping myself safe. I am caring for you and sending the message that I am trying to create a safe environment for you."

Instead of adopting this approach, however, we are clinging to its opposite and the result is, more often than not, fear, not resilience.

From Your Body to the Body Politic

This entire swirl of ideas metaphorically extends to our "body politic."

Let's go back for a moment to strength and resilience in relation to disease. Fear of infection strengthens public support for strong male leaders and authoritarian policies.[20] In 2021, a team of researchers led by Dr. Leor Zmigrod, a University of Cambridge expert in the cognition and psychology of ideology and how groups form, designed a study to test the theory that authoritarianism might reduce people's contact with pathogens, a type of political behavioral immune system.[21]

Analyzing data on the spread of infectious disease in the United States in the 1990s and 2000s, as well as from a large-scale attitudinal survey completed by more than two hundred thousand Americans during 2017 and 2018, the researchers discovered that the more authoritarian a person's beliefs, the more likely the person was to live in an area with higher rates of infectious disease. Zmigrod's team replicated the study in fifty-one countries and found that disease rates from more than two decades in the past were still influencing politics as late as 2016. That year, for example, the higher the past rate of measles and flu in a county or a state, the more votes garnered for Donald Trump.[22] Rates of infectious diseases also correlate to rises in what researchers call "vertical" laws, which target discrete groups with punitive measures such as criminalizing abortion, punishing trans people, or closing borders using painful and cruel measures.

How much is a resilience drawn from a commitment to the narrowest band of performative masculine strength worth to you?

If you conceive of the nation as a body, and you see people who are different from you as invasive pathogens, then being resilient—to weakness, vulnerability, penetration—might lead you to treat those people the way you would a disease. The result is border-patrol mentalities—whether enacted by white women policing bird-watching Black men in Central Park or government agents caging children at the Mexican-U.S. border—that draw on the logics of containment and elimination that have driven America's history of settler colonialism, slavery, internments, and mass incarceration.[23]

Strength and self-sufficiency as resilient virtues have always been used to deflect social and political resources away from investing in a care economy—meaning one that acknowledges the centrality of caregiving, including childcare, eldercare, health care, and other forms of life-sustaining and enhancing activities. Today, these same resilient "virtues" continue to undermine efforts to create care-oriented policies. They are a driving force in growing political polarization.[24]

Precarity, insecurity, and fear—all assured by toxic individualism as the basis for political policy-making—are anti-resilient by any measure. They cause stress, reduce cognitive flexibility, distort risk assessment, and threaten mental, physical, and political security. Feeling safe and cared for fosters more social trust and liberalizes political beliefs, whereas feeling threatened and living with uncertainty and insecurity generates more conservative beliefs.[25] Fear and precarity undermine our adaptability by isolating us from one another.

The Cost of Masculinity to Boys and Men

If resilience has an opposite, it's not weakness or dependence, it's loneliness.

In 2021, the American Psychological Association issued a report on the negative effects of conventional masculinity on boys, men, families, and society. To the enduring chagrin of conservatives, the paper describes how it leads to cognitive inflexibility, emotional repression, and interpersonal stress. Boys, the authors explained, are either explicitly taught or tacitly intuit that being a "real" man means embodying a rigid type of strength and self-sufficiency, both of which can and do lead to emotional withdrawal, hindered self-knowledge and intimacy, and an impaired ability to manage with adversity.[26]

One of the most damaging effects of this problem is pervasive loneliness. In 2017, then–U.S. surgeon general Vivek Murthy declared loneliness a public health epidemic. The following year, the government of the United Kingdom appointed a "minister for loneliness," responsible for generating policies that encouraged community. By 2019, 61 percent of Americans reported being lonely, a trend that has continued every year since.[27] The loneliest, globally: young men living in societies that prioritize individualism above all are the most vulnerable to loneliness. In countries with wide and growing income inequality, the problem is even more pronounced.[28] Social isolation is a collective issue, but due to masculine socialization, loneliness particularly impacts boys and men.

Conversely, one of the resilience advantages that girls and women have is feminine socialization. Women are "naturally" less lonely because we are expected to be rewarded for initiating, cultivating, and maintaining social connections. Because we are taught to preserve and protect relationships, we do so more often. As volunteers, caretakers, and friends, we form rich social networks and are more involved in our communities. Girls are far more likely to be socialized to be other-focused and to develop emotional literacy. Many men's sense of strength and self-sufficiency is based on the women in their lives acting as emotional extensions of themselves, providing relational support and structure that is essential but invisible.

From an early age, girls are taught to think relationally and develop social and care skills not only for their own benefit but on behalf of the boys and men around them. Girls and women do more emotional labor and care work at home and at work, which frequently translates into carrying the burden of both for boys and men, who take it for granted. This allocation of care effort supports a traditional system requiring men's dedication to work and public leadership, but the world has changed, and girls and women are increasingly unwilling and frequently incapable of performing this role. Masculinity, and men, are not adjusting commensurately.

Masculinity, and systems of male power, have effectively out-sourced the cultivation of relationships—the arena of softness, feelings, and vulnerability—to girls and women, to the detriment of us all. One reason for the greater loneliness men experience, for instance, is that heterosexual men still rely too heavily on the women in their lives to provide for most of their emotional needs. Lacking the ability to develop and maintain intimacy—and often confusing it with sex—men are often ill-equipped to form the fulfilling and supportive bonds necessary for resilience and longevity. Widows, for instance, are far more resilient than widowers. During the year after the death of a spouse, men are 70 percent more likely to die than peers whose spouses are alive. For women, sustained by wider relationships, that number is only 27 percent.[29]

It has always been inaccurate, though, to say that girls and women are inherently better suited to relationship building. Boys and men are highly skilled at building relationships, but they are taught to do so in circumscribed ways: in fraternity and hierarchy, usually under the direction of more powerful men. The relational strength of men in groups, whether in sports teams, corporate suites, religious institutions, or the military, comes from bonds with other men acting in mutual interest . . . often to compete with and dominate other groups of men. These bonds allow men to build emotional closeness and enjoy shared activities, but within sanctioned behaviors. These behaviors almost always exclude women as nonsexual intimates, and they often disparage feminine traits, qualities, and behaviors as well as men who exhibit them.

For men, the problem is that so many relationships with other men exist within systems and institutions having an ever-present threat of disconnection and punishment if they fail to conform. When men break fraternal codes—by pushing back against rigid standards, sharing emotions, or holding other men accountable for bullying behaviors—they risk ostracizing, mockery, shaming, and punishment.

Sixty-five percent of eighteen- to twenty-three-year-old men surveyed in 2022 believed "no one really knows me well."[30]

Confused about their roles in society and thrown off course by rapidly changing gender and sexuality norms, many boys and men are turning to communities designed around rejecting the "feminization of society" and "the softening of American men."

A weeklong stint at Man Camp, founded in 2015 by Brian Tome, is a case in point. Tome is the founding and senior pastor of Crossroads Church, and a week in his program, in 2022, cost a cool $10,000.[31] Man Camp promises men will "reclaim what's been stolen" and "move beyond your limits, and find out what you are made of," a discovery that, for some reason, includes defecating in the woods. Promotional videos show men howling, exiting body bags, and bathed in mud. Men wear identical clothes, roughhouse in choke holds, drag each other through high surf, and appear to bask in an orgy of pseudomilitaristic violence—all socially acceptable forms of male bonding—that domestic life denies them.[32] I may personally find the effort an extreme retrenchment of a culture that led to disenchantment with the world to begin with, but there is no doubt that thousands of men are attracted by what Man Camp and other similar programs offer: friendship and identity confirmation that allay confusion over who they are and how they should relate to others without the shame of therapy.

An explosion of podcasts, books, documentaries, and "training programs" promise to provide men with spaces that respect their need to reclaim the responsibilities and privileges of traditional "provide, protect, and preside" masculinity.

Spurred on by pseudo-intellectuals and blunt-force sexists, an expanding and increasingly extremist manosphere promotes dangerous, anti-egalitarian beliefs to millions of boys and men seeking better human connections and relationships. Free online sources of information and friendship take advantage of men's confusion, social disconnection, and despair, all of which contribute to a susceptibility to extremist movements.

Take a popular and absurd green line theory, which asserts no "real man" would angle his body toward his woman partner's or stand facing her because the posture is an indicator of weakness or servitude.[33] While this and other similar suggestions might seem laughable, clearly this content holds appeal for boys and men who feel that they are seen, heard, and can learn. There is comfort and a sense of purpose in falling back on traditional mores and clearly identified roles.

However, conventional manhood has always been the sideshow to what really matters: being in charge. Domination is a stubborn lure with ageless appeal, its harms masked by the benefits of revitalized traditional masculine ideals.

Among eighteen- to thirty-year-olds in the United States, 51 percent of men surveyed in 2022 reported believing that "if a guy has a girlfriend or wife, he deserves to know where she is all the time," a 5-point increase in five years. Forty-one percent said that men "should always have the final say about decisions" in relationships with women, a 7-point increase.[34] Theories of "natural" male domination being promoted to boys and men online may be shaping attitudes such as these, but they certainly aren't helping men form the healthy, loving, and companionable relationships they seem to want, either with women or with other men.

The pressure boys and men feel to be in control and mentally tough, and to bond in ways that involve the denigration and domination of others, is immense. That pressure warps resilience and creates standards that make asking for attention, affection, or help shameful. Worsening the situation for everyone is the ultimately transactional idea that men's roles as providers and protectors form the basis of relationships in which they exchange those services for access to women's bodies, care, and support. Girls and women, as the saying goes, aren't machines you put kindness coins into until sex falls out, and increasing numbers of them no longer have to pretend that they are or ever were. These backward-looking masculinity norms are complicit in why, today, more than 60 percent of young men are single—a number that is double the rate among women,[35] who are much more likely to find healthy connections in queer relations—and the young men mystified by their inability to date or maintain relationships.

Some might say that attitudes such as these simply reflect that men generally have higher levels of social dominance orientation than women, but how are you meaningfully supposed to study social dominance in a system that is based on social dominance for the benefit of some but not others? A system than informs our identities and relationships?

Another aspect of lagging masculinity that affects people's adaptability and resilience is a reluctance or refusal to ask for help or go to therapy.[36] For Black and gay men, proving manhood can be even more vital as a hedge against racism and homophobia, and their mental health risks are commensurately acute: Black men, who report high rates of loneliness, anxiety, and depression, are roughly half as likely as white men to seek therapeutic help.[37] Both loneliness and reluctance to ask for help in understanding emotional distress are factors in soaring rates of death by suicide in boys and men.

It's also the case that masculinity is imposed in ways that strengthen racial discrimination. Black children, for example, are frequently characterized as older—less innocent, stronger, tougher, more capable of doing harm—than white children. Hypermasculinizing Black men is tied to their greater criminalization, and masculinizing Black women is a powerful way of denying them care and traditional patriarchal "protections." The "strong Black woman" stereotype holds that Black women aren't "real," i.e., frail, vulnerable white women. The stereotype hinges on the belief that Black women are brutishly capable of withstanding adversity, enduring feats of bestial labor, and suffering pain. They're expected to carry the physical and emotional burdens of their families and communities and be people who serve the needs of others, not as leaders but as devoted carers.

It's important to point out that women also embrace masculine ideals, especially since demonstrating strength and rationality is one way to counter sexist and racist biases. However, when women do, they can also suffer the negative effects of social disconnection.

Finding Strength in Our Fragility

In the end, this resilience of strength and self-sufficiency is a myth born out of trauma itself.

There is no doubt that self-sufficiency, persistence, and emotional regulation absolutely help us adapt to change and crisis, but what matters is knowing when to use them and when to stop. The real strength that we should be encouraging is cognitive flexibility. That flexibility, for example, allows a person to use, or reject, masculine and feminine behaviors adaptively. Studies show, for instance, that conforming to gender role stereotypes and expectations is emotionally stressful and distressing, whereas androgynous gender expression is protective.[38]

There is nothing specifically or uniquely masculine about being strong or feminine about being emotionally sensitive. Being resilient in healthy and positive ways means accepting that resilience can coexist with wanting and needing care, affection, respect, and love. Unfortunately, as it stands now, gender ideals frequently foreclose this option.

My father was a case in point. He was resilient in all the ways he'd been taught to be a man, but his need to appear strong and self-sufficient proved harmful and unsustainable. It meant he denied his most vulnerable feelings, including sadness and fear. He was not equipped to recognize or address his depression or loneliness. He hid his pain, trauma, social anxiety, isolation, and shame behind a cheerful but corrosive alcoholism. His performance of self-sufficiency meant he routinely took advantage of my mother's energy and nurturing. I don't believe he was unique or rare in these ways.

Had he been able to conceive of resilience in less gendered, more relational ways, he might have been able to develop the compassion and self-compassion that fuel adaptability to change. No one writes "masculinity" as a cause of death on a death certificate, but in my father's case, it should surely be on the list.

We are all strong and fragile. Individuals and part of collectives.

Being resilient, self-sufficient, and capable doesn't have to mean risk, isolation, and emotional repression. It doesn't have to result in taking advantage of, or dominating, others. It helps to start by asking what costs our strength and self-sufficiency impose on others and acknowledging the people and privileges in our lives whose work makes it possible for us to be resilient. Adapting and changing means doing our own emotional labor and sharing in caretaking, valuing those activities and the people who do them. When we think more expansively and understand how reliant our strength and self-sufficiency are on the efforts of others, we cultivate deeper resilience values: social trust, collaborative care, shared knowledge, and collective resources.

The key to reconsidering our myths of strength and self-sufficiency is realizing the anti-adaptability of our cultural contempt for human frailties and the material realities of our interdependent bodies. We are capable of adapting and thriving not despite our frailties and interdependences but because of them. "Strong" can just as easily, if we choose to conceive of it differently, mean mutual care, accepting vulnerability, learning from what we fear, and resisting harmful ideologies.

We adapt most effectively and healthily by appreciating the wonders of the mind *and* of the body, because, at least for now, there is no separating them.

2

RESILIENCE AND THE BODY

The body is not a thing; it is a situation:
it is our grasp on the world and our sketch
of our project.

—Simone de Beauvoir

Dementia is a slow cruelty because of the painful and disorienting ways it chips away at a person's identity and relationships. In my father's case, he was still physically healthy and vital when the basic practicalities of life became confusing and then incomprehensible to him. He began to forget essential numbers. He lost words in English, then Creole and French. He forgot how to play backgammon and poker. He talked to the air, engaging with people long dead while not seeing the person, usually my mother, sitting right next to him.

As he slid into greater dependence, my father didn't lose *himself* so much as he became a different person, which each of us individually and as a family had to adapt to. The problem wasn't that he felt constant loss or pain, because he didn't usually seem to be experiencing either. It was that we no longer shared time in the world as we always had. He lived in one temporal order, and the rest of us lived in another. His perceptions altered our relationships and reality. They altered us. It was confusing emotionally because he was there and not there. After a period of great anxiety, he didn't seem unhappy in his changed state, but when I saw him, I felt a diffuse sadness, an amorphous grief.

I realized one day that he'd probably called me by my name for the last time. I could feel the person I was as his daughter disappearing with his memory, so the more he forgot, the more I tried to remember. I mourned him and the person I had been in relation to him.

In the fall of 2019, when he was hospitalized for the second time, I flew home. I was stunned by his appearance. This formerly six-foot-two man, who weighed at least 185 pounds his entire adult life, was wizened. Whatever physical power he still had was concentrated into the firm grip of his hand.

That Hurricane Dorian descended on the country while he was going through this ordeal compounded my worry and stress. Both his decline and the country's plight intensified my awareness of fragility and the hard, material work that goes into making sure people are comfortable, fed, housed, and cared for with dignity. I struggled intensely to separate the slow creeping loss of my father from the anticipatory distress that Dorian's threat spurred.

When I returned to DC, I was unprepared for how fully grief took possession of my body. During those months, my sorrow surfaced in strange and powerfully physical ways that, without fail, repeatedly caught me off guard. Initially, I thought I was getting sick or was simply exhausted from work, which often required me to travel. My typical reserves of energy evaporated into numbness and detachment. Unwanted memories intruded on my day, derailing me for hours. Unprompted tears seeped from my eyes, and I felt as though I were filled with cement. I couldn't stop sleeping, and when I did, I had terrifying dreams.

At the same time, I was grateful because I knew I had people I trusted and who cared for me. I talked to my spouse, my siblings, my children, and good friends. I read about the stages of grief, mourning, and loss, about resilience and recovery. I took up meditation and structured breathing. I saw my therapist. I wrote page after page of stories from my father's life, trying to recapture aspects of childhood, both his and mine. And yet, everything *ached.*

Somehow, I'd made it through decades of adulthood believing that grief happened in the mind. I had bought hook, line, and sinker the idea that my body was separate, my mind the place where feelings are housed. That I could be resilient through sheer force of will. As a result, I was blindsided, lacking any real understanding of myself and the role the body plays both in responses to traumatic events and in our capacity to adapt to them. How, I asked in retrospect, could I still be surprised that when grief struck, it suffused every cell in my body and was physically painful?

What did I do? Well, for one, I played *Tetris* every night, a calming, lifelong habit.

Hyperfocusing on virtual geometric "pieces" tumbling down the screen not only distracted me but may also have helped reduce the emotional intensity and potentially traumatizing effects of my experiences, a benefit that neither I nor, I imagine, the game's Russian inventor had anticipated. Before I went to sleep, I'd catch up with photo-intensive family news on the hurricane and my mother's updates on my father's daily changes; processing these images and their meanings, I was also often playing the game.

In 2010, researchers in the Department of Psychiatry at Oxford University designed a study that revealed how playing *Tetris* reduced the intensity of traumatic memories and stopped them from intruding involuntarily. Vivid memories and reoccurring thoughts are consistent criteria of post-traumatic stress disorder (PTSD).[1] The researchers described *Tetris* as "a cognitive vaccine" against these types of memories.[2] Studies such as these shed light on what's known as dual-task processing, a way to reroute memories and minimize or even eliminate traumatic stress.

Another example is eye movement desensitization and reprocessing (EMDR), a therapy in which a person recalls, under the direction of a trained therapist, emotionally traumatizing information while simultaneously engaging in a series of rapid lateral eye movements.[3] EMDR alters neurological patterns and mutes emotionally resonant, perception-heavy memories. Reestablishing physical processes and reducing the disruptive traumatic stress in these ways enables us to respond to trying circumstances with more optimism, flexibility, and success.

Until recently, practitioners knew that EMDR worked, sometimes spectacularly quickly, but didn't know how or why. We now understand that taxing working memory or engaging in directed, cognitively demanding tasks—including drawing, focused meditation, intentional breathing, counting backward—can reduce the intrusiveness and intensity of memories.[4]

Both *Tetris* and EMDR are examples of how paying attention to our bodies helps us build resilience. The understanding of trauma *in the body* took decades to establish, only recently gaining widespread popularity, largely due to the success of Dr. Bessel van der Kolk's bestselling book, *The Body Keeps the Score*. While many other practitioners and cultures have advocated for similar understandings of trauma, van der Kolk's work, drawing from neurology, attachment theory, and psychiatry, dominates today's mainstream understanding that trauma lives in our bodies. That we are, in fact, mindbodies.[5]

You Are Your Body

If you, like me, are seduced by the power of the mind, if you believe that your body is a source of weakness and vulnerability, then you, too, are probably *under*invested in understanding why your body matters to resilience. Our powerful preference for "mind only" resilience distracts us from the physical, material realities of being bodies in constant communication with the world. We lose valuable information and miss critical opportunities and solutions as a result.

First, conventional resilience ideas reflect our experiencing the world as "outside" of our "inside" selves. We aren't taught to think about our bodies as porous, as the way we mediate the world. We generally process our circumstances, experiences, and capacities through this split, when in reality a constant flow and flux happens between the two. We don't learn the many ways we self-regulate and *co-regulate* with other bodies and our environment.

All bodies—human and animal—self-regulate to maintain homeostasis, a state of physical stability. We are constantly, involuntarily, and unconsciously balancing the hormones, chemicals, water, and nutrients that maintain our breathing, digestion, blood circulation, and optimal body temperature. Similarly, we are constantly calibrating ourselves to other people, events, and environments. When our bodies are "working," we feel stable and experience a sensation of wholeness in ourselves. Being stressed or traumatized wears away or shatters that sensation.

While homeostasis regulates our bodies to maintain stability, allostasis enables our bodies to adjust to environmental stresses and change. Homeostasis is how our bodies maintain stability to protect against harms; allostasis, on the other hand, involves physiological changes, more immediate and adaptable, that help us respond to danger and threats.

When we live with cumulative stress or experience a shock, our nervous, endocrine, pulmonary, cardiovascular, and gastrointestinal systems shift states. A frightening event, for example, pushes your body into a physical-defense cascade as you release adrenaline, propelling a fight-or-flight response. Another response, one governed by oxytocin release, is to "tend and befriend," more common in women. The most typical response to threat, however, is freezing in place, the most extreme form of which is tonic immobility, a cross-species survival adaptation. A gazelle, for example, might fall limp in the mouth of a lion. Even sharks enter this state when they experience terror.

Biological shifts such as these prioritize our attention and resources—cognitive and physical—on what we need to do next to survive. In these states, our perceptions of time are altered and brain functions that are less immediately useful are limited. Our prefrontal cortex, where rational decision-making happens, is less efficient and effective. This is why, when we are frightened, we feel confusion. As we pay attention only to the most vital information, our ability to form coherent memories is also affected, which is why we can end up with fragmented recall in the aftermath of a shock.

These stress-response mechanisms enable us to survive, but when those same responses are prolonged, they can become debilitating.

While most of us respond to adversity by recovering and being resilient over time, some of us, for a wide variety of reasons, have sustained disruption. In these instances, the body's responses to threat, the ones that perhaps helped a person survive during an intense and difficult situation, don't subside. Many marginalized people, for example, suffer what's called allostatic load, the cumulative body exhaustion that comes from continuously adapting to discrimination, microaggressions, or other adverse situations.[6] Our stress responses can persist well beyond the point of their being needed.

On average, 8 to 10 percent of people suffer these prolonged effects, resulting, for example, in PTSD or long-term grief. People with PTSD experience persistent symptoms, including "flashback" memories, terrifying nightmares, disturbed sleep, feelings of sensory overload, hypervigilance, and sustained fear, depression, anxiety, and anger. Every system in a person's body, from circadian rhythms to nervous to digestive systems, is negatively affected, resulting in chronic exhaustion and stress. Most of the symptoms involve neurophysiological disconnects, such as muscle tension and exhaustion, disassociation, numbness, and even the development of self-harming habits. Over time, this sustained alertness makes it difficult or, for some people, impossible to feel safe, to form and maintain healthy relationships, to work, or to find enjoyment or pleasure in day-to-day activities. To find temporary relief, a person with PTSD more readily turns to substance abuse.

Traditional approaches to PTSD have focused on cognitive and behavioral therapies, which help people analyze and reframe traumatic experiences and challenge disruptive thought processes, but during the past several decades, experts have embraced nontraditional, body-based approaches for self-soothing to create a greater feeling of safety and stability. These somatic techniques and the theories that support them are frequently dubbed "alternative." They take time to be scientifically studied and incorporated into medical and therapeutic practices.

Polyvagal theory, which centers on the role of the meandering vagus nerve, is one such approach. Beginning in the lower part of the brain, this sprawling nerve runs down the entire length of the body, connecting the brain and organs throughout the body. As we process information about changes in our environments, the vagus nerve reacts either by preparing us to meet a threat or by allaying concerns about the threat and signaling that being calm is all right.[7] One popular claim based on this theory is that you can reset an anxious body's state and thereby alleviate overwhelming symptoms such as anxiety by deliberately stimulating the vagus nerve through exposure to cold, medication, or ritualized breathing.[8]

The theory was developed over decades by Dr. Stephen W. Porges, director of Indiana University's Traumatic Stress Research Consortium at the Kinsey Institute and a Distinguished University Scientist. Interest in his work, increasingly intriguing to medicine beyond its origins in behavioral neurobiology and the science of emotion, has expanded alongside neurologist Antonio Damasio's somatic marker theory, showing the crucial role of emotions in our decision-making and choices.[9]

Resilience and Your Sense of Inside

Can you tell what is happening in your body? Do you feel and respond to hunger, or do you eat according to a schedule? As you sit here now, can you feel your pulse and heartbeat? Did anyone teach you to pay attention? Maybe if you were an athlete, but otherwise, chances are good that the answer is no. If you're a woman, the chances are lower still, since self-objectifying, which women are encouraged to do as girls, actively reduces a person's ability to feel their pulse and heartbeat.

Perceiving what is happening in your body is called interoception, one of the lesser-known human senses. Proprioception, a related ability, tells us where our bodies are in space, and imparts our "selfness" in relation to others. These senses are what we mean when we say we have "gut feelings," or that it's important to "listen to what your body is telling you." Homeostasis and allostasis work together not only to respond to but also to forecast reality. Between them there is a constant back-and-forth that creates our feelings of self, agency, time, and understanding of the world.[10]

Interoception, both conscious and unconscious, is therefore essential to resilience because being able to feel and interpret bodily changes and sensations helps us develop emotional awareness and regulate ourselves. One of the advantages of having a good sense of interoception is that it allows you to think ahead so you can focus on options and make optimal decisions.[11]

A large part of the reason mindful practices work is because they reestablish or establish a person's internal awareness. Meditation, yoga, and a focus on better sleep are all examples of ways we regulate our internal selves. These techniques involve using Rhythm, movement, and muscle manipulation to regulate our bodily processes.[12]

Structured breathing is another good technique. How we breathe modulates our cardiac and immune systems, lowers levels of inflammation in our bodies, reduces anxiety, and enhances feelings of emotional well-being.[13]

Like getting enough sleep, proper breathing is now understood as an important tool in recovering from and alleviating PTSD, anxiety, depression, and chronic pain.[14]

Over the past thirty years, Western doctors and researchers have made strides in understanding the relationship between mind and body, but for the most part a fairly strict mind/body split remains stubbornly constant. Yet, all of us have anecdotally heard stories of people who defy traumatic events and devastating diagnoses by using "alternatives" disdained by science and the medical establishment. These people often turn to meditation, breathing, prayer, new diets, exercise, and community connections to build their resistance to illness. These are considered mental and behavioral changes, but they also involve all the body's systems, including, for example, modifying electrical activity related to the growth or disappearance of cancer cells.[15] Today, doctors are more willing to explore mind-body integration impacts such as these as the key to health in ways that would, even a decade ago, have been anathema. Exploring unfamiliar and seemingly "science-defying" approaches requires openness to difference, to not knowing, and to potentially radically changing worldviews.

Many of today's highly promoted resilience traits take for granted and even dismiss the importance of what our bodies do and the role they play in cognition, emotion, and personality. Mental habits tied to resilience—"optimism," "gratitude," "positive feelings," "grit"— assume a baseline of feeling safe and of physical stability. If your heart is racing and you feel chronically anxious or hypervigilant, it is hard to muster the reserves to feel optimistic or grateful. Traits such as optimism or behaviors like being grateful also have placebo effects. In pain regulation, for example, people who feel optimistic feel pain less intensely. Researchers believe that optimism buffers us from feeling threatened or at risk, but don't yet understand the mechanisms be-hind the connection.[16]

We Are Beings *and Interbeings*

Awareness of your internal state isn't only a matter of self-regulation, however. It's also about being more sensitive to the world around you. The more acute and accurate your sense of your own body's workings and feelings, the greater your capacity to tap into *other* people's phys-ical states.[17] A more developed sense of self and others together is the basis for valuable resilience-building tools—from physical stability and emotional competence to feelings of belonging and reciprocal care.

We are getting better at understanding somatic theories of trauma and recovery, yet even within that expansion we remain fixed on our individualism: our separate experiences, feelings, capacities, and re-sponses to challenges. Again, let's think about our skin.

In addition to being a barrier or a container, our skin is also a *bridge*. It may protect and separate us from the world, but it is also a portal and an information system that transposes, absorbs, and con-nects. With emotion, touch, texture, and sensation we expand our bodies into the world and bring the world into our selves. Yet we still have only minimal understanding of how our bodies interact to forge our relationships.

Other bodies influence our nervous systems, emotions, cognition, health, and adaptability. Every interaction we have with others is dense with sensory information and emotional and cognitive calibra-tion. If you have ever held someone's hand while experiencing pain, then you know that just the touch of another human being is remark-ably soothing and reduces your sensitivity to that pain.[18] Simply hold-ing a cup of hot tea elicits feelings of friendliness for the person we are with because we unconsciously associate the physical sensation of warmth with the emotional experience of warmth learned, if we are fortunate enough, as infants and young children.[19]

Touch, ritual, and sound are salves when we are distressed. The same is true of having a supportive listener, a relationship that positively affects cognitive resilience over time. Studies show that, among older adults, having a larger social network is tied to cognitive resilience, memory, sustaining focus, and making decisions. Having nurturing social circles is important, but having a person who listens is particularly meaningful.[20]

In one such study, participants were asked five questions: Is there someone available to you who shows you love and affection? Can you count on anyone to listen to you when you need to talk? Is there someone available to give you good advice about a problem? Can you count on anyone to provide you with emotional support? Lastly, do you have as much contact as you would like with someone you feel close to, someone you can trust and confide in? Researchers found that "low listener" participants were four cognitive years older than those with "high listener" availability. When you "lend an ear" to the people you love, as the lead researcher of the study explained, you are keeping them healthy.

Listening is one way that we humans share our feelings, moods, and habits of mind, but we do this also through empathetic osmosis, unconscious awareness, and physical and virtual connections. Mirror genes, the basis for our ability to understand what other people are doing and why, enable us to act and think as though we are ourselves engaged in an observed activity. We talk to one another with nonverbal gestures, facial expressions, posture, and cues that affect our mental and emotional states, decision-making, and personal judgments. When we use our hands to think, which all humans, including those with sight impairments, do, we invite others to think with us and create understanding jointly. Student learning in a class, for instance, is enhanced when their teacher uses gestures.[21]

We also fall into matching biophysical patterns, what's called interpersonal synchronization. If you are in a meeting and mimic a person's posture or movements, such as tapping on a table in the same rhythm, the chance that the person will support your position if asked doubles.[22] Synchronized arousal is why concertgoers feel "close" to performers and why people will weep together in a theater during a moving performance. The closer you are to a person emotionally, the more powerful these effects, but even between strangers who don't exhibit visible attraction, heart-rate and skin-conductivity synchronization occurs between couples who are attracted to each other.[23]

We also do this collectively in ways that also influence resilience. Traditions and rituals such as swaying, marching, coordinated drills, and singing in unison are all practices of embodied harmony.[24] All national, ethnic, and athletic cultures have well-developed rituals that bring people together in ways that stabilize bodies physically, emotionally, hormonally, and neurologically while bonding participants. As with fans chanting at a soccer game, these physical connections signal affection and rapport and help build connections between people and communities, including those where people culturally differ.[25]

Emotions serve a similar purpose. We think of emotions as existing on the "inside," as personal feelings, but our emotions are social, externalized resources, interpreting information and helping us communicate, adapt, and change in response to what is happening around us. As children, we learn "appropriate" and "inappropriate" emotional behavior, learning to read social cues and adjusting to other people's moods and needs, so that we can join society.

Emily Butler, director of the Health and Interpersonal Systems research group at the University of Arizona, called emotions temporal interpersonal systems. She studied synchrony, arguing that the many ways in which humans pattern themselves is a homeostatic process that helps us achieve a stable and, as much as possible, safe state.[26] While diehards cling to the divisions of "rational" versus "emotional," of "mind" versus "body," emotions are central to cognition, are essential to guiding our thinking, choices, and adaptions.[27]

It's more than cognition and stability, however. When we talk to each other, our brain neurons begin to fire, or sync up, at the same rates. Interbrain synchrony is challenging neurology's focus on individual brains as it becomes more apparent that we *share* our cognition. The closer we are to a person or to members of a group, the more social trust there is between those present, the faster our neural syncing, and the more beneficial the effect on our listening, learning, consensus building, perceptions, and pleasure.[28]

Synchrony works in both positive and negative ways. We "catch" other people's emotions and align ourselves with their behaviors.[29] If your friends are anxious or depressed, your chances of being anxious or depressed increase. You're more likely to smoke, drink, use drugs, or abuse substances if you spend time with people who smoke, drink, use drugs, or abuse substances.

Synchrony can also make our feelings of distress and stress contagious, as illustrated by a 2014 experiment that documented how attuned infants are to their mothers. The study found that when mothers experienced social rejection, their twelve- to fourteen-month-olds' heart rates were higher than the heart rates of infants in a control group. Fathers' stress levels, even more than their possible anxiety or depression, also affect children's development and ability to self-regulate.[30]

Even our tears are chemical social signals. When men are exposed to women's tears, for example, their levels of aggression decline significantly, increasing care and bonding.[31]

Why does all of this matter? Because in our culture—from language and institutions, to laws, education, and medicine—it takes conscious effort not to minimize our bodies and to act instead on the understanding that we relate to everything around us.

Each of us is a body, but together we are interbodies.[32] Your body is yours, but it is also part of everyone else's environment, which has implications for how we respond to stress, hardships, and trauma. By default, however, we are taught and rewarded for overlooking and ignoring these facts, and when we do, we lose valuable insights.

Faith, Safety, and Belonging

When it comes to resilience, religiosity, faith, and spirituality loom large in "how to be resilient" lessons, but their relationship to our bodies is rarely featured as important. The beneficial bodily effects of faith and spirituality are, instead, often associated with otherworldly causes.

Regardless of demographics or context, the greater a sense of faith or spirituality people have, the higher they feel is their quality of life and the more capable they feel of being resilient when hardship strikes.[33] For decades, studies have confirmed the relationship between a person's spirituality and overall resilience. As a result, measurements of faith are included in the Connor-Davidson Resilience Scale (CD-RISC). Available in more than twenty languages, it is the most commonly used resilience-measurement tool globally. The well-documented connection is why faith and spirituality are so frequently included in books, articles, and corporate training materials dedicated to building resilience.

In the United States, most people think of spirituality as religious faith, that is, having a relationship with a higher power, i.e., God. People who are faithful accept that there is more to life than they can see in the material world. To some, this means faith in God, but to others it means faith that things will work out in the long run. Spirituality, likewise, can refer to a belief in divine immanence or, in a more secular sense, in the oneness with the natural world.

Despite that religious and spiritual practices involve the body, these interpretations of faith and spirituality are mainly centered on *disembodied* ideas and forces, including, for example, the idea of a soul, a pantheistic consciousness, or an afterlife.

No matter how or where they are defined, however, spirituality and faith share three powerful resilience-building dimensions that are directly tied to embodiment: shared beliefs, resourceful communities, and valued rituals. When practiced collectively, rituals build bonding and belonging and an awareness of being cared for. Shared beliefs confirm identities and give value to religious relationships, both of which are sources of comfort that help us adjust to change and crisis. Similarly, resourceful communities rally around members in need, providing comfort, food, shelter, and other necessities.

Rituals—such as praying, singing, counting beads, swaying, and chanting—also have powerful physical effects.

Like meditation, ritual prayers or chants create comforting rhythms that help us regulate time, creating a sense of predictability and of control.[34] When people pray or mediate, they are regulating their nervous, cardiovascular, and metabolic systems. Reciting the Ave Maria prayer or a yoga mantra stabilizes our heartbeats. Ritualized breathing as part of a religious rite lowers blood pressure.[35]

Rhythms and rituals also generate feelings of resonance and of transcendence, of being "at one" with yourself and the world. By taking us out of the flow of time, rituals reduce stress and restore predictability even in times that are frightening or overwhelming. Sometimes people describe this sensation as "time collapsing," which also feels like the self dissipating.

So, while "spirituality" and "religion" provide the comfort of care and belonging, they also create opportunities for physical regulation that make us feel safe and stable.

The same is true of practices such as forgiveness and gratitude, both core aspects of religiosity and positive psychology. Although different religious traditions define forgiveness in varying ways, every tradition generally recognizes two aspects: forgiving yourself and forgiving others, both of which have been shown to reduce psychological stress and pain.[36] When we forgive and give thanks, acting compassionately, we forge dense social connections and strong foundations. The complexity of these benefits is frequently, in resilience guides and tool kits, unhelpfully flattened into oversimplified advice such as "build your social support."

It's hard to overstate the effects of belonging that come from faith-based communities. Like other powerful identities—nationalism or political groups, for example—religious belonging is a resilience resource. Studies of political prisoners who have experienced torture show that prisoners who belonged to dedicated activist communities suffered less post-traumatic stress than those who did not have similar political affiliations. In religious contexts, however, these effects can sometimes backfire. Religious people who suffer terrible loss might feel betrayed by the failure of their faith to yield good outcomes. What unites these two examples is that the strength of a person's social identity heavily influences their personal adaptability.

What is also frequently lost in considerations of faith and spirituality is open appreciation for the material resources that faith and spirituality bring in many communities. For decades, social scientists have pondered why women are generally more religious than men and have also explored how their greater religiosity, in turn, builds resilient strength. A lot of time and effort has gone into speculation about whether women's genes, hormones, personalities, or emotionality make their greater faithfulness more likely. Far less attention has been paid to women's pragmatic reliance on faith-based safety nets, necessary to compensate for widespread gaps in political and economic resources. Being part of a religious community often brings access to the care and material provisions that societies don't otherwise provide. The gender gap in faith and religiosity, for example is particularly acute in Christian countries, where it substantively narrows in communities where women join the paid workforce in higher numbers.[37]

In the absence of economic power and financial security, turning toward religious communities, as women are more prone to do, is a resilience response that has less to do with their being predisposed to believe in a divine being, a suggestion that contributes to the idea of women's relative lack of rationality, than it does with their pragmatically, and rationally, needing, and seeking out, care, support, and belonging. It's not a matter of God so much as social goods and protective community.

Place, Nature, and Belonging

Those same vital feelings of safety, stability, and care that come from belonging and faith also come from other spaces we move through. In the same way that our resilience is tied to mind-body and body-to-body connections, it is tied to body-environment connections.

We are nurtured by the spaces we nurture.

During the pandemic, many people, otherwise largely unaware, realized how much they missed and loved nature. A 2022 study of COVID-life habits showed that people, especially those living in cities, sought out and enjoyed the outdoors in ways that far exceeded their pre-COVID levels. They suddenly had time for nature-based recreation and used nearby parks and distant trails to spend prolonged time in green spaces.

Not only did people go outdoors more during the height of the pandemic, but they were quieter and more attentive to what was happening around them, gravitating more toward naturalistic parts of parks than to more formal playgrounds and sitting areas. They expressed gratitude and appreciation for nature, a resilient and spiritual response to an altered world. A *lack* of access to green space during the worst of the crisis also correlated to housing and health inequalities that resulted in higher mortality rates.[38]

Research, including studies of more than 290 million participants in more than twenty countries across Europe and Japan, has correlated time spent in nature with more than one hundred positive health outcomes.[39] These positive effects come from slow and deliberate interactions between people, trees, the air, and ambient sounds. A regular twenty- to thirty-minute walk through the woods lowers your cortisol levels, improves immunity, and reduces the incidence of chronic illness. As of February 2022, doctors in Canada prescribe passes to national parks as a way for patients to manage hypervigilance and anxiety and to improve overall health.

Our Alienation from the World

Mind-over-body beliefs go hand in hand with Man-over-Nature beliefs. The Western world's rise to power stemmed, in no small part, from the assertion that nature exists outside and apart from humans, a hierarchy that categorically isolates us from other life, our environments, and one another. Being alienated from the natural world—believing we are separate from and in control of that world—has serious harmful effects on all of us. This divide in particular masks our exquisite interdependencies and fragile set points.

Europeans who colonized the United States, for example, understood faith and spirituality as a function of the mind, so their religions could be carried inside people's minds and communicated through a book of ideas—the Bible—both capable of being transported across oceans and continents. To the Indigenous peoples they encountered, these approaches to nature, faith, and spirituality were unfathomable. The Western world sees nature as something to be dominated and exploited, whereas Indigenous cultures understand the natural world relationally, through mutually nurturing connection: filled with relatives to be cared for, respected, and honored.

So, when the U.S. government displaced, and continues to displace, Native Americans, it didn't simply relocate them to new environments where they could transplant their lifeways. It destroyed their resilience-building tools: identities, rituals, relationships with nurturing environments, and sense of belonging to the world.

The Trail of Tears is a case in point. In 1830, more than 125,000 members of the Eastern Woodlands nations lived in territories across Alabama, Florida, Georgia, North Carolina, and Tennessee. In 1830, under the direction of President Andrew Jackson, a man known for his vicious campaigns against Creeks and Seminoles, the U.S. government passed the Indian Removal Act, legalizing a mass expulsion of Indigenous peoples from tribal lands to an "Indian territory," now Oklahoma. People of all ages, some in chains, traveled by foot, initially without water and food, a forced march that an unnamed Chahta (Choctaw) leader described as a "trail of tears" in which between three thousand and six thousand people are estimated to have died while marching.[40] A forced and brutal separation from land to be sure, but, even more importantly, from relationships, memory, and knowledge. A highly effective tactic of war that we see playing out in ongoing settler colonial violence around the world.

Clashing Worldviews

Our mind/body problem and the many alienations it produces— separation from our selves, nature, and people closely affiliated with nature—stem from an unremittingly oppositional, dualistic worldview. We think in terms of distinct and oppositional binaries—such as male/female, white/Black, Man/Nature. We also think of these pairings hierarchically, one side being superior, the other inferior.

You may not think about dualism during your day, but when you're a woman and your doctor dismisses your pain or your concerns, that is dualism. When someone, or the government, refuses to use a person's chosen pronouns, dualism. When your insurance company denies coverage for mental-health care, dualism. That gas we pump into our cars, produced in reckless endangerment of nature, the same.

Our medical, educational, social, and legal systems continue to institutionalize deep-seated, binary beliefs, hindering our appreciation for bodies and their abilities. Yet, we still learn to think today, including through our resilience myths, that our minds rule and the body is a stupid but necessary appendage. Instead of being curious about our potential for connection, we minimize ourselves and pathologize the many complex ways our bodies communicate valuable information— including, for example, anxiety, depression, and even loneliness.

When seventeenth-century philosopher and mathematician René Descartes exclaimed, "I think, therefore I am," articulating his theory of mind/body separation, chances are he didn't anticipate its far-ranging negative effects. We pathologize to capitalize in ways that compromise connection and care. A vivid example: "Can Loneliness Be Cured with a Pill?" asks a recent *Guardian* headline. "Scientists Are Now Asking the Question."[41] We know the cure for loneliness. It's self-compassion, mutual care, and the loving of other people and living beings.

But, as Spanish Jewish poet and philosopher Yehuda Halevi said, "'Tis a fearful thing to love what death can touch."

Dualism, Terror Management, and Resilience

Dualism isn't all bad. For one, it is a useful cognitive shortcut. When we are faced with complexity, our ability to quickly flatten information into oppositions, such as male/female, white/Black, rational/irrational, thinking/feeling, can be a genuine advantage. Secondly, and importantly for resilience, the mind/body dualism I've just critiqued helps us manage terror. Believing in it is one way humans reduce the anxiety that comes with our awareness of our finitude. The resilience we've constructed around radically separate minds and bodies serves this purpose well.

Descartes himself, for example, was a fragile child with a weak chest who suffered poor health his whole life. He lived through an era of endless vicious wars and was also, for a time, a mercenary who studied military engineering for the Dutch. He lost a young daughter and did his expansive thinking against a perpetual backdrop of virulent, recurring plague. He eventually died of pneumonia at fifty-three.

While splitting the mind from the body can be a useful short-term good coping mechanism in the face of mass deaths and constant physical threats, it is a spectacularly poor intellectual and philosophical structure on which to build a society or a theory of long-term adaptivity and resilience.

Descartes's elaboration of mind/body theories, the basis of so much of modern philosophy, informed colonial expansion through extensions such as male/female, "civilized"/"savage," Man/Nature. Its structure was used to ascribe inferiority to certain minds and bodies and then to justify hierarchical orders for exploiting them.[42]

Every day we learn more about how complex and remarkable we are, but what we learn is constantly hampered by a stubborn cultural suspicion of our fluid, porous, and dynamic natures. We remain proverbially blindfolded, each discipline expertly describing a different part of an elephant but incapable of understanding the wonder of the whole.

While we remain mysteries to ourselves, there is no doubt that our mind*fulness* is inseparable from our embodiment. Resilience flows from our material interactions and our social natures, it is built into our cognition, neurology, emotions, and physical states.

Clinging to the idea that bodies are dumb vessels and that we dominate Nature prevents us from understanding ourselves, our relationships, and our environments. It prevents us from finding ways to positively adapt to change and crisis.

Advances in neurology, molecular biology, endocrinology, and more increasingly reveal that our emotions, our cognition, and our physical health are entwined and that our health as individuals—mental and physical—is deeply related to the safety and well-being of other people and to our places.

Our individual capacities for resilience are born of our social identities. Our self-conceptions, empathy, and compassion, the care and purpose we need—all derive from these identities. Our strengths as individuals can't be teased out from our social bonds and our group identifications. How we relate to others influences our sense of self, our perceptions of harm, and our ability to cope, survive, and thrive.

If we want to better understand how to weather stress and trauma, we have to think more deeply and expansively about the relational resources that feed our "individual capacities" and that stem from our belonging to families, places, communities, and larger collectives.[43] This lens provides rich insights into the vast array of responses we humans have to potentially traumatizing experiences.

We are indivisible, and we should celebrate this fact.

3

THE IMPORTANCE OF FORMATIVE EXPERIENCES

Because every time you say, "Oh, they're
resilient," that means you can do something
else to me.

—Tracie Washington

My father loved talking about his childhood. He and a close circle
of cousins and friends ran as a pack through their Port-au-Prince
neighborhood. They did errands at the behest of a bevy of aunts,
and, as young as eleven, stole cigarettes to smoke in hidden alley-
ways. In the summers, my father and his tribe decamped to the
mountains of Kenscoff, a cool retreat away from the city's stewing
heat. As he grew older, they caroused through nights, returning
home at dawn, where, to his mother's ire, he would collapse on a
sofa to sleep away the day.

These memories often brought tears of laughter to his eyes, and
in his retellings he sounded almost giddy with happiness. He even
relished episodes that seemed distinctly not funny. He became
ambidextrous, for example, because his Jesuit teachers thought
left-handedness was a sign of the devil, so they tied his hand behind

his back, forcing him to use his right. Even stories like this one sustained him.

In his recollections, he made essential choices, preferring positive memories over negative ones. He rarely talked about his family's poverty, his childhood physical insecurity, or circumstances that caused shame or anxiety. Not until I was a prodding teenager did he begin to describe his early life with more nuance and detail.

He was the son of Arab migrants, growing up in the difficult realities of Haiti's social and political chaos. He came of age in the shadow of François "Papa Doc" Duvalier's 1956 military coup and the menace of his paramilitary force, the Tonton Macoutes. His father, who was already fifty-three when my father was born, was left penniless when two brothers absconded with their joint family assets. My grandfather plunged into a depression and was unable to work, so my grandmother became a seamstress and my father left school at fourteen to help support them. All my father ever said about this time of his life was that nothing we children ever complained about could compare to the abject boredom of years of nightly curfews without electricity. Words such as *poverty, violence, sexual assault, anxiety,* and *fear* never came up in my father's stories, but his childhood was filled with these realities and as an adult he struggled to trust people. Throughout his life he had social anxiety and terrible night terrors.

If asked, however, he'd relate happy memories and say that his childhood was "normal." Today, we'd say that my father had a high ACE score and had transcended these difficulties.

Adverse Childhood Experiences

ACEs is an acronym for "adverse childhood experiences," potentially traumatizing events or circumstances that people experience as children. The term was coined in a 1998 study that linked childhood experiences and the adult onset of chronic diseases, mental illness, and violence. Roughly 61 percent of adults surveyed report at least one type of ACE. Almost one in six people, more likely to be women and minorities, register four or more ACEs.[1]

The more ACEs a person has, the higher the person's risk of developing mental illness, substance abuse, and chronic health problems, including alcoholism and depression. ACEs are associated with having a greater chance of smoking, dropping out of school, having difficulty keeping a job, perpetrating or becoming a victim of intimate violence, crime, or sexual assault. Six or more ACEs can reduce a person's life span up to twenty years.[2] Because there's a price tag: the CDC estimates that the economic and social costs of ACEs is in the hundreds of billions of dollars each year.[3]

The first ACE study, involving seventeen thousand participants, was conducted between 1995 and 1997 and was initiated to study the relationships between negative childhood experiences such as parental abuse, household dysfunction, or other traumatic events and later outcomes. Today, ACE science informs growing public awareness of the childhood roots of resilience and trauma-informed programs for families, schools, workplaces, and the medical and justice systems.

ACEs are an insightful way to measure how troubling and violent life is for tens of millions of children, but perhaps the framework's greatest virtue is that it reveals what our society considers harmful. What, after all, is "normal" for children in terms of stress or crisis? What does our society expect them to adjust *to* and be resilient in the face of? That consideration isn't about individual capacity, experience, health, or psychology, but about our collective values.

Despite the framework's usefulness, it has known problems and biases. The original group of ACEs was a subset of potential adversities chosen by the founders and normalized by the study's participants, a survey pool made up of almost all white, college-educated, middle- and upper-middle-class people living in San Diego. They were employed and had health care and were all affiliated with Kaiser Permanente.[4]

The heavy presumption seemed to be that a heathy and normal childhood could only take place within the parameters of a white and conventionally patriarchal, heterosexual marriage. Having divorced parents, for example, was one ACE. On the other hand, many social and political vulnerabilities fell outside the purview of the study. Dominant social norms and harsh political realities weren't identified as sources of hardship. Sexism, as a component of street harassment, sexual abuse, or intimate violence, didn't make the cut as a source of insidious trauma. Neither did systemic racism, trans- and homophobia, school bullying, gun violence, or xenophobia. Today, researchers are developing "C-ACEs," more culturally informed models to, for instance, include the lifetime impacts of microaggressions and systemic racism on Black children and the impacts of ACE interactions with gender discrimination.[5]

Today, ACEs are often used as individual assessment tools, despite the founders of the ACE study never intending it to be used this way. You can, for instance, take a three-minute personalized ACE test online, and various institutions use ACE scores to implement trauma-informed care practices. In 2020, alarmed by misapplications of their work, including the use of ACE scores in algorithms, the scientists publicly urged rigor and caution.[6]

The Banality of Childhood Trauma

Michael Barr lives in the small town of Belmont, Iowa. In the spring of 2022, he was sitting at work, in an open-floor-plan office, when an armed man walked in, said, "Good night," to Michael's boss, and fired an AR-15, spraying the room with bullets. Barr, shot in the thigh, lay on the ground bathed in blood until the shooting stopped. He survived, but twenty-two of his coworkers did not.

After terrorizing the office for more than an hour, the shooter, Silas Pike, eighteen, was killed by law enforcement officers. Media described him as a lonely young man. He was also known for violently threatening girls online, behavior that, though reported by his victims, went unchecked. In the months after the attack, Barr was sad and angry. But, according to news reports, he did a lot of "physical therapy" to recover. His family also urged him to have faith and be strong when he felt anxious, depressed, or scared.

Three months later, after his company had renovated their offices—putting up protective barriers, adding security locks, and hiring a full-time private security force—Barr returned to work, albeit at a different location. Many of his coworkers refused to do the same. On the day he went back, he was lauded for his strength, determination, and positive attitude. One article even called him "buoyant." CNN ran a piece with the headline "Belmont Man Shows Exceptional Resilience."

This is a true story, but I've altered some of the details in a way that will almost certainly leave a bad taste. Michael Barr is a pseudonym for AJ, a ten-year-old boy shot at his school in Uvalde, Texas, on May 24, 2022. His "boss" was his teacher, and his "coworkers" were nineteen schoolmates and another teacher killed by eighteen-year-old Salvador Ramos. Prior to the shooting, Ramos had in fact threatened women online, only they were young teenage girls who felt that reporting him wouldn't change anything for them. He also shot his grandmother prior to going to the school, becoming one of the 66 percent of shooters, 98 percent of whom are men, whose mass killings begin with a family member.[7] AJ lay wounded as the killer moved through the school. AJ listened for the police and law enforcement officers, who waited, a now-infamous seventy-seven minutes, to enter.

A news story about AJ's return to school did run with the gob-smacking headline "Uvalde Boy Shows Exceptional Resilience as He Goes Back to School with a Smile on His Face and Photos of His Massacred Classmates on His Chest."[8] The article ended, with no basis for the claim, on a note of better and boundless opportunity: "Wearing their images proudly on his chest, AJ got ready for school. And with the excitement and trepidation of any first day, he walked into fifth grade."

"You have to be strong . . . ," explained the young boy in the article, "like they would want you to do."

On a standardized resilience test, the piece seemed to suggest, this child would pass with flying colors. He might positively respond, for instance, to the following CD-RISC categories: "Coping with stress makes me stronger," "I think of myself as a strong person," "I deal with everything," "I handle unpleasant feelings," and "I have a strong sense of purpose in life."

An entire generation of American children, now known as "Generation Resilient," have never known a world where the threat of mass murder isn't a daily reality. If resilient children are "strong" and "smile" as they walk back into a classroom after a mass shooting that injured them and killed their teachers and friends, then children who are anxious and angry and refuse to return might be considered the opposite: lacking in resilience, weak, and fragile. Not gritty enough.

Sadly, AJ's example is now common, as is the imposition of an adult "hardening" mentality on children. All we really know about AJ is that a young boy was brave enough to walk through the doors of a school and that his anxious parents managed to let go of him, despite their experiences of violence and incompetence. Given the lessons learned by the more than 250,000 American children who have been exposed to school shootings in the past thirty years, we also know that their lives have been irrevocably altered, and probably *not* for the better. This boy's sense of safety and self, the relationships he was building, his social trust, and his family and community were harmed in innumerable ways that have multigenerational consequences.

By now, most of us are appalled and enraged by America's cruel sacrifice of children to gun culture. But part of the problem we face in ending the savagery is that we repeatedly fall back on notions of resilience that are implicated in this very violence.

During this same period, for instance, another story featured a nine-year-old girl who hid in a classroom where her cousin was killed. When it was time for her to go back to school, she was afraid, clearly struggling with anxiety, depression, and trauma. The article mentioned her going to therapy, having nightmares, and crying herself to sleep before the first day of school. The words *strong* and *resilient* don't appear once in the piece, although, arguably, the child's refusal to return to a traumatizing place where risks seemed high shows both strength and resilience. [9]

Children aren't only traumatized by mass shootings but by having to think about them constantly. A study published in *Nature* magazine found that after school drills, expressions of students' anxiety and depression increased by 39 to 42 percent.[10] In the case of Uvalde, children had gone through drills, but now also know that even the hour-long presence of parents and 376 law enforcement officers didn't save them.

Exactly one year after Uvalde, on May 24, 2023, a neo-Nazi gunman injured seven and killed eight people, ranging in age from five to sixty-one, at a Texas shopping mall. An expert guest appearing on Fox News to discuss what happened shared this advice for Americans worried about being victims of a mass shooting: "Be polite and professional, but plan to kill everyone you meet."[11]

That isn't resilient adaptation. It's the mantra of a death cult. The absence of reasonable safeguards against gun violence, the fortressing of schools, lockdown exercises, and the nonstop vigilance they produce is now a type of state terrorism perpetrated against children.

Raising Resilient Children: New World, Old Rules

Gun violence is only one reason why parents and educators are deeply interested in helping children to be resilient. Pre-pandemic, children and adolescents had high levels of anxiety and sadness and reported feeling stress about problems ranging from academic pressure and fraught social lives to fears about terrorism, mass shootings, and climate disasters. In addition to these macro concerns, one in six children living in under-resourced neighborhoods were worried about where they might get their next meal.[12] For these reasons and more, teaching children to adapt to crises and stay happy and hopeful was already an urgent necessity.

COVID pushed all of these "normal" worries into overdrive and demonstrated the importance of conditions in children's early development. During the first several years of the pandemic, teenagers who reported four or more ACEs were four times more likely to be anxious and depressed. Their rates of attempted suicide were twenty-five times higher than among children without ACEs.[13]

One of the most devastating problems that children face is intimate abuse in homes, with American children having more exposure to violence than American adults.[14] The pandemic resulted in a dramatic spike in home violence, but only the most extreme cases ended up in emergency rooms, meaning that children were hurt and dying of injuries at higher rates.[15]

As soon as the early chaos of the pandemic settled down, resilience advice began to proliferate, especially advice about how to help kids. In search of some remedy or meaningful lessons, many adults—and media—turned to personal experience and childhood lessons to find answers. In September 2021, as it became clear that no child was going to participate in anything resembling a "normal" school year, the *New York Times* parenting newsletter published "The Secret to Raising a Resilient Kid."

When he was a boy, the author wrote, his father took him, his best friend, and a neighbor on a grueling backpacking hike to the top of a mountain. By day two, the boys grew exhausted and asked to turn back. The author's father said that the two friends could stay behind, but the son had to continue, an important lesson in resilience, which the author defined as a psychological principle that included being motivated, flexible, and optimistic. "Dad," the author explained, called it "character," concluding that the experience was a valuable lesson he later described as an "epic victory of teenager over nature."

Even though the writer went on to stress the importance of flexibility, stability, and unconditional love, he didn't explore the quality of his father's example or the effects of conforming to patriarchal expectations and the demands of extreme physical rigor. A father's attention and trust are powerful contributors to character development, for instance, with or without the addition of a physical endurance test or emotional repression. There are also resilience lessons in teaching a child how to listen to the needs of others, recognize and respect limits, or consider risk from differing perspectives. Maybe, for reasons we'll explore later, associating resilience with a young man's victory over nature contributes to anti-resilient problems. It's not a useful solution.

The idea behind "character" lessons like the one described above is to micro-dose children with manageable challenges so they incrementally build resilience "muscles." Instead of meeting the needs of developing children, however, they muddy the waters by eliding parental care, trust, and nurture with experiences of emotional discomfort, striving for heroic behaviors, and sacrificing to take control of circumstances.

As COVID crises stretched on, advice along these lines—a privatized resilience of toughness and good character—could seem smug and glib; detached from the reality of many, if not most, children's lives, resilience had less to do with character and determination than with craven and deadly policies. Were children really supposed to stare the ravages of the pandemic down by working on their character, drive, and ability to defeat nature?

By the time "The Secret to Raising a Resilient Kid" ran in the *New York Times,* more than 120,000 American children had lost a primary or secondary caregiver to the virus. That number doubled in the next year, with losses borne primarily by low-income children living in impoverished neighborhoods blighted by racism.[16] By May 2022, 8 million children globally had lost a primary caregiver.

In 2021, the American Academy of Pediatrics declared the state of children's and adolescents' mental distress a national emergency.[17] In addition to sharp increases in anxiety and depression, suspected suicide attempts among boys had risen by 3.7 percent. Escalating a trend that began years before COVID, suicide attempts by girls rose by 50.6 percent.[18] Researchers concluded that during a studied ten-month period, adolescent brains underwent accelerated aging, particularly in girls.[19]

Children aren't little adults. They are, by definition, dependent, developing, learning, and often helpless. Even the most capable child is not in actual control of much at all.

Taking Resilience to School

According to the American Psychological Association, resilience is now the education sector's fourth *R*, snugly nestled alongside reading, writing, and arithmetic.[20]

Today, students are taught to be resilient not as a response to adversity or trauma but as a generalized life skill that cuts across many domains. Resilience is a path to academic success, athletic prowess, character development, and mental health, all of which are included in the purview of positive education, the application of positive psychology in schools.[21] Schools hold resilience workshops, provide resilience training for teachers and administrators, and use lesson plans and games to coach children in desirable and beneficial habits.

Teaching resilience, frequently in terms of "values in action," has the added benefit of appealing to parents. What parent could, after all, possibly object to children learning coping skills in lessons about self-care, optimism, empathy, strength, perseverance, kindness, gratitude, forgiveness, and life success?[22]

Despite these efforts, however, there is little to no agreement or factual consistency about what teaching children resilience *means*. The broader prevailing vagueness of the word means that different types of resilience—of individual mental and emotional adaptability, of public health, of physical survival, and of moral development—are confused in a variety of contexts and applications. In schools, resilience is a sprawling mash-up of positive psychology, trauma-informed approaches, and virtue-based education that has more to do with adult fears and enforcement of social norms than with children's adaptability and well-being. As a result, for kids, "being resilient" easily ends up confusing, stressful, and counter to even the best intentions.

Take grit, a universally admired trait. Like *strength*, grit is synonymous with *resilience*. Defined by the *Oxford English Dictionary* as "strength of character," grit is thought of as a teachable mindset that anyone can develop over time and with some diligence. The past decade's iteration of perennial grit lessons was launched into the educational stratosphere in 2016 with the publication of Angela Duckworth's bestselling book, *Grit: The Power of Passion and Perseverance.*[23]

Duckworth, a popular professor of psychology at the University of Pennsylvania, conducted an array of studies in multiple contexts—such as military academies, private schools, spelling bees—which revealed the many benefits of being persistent, goal oriented, and disciplined.

In one study, Duckworth and her colleagues identified cadets at West Point who scored high on a survey measuring grit: cadets with high scores were less likely to drop out of a challenging training program. Those who persisted through the program were far more likely to say they agreed with the statement "I finish what I begin." Students who dropped out, for whatever reason and regardless of their satisfaction with their choice and its effects, lacked the ability to persevere and failed. The conclusion was that they lacked the grit necessary to succeed in an intensely competitive and potentially violent environment.

It's unsavory to contemplate, I know, but what if you're a military cadet, have the requisite grit, and your goal is sex? What if you begin an unwanted sexual encounter and you believe failure isn't an option? What if you see resistance to your actions as a challenge to overcome? It may seem like a harsh comparison, but grit, confidence, having a challenge orientation, commitment to task, and exercising control— all valued in resilience lessons—are also central to how rapists think and act.[24]

Clearly, grit is *not* the root cause of escalating sexual violence in American military institutions, but the promotion of grit as an indicator of strength, character, and successful achievement is usually accepted as an unadulterated good, whereas it has both positive and comparatively rarely discussed negative consequences.

Another approach to resilience that's popular in schools and parenting forums is teaching children to have growth mindsets as opposed to fixed ones. The idea, developed by Stanford psychologist Carol Dweck in 2006, is that all can hone their mental skills to recast problems as opportunities to learn and grow. She dubbed this orientation a growth mindset. A fixed mindset, conversely, leads people to think they can't change, learn, or develop over time. In the years since, Dweck's mindset approach has gained a tremendous following in schools, where it's been positively linked to improved academic performance, motivation, behavior, and outcomes, despite ongoing research that casts substantive doubt on the efficacy of the model.[25]

Researchers such as Duckworth and Dweck are well aware of the nuances and limitations of their findings and, as researchers, constantly revisit and refine their ideas, but it's difficult to control how people use concepts such as these once they are widely proliferated. Like others before her, Duckworth has faced criticism for the ways that grit as resilience in school tends to fall on the shoulders of low-income, minority students who are told that they can overcome difficult circumstances through perseverance. Instead of building a culture where children's vulnerability and precarity are considered unacceptable, grit agendas easily turn both into troubling tools.[26]

Think about how parents and educators embrace mindset resilience as a way to improve students' academic performance, despite academic achievement being a questionable marker for positive adaptability over a lifetime. Many children can excel academically but not be adapting in healthy ways to stress. Displays of the kind of behaviors we reward in children—the ability to sit in class, concentrate, and get good grades—often mask covert distress, including among students who don't want to further stress parents already stretched to their limits. For example, more than 60 percent of children who live with abusive parents perform well academically; those same children don't score high on social competence factors or other indicators of cognitive flexibility and emotional regulation.

A child who gets good grades, is popular, and athletic is more likely to be thought of as *well-adjusted*, a term that might lead you to think they have a resilience leg up. When adults—parents, teachers, counselors—evaluate children to determine their levels of resilience or to think about how to help them academically, a child's ability to self-regulate looms large. But an inability to self-regulate isn't only about control or maturity. It's relational, because when children persist in unregulated ways, it's often the case that they are asking for something: attention, help, quiet. Cheery children who diligently apply themselves might not feel safe but have instead learned to ignore their feelings and needs to do what they think will make the adults around them happy. Their good grades and never-quit attitudes allow schools to compile glowing statistics, but don't genuinely help them adapt, cope with stress, or be healthy. [27]

The expression *well-adjusted child* conveys positive regard, but it also describes a child who doesn't rock the boat and is more likely to conform to societal norms and expectations. Being *well-adjusted* may lead children to hide their vulnerabilities, pursue unrealistic standards of success and happiness, and feel shame. In this way, in their perceptions, their anxieties or sadness become "maladjustments." If they feel outrage over injustice and get angry, their behavior becomes the problem instead of a cry for help or a legitimate demand for communal support and change.

"Gritty people are *more* dependent on other people, not less," explained Duckworth in 2023, writing about what teachers get wrong about grit and how her thinking has evolved over time. "They rely more on their coaches, mentors, and teachers. They are more likely to ask for help. They are more likely to ask for feedback." So while grit sounds like a trait that individual children can be taught, its essence is relational: they find help and support, cultivate meaningful connections.[28]

Community schools that provide broader social supports and opportunities for students, their families, and neighborhoods understand differences and tensions such as these. Instead of emphasizing measurements of academic success, they focus on learning environments that recognize what students' day-to-day lives look like. They prepare children for life, relationships, and not just workplace needs by emphasizing dignity, citizenship, democracy, and environmental stewardship. They often drop the idea of grades entirely. In these spaces, children whose families or neighborhoods might be struggling find safety and belonging, providing the foundation for resilient outcomes.

Resilience and Athletics: Fit for Life?

In addition to academics, athletics are a major nexus for teaching resilience, in schools and out. In the United States, 60 million children and teenagers participate in organized sports every year, and when they do, they are immersed in cultures of resilience such as mental toughness, grit, personal growth, high performance, and winning.

Athletics undoubtedly offer many benefits. Leadership, social competence, health, and feelings of purpose and belonging are all enhanced. Sports help children mentally and physically, reducing stress and mental distress. But these benefits exist alongside serious downsides: pervasive physical overwork, psychological burnout, feelings of failure and shame, and an inability to know when and when *not* to apply resilience lessons.

For many athletes, leaving lessons about strength, grit, challenge, dominance, and perseverance on the field can be difficult, especially when resilience is taught as a skill to carry into all aspects of life.

On October 29, 2022, the Michigan State Spartans, a college football team, played a game against the University of Michigan. Only two weeks before the game, media applauded the Spartans for "finally showing resilience" and breaking a four-game losing streak. But on the 29th, they lost again. As the teams withdrew from the field and entered a stadium tunnel, up to ten Spartan team members attacked a Michigan player. Some hit him repeatedly in the head with their helmets. After the incident, which was caught on video, Michigan State was fined $100,000, six players were suspended, and five were subsequently charged with aggravated assault.[29] Sometimes, knowing when to abandon a goal is the resilience skill worth cultivating.

Like grit, having a growth mindset also applies to athletics. But what happens when children—even strapping adolescents—want to stop, rest, or opt out because they are tired or no longer find pleasure in sports? Parents and coaches often encourage students to "stick with it," teaching, in effect, that they should overlook their feelings, desires, or discomforts, prioritize specialization and performance, and sacrifice for the win. Every year, for almost fifteen years straight, a period that coincides with the rise of resilience and performance programming in schools and sports, sports-related injuries among children have increased. Experts cite specialization, overtraining, and overuse as all contributing to injuries and to burnout.[30] Children who want to stop a sport or "give up" a pursuit often feel like failures.

What do we even call the virtue of knowing when to stop? Curious, I searched TED Talks, a reasonable barometer, considering that Duckworth's TED Talk has garnered more than 25 million views. The only one I could find that seemed related was made in 2012 and titled *Forbearance*. In it, eighty-five-year-old Thelma Gibson, who, fate would have it, is also of Bahamian descent, uses *forbearance* to affably describe how she resisted decades of systemic and interpersonal racism.[31] It has 1,247 views.

If every obstacle, problem, or hardship can be turned into an opportunity to learn and do better next time, when does your improving end? Are you ever enough as you are?

The older children get, the more pressure they feel to succeed, which means not just doing your best, but being the best. In recent years, perfectionism among adolescents has been on the rise, a problem, researchers believe, tied to growing parental pressure in an increasingly individualistic and competitive society.[32] One of the reasons that 70 percent of kids drop out of sports by the age of thirteen is that both school and extracurricular sports are designed to filter them out in order to cultivate high-performing athletes.

Children who swim against the tide and change course often think deeply about their decisions, coming to know themselves better. They gain agency and self-efficacy, learn to be satisfied by their choices, and frequently achieve happiness. It takes bravery and confidence to make these decisions.

Choosing change also teaches children the valuable lesson that resilience is variable over time and context. As with adults, children can be resilient in one part of life—academics, for example—but not in another—forming strong friendships. They are capable of coping at certain times, but not at others. Changing paths is a risk, and when supported, they learn that people around them value them regardless of how they perform. When they take risks, they gain the insight that relying on others for support when they need it isn't only acceptable but necessary.[33]

A Resilience of Inequality

Whether taught through self-care, academics, or athletics, resilience often shows up as an indicator of virtue, of good character, a moral standard of behavior that, through grades and performance, becomes a measure of human potential. This emphasis detaches adaptability from adversity and context and instead associates it with maturation defined by conformity, self-optimization, and, too often, the belief that suffering leads to growth. As one educator puts it in a letter to his school community, "Resilience isn't really learned, instead it has to be earned."[34]

When we teach children that there is a standard, individual way to be resilient, several vital components of resilience fly out the window as priorities: cognitive flexibility, respect for difference, the importance of belonging, and social trust. What kids are unhelpfully left with is a tremendous burden of responsibility coupled with a distrust of the adults tasked with caring for them.

ACEs and trauma-informed approaches, for example, resonate with teachers and school administrators because they accurately capture the experiences of many children and teachers. In well-meaning efforts, many schools are now using ACEs in educational programming. However, even the most thoughtful teacher can unintentionally stigmatize students and misapply ACEs, with counterproductive outcomes.

In 2020, concerned with the uncritical adoption of ACEs in schools, educator Alex Winninghoff analyzed a Washington State high school class discussion of trauma. During the lesson, students took an individualized ACE test, and their teacher made a presentation about the impacts of ACEs, including increases in the likelihood of illness, sexual assault, and criminalization. He then showed brain scans comparing images of "normal" and ACE-"damaged" brains. "How," asked one of the slides, "are you going to be different?" It's a question that encapsulates ideals of future transformation, optimism, growth, and hard work while squarely putting the onus of accountability for change on the children, as well as implicitly criticizing their caregivers. Given what seemed like a screening test by an unprepared teacher, some children could legitimately have been left with the impression that they might have brain damage and were personally responsible for overcoming the inadequacies of their parents and homes.[35]

In theory, when students walk into schools they are supposed to be equals, and it's a delicate balance to convey the ideal of equality while having to navigate, daily, the reality of inequality. When teachers, parents, and administrators pretend that everyone is the same, they don't convince students. Instead, they give them grounds to distrust adults. Individualistic, future-focused curricula that ignore the realities of children's lives and histories alienate millions of students, *who need help being resilient in the here and now.*[36] Children undoubtedly can and do benefit from learning cognitive, social, and emotional skills that enhance their adaptability and well-being, but depicting structural injustices as matters of personal responsibility has never been the answer.[37] It's a power play that children well understand.

One of the more ironic twists of the rise of resilience ideologies in schools is that social vulnerabilities—such as poverty—have been turned into a "resilience advantage." For years, research has shown that children in affluent communities are "less resilient" to stress than their less privileged peers, leading one psychologist to dub them, in 2006, "America's newly identified at-risk group."[38] Since then, annual studies have routinely revealed class-based gaps in resilience, mental health, and empathy. What if what's going on is that children in these affluent environments are entitled in other ways not measured by resilience studies?

What if they are doing what they have been taught: labeling and articulating their emotions, excessively striving for growth and improvement, and orienting themselves toward success that is understood in terms of winning and domination, neither of which is conducive to empathy? What if their "lack of resilience" is how they can achieve the change that they need?

Studies revealing affluence gaps mainly agree that there are two primary causes, neither of which can be solved through individualized behavioral approaches to resilience: one, kids who score low on measures of resilience are often under extreme pressure to perform, and, two, they report parental inaccessibility, depression, and distance, particularly for boys, among fathers, a known risk factor.[39]

Instead of pushing back against norms or encouraging parents to be more involved with their children, schools continue to stress the need for students to be more personally resilient in strength of purpose, heightened productivity, and positive mindsets. This encourages students to double down and conform to the very standards causing them distress.

It's not only parents or educators who embrace highly individualized paths to children's resilience. Therapy is also focused on personal behavioral approaches. A recent study of the efficacy of teaching teens to recast their stories, learn mindfulness techniques, and develop gratitude practices, known as dialectical behavioral theory, revealed that the mental health of kids exposed to this therapy, many of whom did not start off with depression or anxiety, *worsened*. Overall, depression and anxiety were *more* pronounced in the more than one thousand students in the study, and their relationships with parents *had degraded not improved*. The students were unhappier and less capable of self-regulation than before the program. These conclusions are supported by a range of similar studies.[40]

Findings such as these can mystify educators, parents, and counselors, but it makes sense that teaching children to ruminate on worries, problems, and anxieties in terms of personal responsibility might not be the best idea. It may, indeed, appear to leave them feeling isolated, scared, disoriented, and angry. Instead of appreciating that children's day-to-day experiences and immersive media exposure might be truly unsustainable and cruel, the response to children, as Parul Sehgal writes, is to assert "that these young people are terribly touchy nowadays."[41]

I'm not suggesting that teaching children how to cope with life's adversities is a bad idea or impossible. However, so much of the lessons that children learn seem to be informed more by tradition, convention, and an interest in preserving the status quo than by what we know is important to cultivating resilience. Most of the time, this involves teaching kids endless ways to improve and *change themselves*— be mindful, change mindsets, develop healthy habits. These certainly help, but they are, in essence, window dressing.

If communities are genuinely interested in building resilience in children, it might be more effective to offer mandatory classes for parents and adults, urging them to consider healthier collective norms and standards for what happiness looks like and what constitutes success.

The question isn't how we can help children learn to be resilient but what are we doing, as a society, to undermine their well-being and innate ability to adapt.

Care, Trust, and Resources

So, what works?

Successful resilience-oriented programs for students are characterized by two things: good relationships with teachers and administrators and programs that validate student experience. Students respond well when they trust adults and when resilience lessons and guidance are adapted in substantive and meaningful ways to the circumstances of their lives. These demonstrations of understanding signal to children that they are important to the communities they belong to.[42]

Here's a striking fact: despite the prevalence of ACEs and other chronic childhood stressors, most people go on to lead happy and purposeful lives. How does this happen?

In the mid-1970s, psychology professor Emmy Werner and Ruth Smith, a psychologist living on the island of Kauai, set out to study the life outcomes of 698 Hawaiian children. The landmark study, still considered the most important in the field of childhood resilience, ran for thirty-two years, making it possible to distinguish between short-term distress and long-term adaptability in ways that would otherwise have been obscured. Most of the participants were considered "at-risk" children living in harsh and challenging conditions. Initially, the researchers were interested in how individual traits and behaviors affected life outcomes, but in a major shift in how resilience was thought of at the time, they also included measures of biology, demographics, sociology, and environment inputs. As a result, they effectively shifted the conceptual emphasis of resilience from individual factors to relational and ecological ones, from the harms of negative inputs to the value of positive ones.[43]

What they found surprised everyone: despite living with toxic levels of stress and trauma, most children in the study became capable and often happy adults. Children who formed strong relationships with adults and peers and who had access to social and material support in their communities transcended their difficult childhoods.

Having trusted caretakers, supportive relationships, and well-resourced, nurturing communities and spaces—known as positive childhood experiences (PCEs)—enables children to problem solve, self-regulate, and envision purposeful futures. Having even just one caring person in your childhood, for example, lowers your lifetime risk of physical, mental, emotional, economic, or social problems. A person with ACEs who has such a person is far more likely to have a good life outcome than a person with no ACEs and no such person.[44]

One researcher who realized the power of positive experiences, influences, environments, and relationships to offset harms was Dr. Ann Masten. A pioneering professor of child development at the University of Minnesota, Masten has spent decades studying what she calls "multisystem resilience," proving that most children have the capacity for resilience once they have access to care, resources, and social assets, such as targeted educational programs and professional opportunities. Children who are nurtured act from a foundation of worth and purpose; they can be more optimistic about their own skills and competence and can risk humor as a way to build friendships and relationships. Much current thinking about children's resilience as contextual and not a fixed trait, and of protective factors that shield children from negative long-term impacts, comes from her work.[45]

Broadly speaking, critical protective factors fall into three categories: individual, familial, and environmental; supportive peer friendships are also vital to resilience over time.

As individuals, we all have different traits and capacities that help us adapt . . . or struggle to adapt. Our levels of extroversion, sensory perceptions, emotional sensitivities, and ability to find resources in our environments all affect how we respond to change and stress. Some children, for example, have propensities that protect them from some of the worst examples of childhood neglect and maltreatment: high self-esteem, self-regulation, optimism, charisma, and a disinclination to ruminate. Their traits and habits result in important social benefits such as making friends easily and engaging with adults. These in turn lead to strong and resourceful relationships.[46] For other children, however, these behaviors don't come naturally and are even anxiety provoking.

Like Masten, Dr. Thomas Boyce, emeritus professor of pediatrics and psychiatry at the University of California, San Francisco, has focused his efforts on understanding children's stress responses. In 1995, he and fellow psychologist University of Utah professor Bruce Ellis conducted research that led them to describe children's responses to stress using two metaphorical categories: orchids and dandelions. In follow-up studies, a third category was identified, tulips, who land somewhere in between orchids and dandelions. Tulips show medium environmental sensitivity. Roughly 30 percent of people fall into each of the two outlier categories, with 40 percent of us, the tulips, residing in the middle.[47]

"The orchid child," Boyce explains, "is the child who shows great sensitivity and susceptibility to both bad and good environments in which he or she finds herself or himself." When exposed to stressors, orchid children, more likely to experience anxiety and depression and to feel emotions strongly, experience high reactivity in their fight-or-flight systems. These children, however, also experience higher and more intense pleasure, joy, and awe.

Children who fall into this category need more intense nurturing to process stress and manage environmental chaos. Schedules, routines, and consistency are more important to them.[48] Some children, however, don't adapt positively even when nurtured.[49]

Dandelions show almost no reactivity at all. They are resilient in the ways we traditionally think of resilience: "strong," "not sensitive," "optimistic." They barrel through stress and potentially traumatic events and circumstances, an advantage enhanced because their genetic predispositions are generally more aligned with what our culture values.

Teaching resilience as a universal capacity that any child can build can easily ignore these differences, actually hurting children's adaptability. For tulips or dandelions, standard resilience advice makes sense. These children's more likely traits and behaviors—extroversion, confidence, imperviousness, less pronounced emotionality, optimism—suit resilience norms that reward grit, extroversion, being thick-skinned, and optimism.

For more sensitive children, the same ideals are likely to aggravate anxiety and stress, contributing to perfectionism, shame, and feelings of failure. The sensitivities and emotional dispositions of orchids mean they withdraw from interactions that might yield nurturing connections. Their ways of being *aren't* valued by a society that recoils from emotions, and what is considered antisocial introversion. Because of their behaviors, they are more likely to be bullied and scolded for their sensitivities. Instead of acknowledging a sensitive child's needs, many adults press children to try harder, feel optimistic, and be more sociable.

Because "sensitivity" and "emotional frailty" are considered feminine and weaknesses, orchid boys often pay an especially high price for failing to buck up. Prone to introspection, gravitating toward the arts instead of sports, sensitive boys come under intense pressure to overcome . . . themselves. Their violation of traditional masculinity norms—the ones that align with resilience expectations—means they are more likely to experience social rejection and parental pressure. The way toward resilience isn't in imposing standards but meeting children where they are. These findings further strengthen the argument that applying universal standards, such as set-in-stone developmental guidelines or resource models, can do far more harm than good.

These aren't cut-and-dried categories that children can be scientifically slotted into. Ongoing research finds that most of us are mosaics, whose stress sensitivity and resilience responses change in relation to combinations of nature, nurture, environments, timing, relationships—all are important.

With proper love and attention, for instance, orchid children are also resilient, in fact *more* resilient over time than others. What our culture tends to abhor as weakness and vulnerability—"sensitivity," emotionality, anxiety, or depression—actually enhances a certain kind of cognition. The "risky genes" that generate propensities for behaviors considered dysfunctional or signs of a lack of resilience are often the same ones that lead to greater openness, flexibility, and adaptability.

Children are positively responsive to positive *responsiveness*. Boyce's research found, for example, that highly sensitive and sometimes demanding children, prone to mental distress, become the most generous and adaptable when their needs are acknowledged.

Our differences in sensitivity and emotionality—those that result in our depression, anxiety, and other "negative" feelings—are critical to our success as a species. Exposed to unknowns, new and unpredictable settings, and potentially dangerous circumstances, sensitive people recognize early signs of threats, risks, and opportunities, imparting a distinct advantage to their community. Highly sensitive people are an early-warning system for both good and bad possibilities.[50]

Which gets us to the remaining category of protective factors: families and larger environments, ways that provide nurturing opportunities for children and create environments that give them critical relief from stress and fear.

If you are the primary caretaker of a child, how you approach raising children is an important source of support or a substantial risk to a child. Having a tolerant, authoritative parent, for example, increases the likelihood of a child's being resilient.[51] Children of firm and responsive parents develop healthier autonomy, seeing themselves as independent but accepted, cared for, and connected. Authoritative parenting combines emotional intelligence, stress support, encouragement, and communication of confidence in a child's abilities. It more often models behavior that teaches kids how to manage tension, know themselves, and persevere with a pragmatic and generally positive outlook.[52]

By comparison, children raised by more rule-driven, authoritarian parents are less able to manage change and self-regulate when stressed. Authoritarian parents value hierarchy and expect obedience and so are often impatient with emotional displays, making them less attuned to children's needs or responsive to their distress. They are more likely to model rigidity, and as a result, children's emotional competence suffers. Authoritarian parenting is more likely to traumatize children because it results in a higher likelihood of emotional repression, cognitive inflexibility, and fear-based reasoning.[53]

A child's resilience is also directly related to their *family's* level of connection, cohesion, and overall resilience, meaning that families also need social acceptance and support.[54] This support includes community well-being and the availability of opportunities to pursue fun, professional success, creative endeavors, and engaging social lives.

It Actually Does Take a Village

If you find yourself thinking, "Why aren't today's children more resilient?," consider asking instead, "Why are resources dedicated to children in our society so scarce?"

Interviews of the Kauai study participants when they were in their forties, for example, showed that the availability of continued education through community college, joining a religious institution or the military, finding a supportive life partner, and having access to psychotherapy all contributed to positive life trajectories.[55]

Helping children develop resilience requires investing in their families' well-being and in their communities. Safe and supportive communities require dedicated economic and political resources that also include making sure that parents and grandparents have access to mental health resources, economic opportunities, parental training, and ways of learning social and emotional skills that may never have been passed on to them in the first place.

"Supportive" can mean many different things to different people, but in terms of resilience, it translates to, in addition to public investments, positive social norms that promote openness to difference, respect for diversity, and a commitment to education that includes the availability of enrichment programs, after-school activities, and more.

Trauma-informed approaches pursue collective care and support for children to give them a greater chance of lifetime resilience and positive outcomes. Growing resilient children means recognizing the fluid and dynamic exchange between nature and nurture, children and their families and societies. It takes dedicated will, time, space, and a great deal of money.

For example, just months before the pandemic struck, Dr. Nadine Burke Harris, California's first surgeon general and author of *The Deepest Well*, a book about the impacts of childhood adversity, established an institutional goal: to reduce ACEs and toxic childhood stress by half within one generation. She introduced trauma-informed approaches to social services, education, and health care, emphasizing the importance of early interventions.

Resistance Is Resilience

In the past decade, criticizing Gen Y and Gen Z for their lack of resilience has become a virtual parlor game in conservative and, increasingly, even liberal circles. A cottage industry of books, articles, and podcasts asserts that today's youth are fragile, "coddled," weak, and even, to many, irreparably *feminized*. They are cast this way whether they argue in favor of trigger warnings or protecting their well-being, personal interests, or their visions of the future.

In a classic example of generational disconnect, a 2021 World Economic Forum study of five thousand adolescents unironically labeled the "disillusionment of Gen Z" a global "risk to the future."[56] The authors of the paper announced it was time to "equip young people to meet the challenges they face," if they were "ready to learn" how to be resilient. The paper defined resilience as a "person's ability to bounce back quickly from failure, time and time again, without experiencing a loss of enthusiasm for the task or challenge at hand" and tied resilience to "self-efficacy, grit, toughness, growth-mindset, and adaptability." As with other paternalistic takes, the authors seemed to go out of their way to ignore how younger people effectively adapt to adversity: subverting norms, systems, and institutions that traditional resilience ideologies harmfully sustain.

If *coddled* has appeal as a criticism, it helps to remember that the word originally referred to being immersed in an increasingly hot and hostile environment, one threatening disintegration. Younger people aren't distressed because they lack the right mindset or don't understand what is happening around them. They are distressed because the world is distressing, and adults have failed them.

American children are drowning in violence, to a degree that the rest of the world understandably finds staggering. They are living through climate disasters even as aged leaders stubbornly refuse to take the steps necessary to avoid critical tipping points. Their schools have turned into militarized fortresses and their streets can feel like war zones. They have grown up with a nonstop flood of cruel and terrorizing images of Black death. Misogyny is rife in the public sphere, and sexual violence is on the rise. Xenophobia and hate crimes begin in schoolyard and social media bullying. These children have additionally spent their formative years watching millions of adults descend into irrationality and authoritarianism. Children who have lost people to suicide can now attend bereavement camp to learn to grieve in healthy ways.[57]

Adapting in this environment can't mean you aren't sad or angry; in fact, those emotions are often what makes pragmatism, adaptability, and survival possible. Young people are simultaneously capable of feeling distress and positively adapting to crises and adversity because they have to be.

Resilience Is Everywhere in Youth Cultures

Post-millennials, especially girls and women, are rejecting performative resilience. They are leading global justice movements against climate-change denial, gun violence, and white supremacy. They embrace Black Lives Matter, Indigenous rights, and antiracist and anticolonial worldviews and compassionately accept gender and sexual fluidity. But perhaps what is most incomprehensible to their elders, their ways of being resilient call capitalism into question on personal and political levels.

In an environment of abandonment, in terms of our society's failures to prioritize children, they find support, validation, belonging, and purpose in one another and often behaviors that adults think of as maladaptive, antisocial, and hostile. In the absence of care, they adapt as well as possible to their environments and find people who, despite risks and dangers, make them safer and give them belonging and purpose that their wider society denies them.

For instance, girls who advocate for themselves armed with intersectional feminist theory are more resilient to a culture that objectifies them and exposes them to high rates of discrimination and sexualized and racialized violence. Yet, despite our knowing this, feminism isn't taught as a resilience resource in schools, and there is still an overt backlash, even in many liberal environments, to the talking points of feminism. Minoritized kids—LGBTQ students, the children of immigrants, and those from Indigenous communities—similarly find ways to come together to affirm specific values and find purpose, meaning, and security. Black students who build supportive communities within communities, such as sitting together at lunch or forming affinity groups, are acting resiliently, but are often belittled or barred from creating these protective environments.[58]

When children in under-resourced neighborhoods join gangs, they encounter risk and harm, but they also find people who understand, accept, and protect them. Gangs also offer access to valuable material resources. Teen mothers likewise demonstrate characteristics associated with resilience and agency, making decisions that go against the tide of the dominant culture's expectations but acting in ways that confirm self-worth, feelings of control, and efficacy.

One aspect of the World Economic Forum survey of five thousand Gen Z adolescents surprised the authors. Eighty percent of respondents said they felt hopeful about their futures and meeting global challenges. When asked, they identified their school as the most important institution preparing them for the future and wished that educators focus more on how the world is changing.[59] Other research similarly indicates that, even as rates of anxiety and depression climb in this cohort, they are managing the tension between pessimism and optimism. As a result, they frequently understand what they are experiencing with hopefulness and not despair.

Gen Y and Z are demonstrating types of resilience that don't fit traditional ideas about success, happiness, work, or profit. Their pessimism is pragmatic because being honest about the state of their world is the best possible way to adapt to it. They are inclined to be accepting of their world's diversity instead of interested in conforming to standards, and they appear to be more comfortable with the fluidity of existence. They often approach politics with empathy and compassion; respect feelings and dignity; value community and working across differences. Digital natives, they understand social media and technology, both their good and bad uses, effectively using both to build bridges and overcome obstacles. Politically, they are more interested in practical solutions than party identity.[60]

What really worries people who are critical of children's loud despair, emotionality, and rejection of norms is that their way of being resilient is having a specific effect: *it makes them ungovernable.* Pearl-clutching critics of younger generations aren't dedicated to helping children thrive but rather to failing systems and corrupt power.

So, while there are many good reasons to be concerned about children's mental health, and to want to teach them how to develop resilience, there is also a great deal to learn from them. The difference between approbation and admiration is a matter of power and world-view. As a teacher or parent perhaps worrying about children's emotional distress, "failures to launch," or "allergic to work" attitudes, can you step back to consider that for younger generations being resilient requires a necessary blend of resilient optimism and strategic pessimism? That it might lead them to see that democracy and unbridled capitalism are incompatible?

4

THE NECESSITY OF NEGATIVITY

I'm a pessimist because of intelligence, but an
optimist because of will.

—Antonio Gramsci

As a person whose family has lived on islands for centuries, my breath
catches in my throat when I consider entire archipelagos disappearing
into the sea. When I see the words "a world with no beaches" and
"tens of millions of climate refugees," my brain shuts down. It's not
that I am unfamiliar with the ravaging, destructive power of water or
storms, however.

I was brought up to have a healthy respect for hurricanes, but at a
time when hurricanes and sea rise didn't pose today's levels of threat.
By comparison, my father was remarkably cavalier about hurricanes.
He'd grown up in Haiti, spending far more time on mountains than
seashores. Not even more than half a century in The Bahamas convinced him to either love the ocean or dread its might. Each year,
he and my Bahamian grandfather, who was scarred by the effects of
multiple catastrophic storms, sparred over if and how to prepare for
potential devastation. Either way, no matter how terrible a hurricane
was, we were lucky enough to always stay safe, suffer minimal losses,

and, particularly as children, even be excited by the drama and disruptions.

As a result, I always held the optimistic belief that we'd forever figure out a way to make that true whatever might happen. My faith was an example of optimism bias, a tendency humans have to believe things will work out and that we are less likely to have bad experiences than is probably the case. It is an especially common cognitive response when we are forced to consider atypical scenarios, such as a storm of the century.[1]

Hurricane Dorian destroyed my faith in the inevitability of good outcomes.

Dorian was staggering and fierce; beautiful and immense. Photos of the storm show miles of the vertiginous cumulus clouds that made up the hurricane's deep, almost perfectly circular eye wall. Above the peaceful eye, the bright blue sky was clear; below it, the deep blue sea appeared calm. As it neared landfall, Dorian quickly met the criteria for a Category 5 hurricane, the most dangerous and intense on the Saffir-Simpson Scale. But Dorian's massive water volume moved it beyond the standards of a scale optimized to measure wind speed.

For people who experienced Dorian on the ground, there is now a clear before and after. Before September 1, the town of Marsh Harbour in the Abacos, a chain of islands in the north of the country, *existed*. After September 1, it didn't. Before that day, six thousand Bahamians lived cheek by jowl in the town, alongside an unknown but significant number of undocumented Haitians and Haitian Bahamians. People woke up, got ready for work, took kids to school, and thought about what to get for dinner and how to spend the weekend. They could rely on a thriving tourist industry, busy marinas, a fleet of local ferries, communities of worship, packed resorts, a new airport, cell phones, and the internet. Within hours, everything was gone. An unknowable number of people, entire families, were gone, tangled into rubble or swept out to sea.

As the hurricane approached, our far-flung family relied on a never quiet WhatsApp thread to share preparations and status updates. Those of us who were far away watched as loved ones went about the familiar routines of hurricane prep, everyone feeling increasing dread. Once the storm hit, we kept up with news, images, messages, and then live feeds. Eventually our chat took a dark turn, first because updates became impossible and then because, once communications were restored, the thread turned into a fire hose of incomprehensible images and videos: families escaping to rooftops, cars careening erratically over floodwaters, trucks lodged in trees, people clinging to lampposts, rain-filled boats crowded with disoriented survivors, and parents ferrying children to safety.

It took days for phone and internet services to be restored, after which aerial photos of devastation emerged. With only scant exception, nothing was left of what had existed only days before. Hills and valleys of wood, plastic, steel, and dirt interrupted by pools of water of unknown depths formed a new landscape. Almost a week passed, during which survivors hid under rubble for shelter, before rescuers could make landfall. Because the government prioritized rescues, shelter, water, and medical care over counting the dead, there is no reliable official count of losses.[2]

During this period, Dorian moved toward the much more densely populated island of Grand Bahama, where more than fifty thousand people were battened down. Pummeled by eighteen- to twenty-three-foot storm surges and sustained 180-mile-per-hour-plus winds, more than 70 percent of Grand Bahama's landmass eventually disappeared into the raging ocean as families fought their way to higher ground and shelter.[3] The excessive damage caused by the storm resulted not only from its intensity but from its slowness—it hovered over the island, moving at just one mile per hour for more than forty-eight hours—both effects of climate change.

Today, we know that Bahamians lived through the fiercest and most prolonged exposure to a catastrophic hurricane in recorded history.[4] More than seventy thousand people were left homeless and damage exceeded $7 billion, an amount greater than 50 percent of the country's $12 billion gross domestic product.

Support from all quarters was immediate. Before government agencies could mobilize, Bahamians, in a fleet of private boats, fanned out, rescuing stranded and injured people and their pets. An anonymous man in Florida walked into a Costco and bought one hundred generators. A woman gathered more than one hundred dogs in her home. Rihanna dedicated a channel of Fenty sales revenues to relief efforts. Michael Jordan pledged $1 million and Ludacris pledged $100,000.

Global aid organizations sent donations, set up relief pipelines, and established emergency medical services. A cruise company re-routed a ship to rescue, feed, and transport thousands left homeless to the U.S. mainland. World Central Kitchen, founded by chef José Andrés, sent its Resilience Programs team into the country to serve tens of thousands of meals.

How resilient were people directly impacted? By most typical estimations, very. Like so many other communities picking up the pieces after a catastrophe, people helped one another find food, water, shelter. The government prioritized getting children back into school. Incredibly quickly, the trauma of the storm receded, and within a scant few weeks the government made it clear that the country was back on its feet, calling for tourists to visit unaffected islands to help fuel recovery and reconstruction.

After initial coverage of devastation and dramatic rescues, relief and resilience narratives quickly surfaced, and in these, survivors were often depicted as shell-shocked and bereft of personal belongings but staying positive and grateful to be alive.

"I reminded my wife that when we got married, we had no house, but we had a little fifteen-foot whaler," said Abaco resident Michael Albury a week after the storm. "Today, we have the fifteen-foot whaler, no house, no business. We're starting out fresh. But it's a clean slate and we can do whatever we want."[5] Despite being at the epicenter of a complex disaster and rescue, Albury seemed confident that his family could and would rebuild.

Many of us are in the face of global crises. We know, based on years of study, that having an optimistic attitude is a proven dimension of resilience. But why does it work? What enables a positive attitude to begin with?

The Power of Positivity

If optimism as we've come to know it had a birthdate, it would be 1952, the year Norman Vincent Peale published his bestselling book *The Power of Positive Thinking*. In self-empowering nuggets of wisdom instructing readers in "how to create your own happiness" and "how to have constant energy," Peale assured people that happiness and optimism are choices available to anyone.

"Whenever a negative thought concerning your personal powers comes to mind, deliberately voice a positive thought," Peale urged readers. "Scatter sunshine, forget self, think of others," he explained, while telling them, simultaneously, how to think almost entirely about themselves. Always look on the bright side. Count your blessings. Take control of your future. If feeling bad weakens you, don't feel bad.

His slim volume, translated into more than forty languages, is one of the bestselling books of all time. Decades after its publication, people continue to trade in his motivational aphorisms, the principles of which dovetail perfectly with the explosively popular school of positive psychology. Like Peale's gospel, the science promotes optimism, gratitude, perseverance, spirituality, and resilience as individual strengths that lead to personal happiness.

It's impossible to overstate the influence of Peale's gospel on American culture. While optimism is a human trait, being optimistic is often seen as peculiarly American. As an attitude toward life, it aligns well with a culture dedicated to individual happiness, personal success, and the pursuit of wealth. In this context, optimism has less to do with personality or cognition and is more about claiming the power to control your destiny.

Donald Trump, for instance, is one of Peale's most influential acolytes. Trump was six years old when Peale published his book, which inspired Trump's parents to join the Protestant pastor's congregation at the Marble Collegiate Church in Manhattan. Every Sunday the family drove from Queens into the city to hear Peale preach, which he did there for more than fifty years. Peale became a lifelong mentor and friend of Trump's, officiating at two of his weddings. Trump calls Peale "one of the greatest speakers" and credits the pastor with inspiring his self-confidence, resilience, and success. For his part, Peale returned the admiration, describing Trump as possessing "a profound streak of honesty and humility."[6]

Trump's brand of optimism, confidence, and gratitude comes straight from the pages of Peale's work, and it doesn't typically reflect a deep reservoir of honesty and humility. "I feel so powerful," Donald Trump exclaimed in 2020 while recovering from a case of COVID that was much more serious than he or his administration admitted. His advice to Americans at risk of getting COVID or who already had it was "Don't let it dominate you." Having COVID, said Trump, handily erasing the work of countless researchers, doctors, nurses, and health-care workers who helped keep him alive, was "a blessing from God."

Peale's lessons inform Trump's life. For Trump, optimism and persistence are matters of faith and family.[7] Thinking positively and refusing to give in to negative circumstances, according to Peale and Trump both, are applicable regardless of circumstances. Including, apparently, electoral disappointment. Trump's refusal to accept his 2020 presidential-race loss is part and parcel of this commitment to thinking good thoughts always and to Peale, his spiritual mentor.

Having a positive attitude *is* linked to better coping, higher self-confidence, improved health, happier relationships, and increased life satisfaction. Positive thinking helps us have a sense of purpose and control. If you feel rosy about your future, you might take more steps to ensure it by exercising and eating more nutritious foods. Additionally, and importantly vis-à-vis resilience, having a positive and optimistic attitude makes you attractive to other people, facilitating friendships and valuable social connections.[8]

Some of us are born with a propensity for optimism. One study of five hundred pairs of identical twins, for example, found that optimism is roughly 25 percent genetic. As positive psychology urges us all to consider, though, anyone can adopt ways of thinking that are more positive and, in so doing, learn to moderate the negative effects of distressing thoughts and feelings.

A great deal of what we think and learn about optimism today comes from Peale's mission and also significantly from its scientific counterpart, positive psychology. The domain is concerned with improving life outcomes by focusing not on what's not working—pathology, distress, traumatic responses—but on what is working: the positive traits, characteristics, and habits that either protect a person from suffering or enable the person to adapt most effectively and positively to adversity. The field's perennially controversial father, Martin Seligman, wanted to "steer psychology away from the darkness and toward light."[9]

Seligman and others go to lengths to describe positive psychology's scientific grounding and make clear the differences between Peale's theology of positivity and prosperity and their field, but Peale's optimism-based truisms map well onto positive psychology's life-skills, happiness-enhancing, and resilience-building habits. Both include ritualistic practices and concepts such as forgiveness, gratitude, faith that good will come, and spiritual meditation.

"Positive psychology," Seligman, a charismatic leader in his own right, has explained, called to him "just as the burning bush called to Moses."[10]

Optimism and Resilience

Positive psychology's explosive growth in the early years of this century coincided with the events and effects of 9/11, a touchstone in the rise of resilience as a normalized trait and, importantly, a refusal of helplessness in the face of threat and trauma.

In Seligman's early research on depression, which paved the way for positive psychology as a discipline, he found that pessimists are more likely to think of adverse events as permanent and pervasive, blaming themselves and falling into unhelpful patterns of helplessness and passivity. In contrast, optimists see negative events as temporary and are more likely to maintain a sense of agency over their lives. How a person thinks about their problems, their attribution, is critical. He went on to describe the beneficial effects of what he called "learned optimism," a way to offset learned helplessness and feelings of a lack of agency and control, and published a book by that name in 1991. In this way, optimism and a reslience wrapped up in it, was as much, if not more, about feelings of control than adaptability.

As we've discussed, in the years after 9/11, demonstrating the "steel of American resolve" was a collective desire.[11] Information about how to develop resilience proliferated as individuals and institutions adapted to a new world in which the meaning and reality of vulnerability had been redefined in minutes. Optimism and resilience became markers of American virtue and character in the clear belief that resilient citizens add up to make a resilient country.

Resilient strength and optimism became the keys to our self-defense and self-worth, a shield, a virtue, a strength, a sign of superior character and culture. We found evidence of it in acts of heroism, suffering, survival, mourning, and self-sacrifice. There was resilience, as George W. Bush infamously put it, in shopping in defense of our cultural values.

In 2004, Seligman and Christopher Peterson, another pioneer of positive psychology, published a weighty tome, titled *Character*

Strengths and Virtues: A Handbook and Classification, a taxonomy designed "to help people evolve toward their highest potential." In it, optimism, one of twenty-four character strengths, is defined as having a positive and hopeful perspective and the belief that good things will come. Resilience falls under the virtue of courage. The book has since become the basis of a program that is used in schools and other institutions the world over. [12]

In theory, the identified virtues are shared across the world's diverse religious and philosophical traditions, but that doesn't inspire much confidence if you consider that most of those traditions were defined, over millennia, by and for men in the near complete absence of women, interpreted through a lens of Western culture, and then refined into this particular product at this particular time.

Optimism and Entitlement

Research shows that optimism, as a personality attribute, helps an individual cope with stress and adapt to change. It is also shaped by social influences and life events and experience.[13] It can, to an extent, be learned, a resilience-enhancing habit.

In our mainstream script, however, little suggests the degree to which context, environment, and experience can affect a person's ability to be optimistic or develop optimistic attitudes. Instead, resilient people are often depicted as naturally more optimistic, a trait that, furthermore, is linked to being gritty, strong, honorable, and, even, prominent. That connection ignores how power, entitlement, and privilege *make* optimistic resilience possible for some, but not others.

For example, one of Martin Seligman's earliest and most generous financial backers was self-made billionaire philanthropist John Templeton. Lauded for his good works, Templeton, like Trump, credited Norman Vincent Peale's *Power of Positive Thinking* with inspiring him to adopt the positive mindset that made him successful.[14]

Templeton was curious, intelligent, and generous, and, by all accounts, worked hard to achieve his goals. He was also white and conservative and spent his formative years in Jim Crow Tennessee, where he grew up on what was once Native American ancestral lands. As a young man, he attended a racially, religiously, and gender-segregated Ivy League college, his education funded by grants and scholarships that he raised himself. Despite his curiosity and intelligence, Templeton didn't appear to recognize the many ways that his environment and identity helped him overcome poverty and hardship to become as wealthy and powerful as he was. Instead of considering how circumstances and resources facilitated his optimism and success, he thanked Peale for showing him that "what I had become in my short lifetime was mainly dependent on my mental attitudes."[15] He went on to commit himself and his amassed fortune to the reconciliation of science with religion and the exploration of mind-over-matter philosophies, often related to the power of the individual to succeed with the right attitude.

A conservative Presbyterian who invested tens of millions of dollars in the development of psychology research programs, he established the Templeton Foundation, a multibillion-dollar undertaking, to bring science and religion into alignment. One of his passion projects was expanding the reach and impact of positive psychology. The Templeton Prize for Positive Psychology is probably the single biggest financial award in the field of psychology.[16] Since the foundation's inception, critics have warned of the organization's questionable goals, religious agenda, and treatment and definition of science.[17]

In 1964, Templeton traded American for British citizenship and moved to The Bahamas in what many considered a self-imposed tax exile. At ninety-five, he died there in 2008. He died during a period, between 2003 and 2010, in which more than $20 million of Templeton funds financed the work of deniers of anthropogenic climate change.[18] In 2020, alongside the Koch brothers, the oil industry, and countless anonymous others, the Templeton Foundation contributed to a "research integrity" conference notoriously attended only by white male scholars[19] who appear to believe that climate change is a problem of political correctness run amok.[20]

The words *white male scholars*, like *white supremacy*, cause great discomfort and defensiveness in many people. This is as true today as it was in the 1950s, when Peale's homespun positivity was embraced by millions of white evangelicals and highly visible and prominent business leaders.

In the years immediately leading to and surrounding the publication of Peale's gospel of optimism, jarring changes were taking place in the world: fourteen-year-old Emmett Till was tortured and lynched; Malcolm Little threw off a slave owner's last name and changed it to X; the psychotherapist of colonialism, Frantz Fanon, wrote *Black Skin, White Masks*; and Ralph Ellison published *Invisible Man*. *The Diary of Anne Frank* was published in English. Planned Parenthood began funding research into oral birth control and founded the International Planned Parenthood Federation. The birth control pill, a world transformative biotechnology, was invented. Hugh Hefner's *Playboy* magazine was published. *Brown v. Board of Education*, the landmark Supreme Court case that ended legalized racial segregation in U.S. schools in 1954, began. The United States tested its first thermonuclear device on the Marshall Islands. The Great Acceleration, a radical change in the relationship between humans and other living systems on Earth, is dated to the years between 1950 and 1955.

This was the backdrop of Peale's politically edifying and emotionally palliative "don't look back" ideology. Then, as is the case now, embracing an optimism of personal strength, resilience, and power to overcome hardship enabled millions of people to ignore history and the difficult feelings that public scrutiny and social change elicit. His madly successful ideas about positive thinking can't be divorced from a national refusal to feel discomfort and acknowledge privileges enjoyed by men such as Fred Trump, John Templeton, and Peale himself.

But resilience often requires us to feel *discomfort*, sit with it, and parse what it means. Adapting positively involves accepting the unsettling feelings and engaging in careful listening. It takes changing and accountability. Instead, "if it doesn't feel good, you can choose not to feel it" has somehow come to define resilience. Learned optimism suffers from the potential to similarly slide into denialism. In theory, learned optimism takes acknowledging both negative and positive experiences, but in practice and nomenclature, that distinction is easily lost in favor of looking away from difficult truths. In many circumstances, *optimism* is a serious misnomer because what is being demonstrated is denialism, entitlement, and narcissism at scale. In this thinking, positivity means minimizing truth, history, and the advantages of power. It makes it *probable* that you ignore wider circumstances enabling your positivity, and shame and blame others who don't share your good fortune.

It's easy, if you are fortunate enough to belong to a caring family, well-resourced communities, and politically empowered classes, to take optimism for granted when tragedies or shocks occur. It's when we lack resources and those networks of families and communities that we become acutely aware of their importance to personal resilience and recovery.

Media constantly reinforce this dynamic. Take Michael Albury, the man in Marsh Harbour whose personal possessions were reduced to his fifteen-foot boat. He and his family clearly suffered terribly; however, when Albury was interviewed by the media, he explained, "I'm smiling because I have the important stuff," and expressed his eagerness to rebuild his family's lives. He provided an ideal image of optimistic resilience: even as he faced tremendous loss, he was hopeful, optimistic, grateful, and forward facing. In fact, the title of the article was "Bahamas Strong: After Hurricane Dorian, Hope Emerges."[21]

Another resident of Marsh Harbour, Lavita Altima, on the other hand, was none of those and didn't seem at all hopeful. A Haitian immigrant to The Bahamas and a single mother, Altima was also left completely ruined by the mega-storm. She and her child were taken in by a church, which provided them with much-needed food and shelter. This was the *second* catastrophic disaster that Altima had lived through. She was in Haiti in 2010 when it was hit by a devastating earthquake that killed more than 250,000 people and injured another 300,000. UN peacekeepers and aid workers, sent to help, then introduced cholera to the island, spurring the first deadly epidemic of the deadly disease in the modern era.

Like Albury, Altima also understood her situation. "I would like for somebody to help me and my baby," said Altima, thirty-nine, as her two-year-old played a few yards away. "I don't have anyplace to go and nobody here."[22]

It's easy to think a person such as Altima is less resilient than a person like Albury. She didn't sound optimistic or confident and didn't express thanks. The news story portrayed her as helpless, despondent, and dependent. Many people would disdain her passivity and see her asking for help as a form of laziness, of sitting around waiting for "free stuff." Like that of other Haitians, Altima's position in The Bahamas was precarious even before the storm. Isolated, poor, and a foreigner, a "nobody" as she described herself, she had zero social or political capital. In fact, she had *negative* social capital. In the immediate aftermath of the hurricane, a vicious tide of xenophobia swept through the nation as people scrambling for resources focused their fears and rage on Haitians, even those who were longtime residents or born in The Bahamas.

Altima's despondence was almost inevitably related to exhaustion and pragmatism, as opposed to not having an optimistic mindset or lacking agency. In her situation, asking for help *is* agency and self-efficacy, a way to exert some control over the future in difficult circumstances when status, power, resources, and relationships are frayed or nonexistent.

Albury's self-sufficiency and optimism, hopefulness, and determination were facilitated by his being embedded in a community, culture, and country. He enjoyed citizenship, political efficacy, a sense of belonging, access to connections and networks, and full-fledged knowledge of how to navigate his milieu to get back on his feet. He could almost certainly tap into the kind of social compassion, support, and collective mutual aid that buffer us as individuals from risks and threats and generate resilience as a communal asset.

Most of what we read about optimism strongly suggests that it's possible to work hard, shed pessimism, and be more positive. You can, according to *Men's Health*, for instance, undertake an "Optimism Training Plan" that promises to "Improve Your Outlook in Just 5 Days." Not only your outlook, but, with it, your moods and, eventually, your health, confidence, and longevity.[23]

Optimism may be a mindset that you can cultivate, but it's likelihood is also correlated to social resources, status, and wealth. A 2014 study revealed that among people who were asked to lift the same heavy object, those who felt they had lower levels of power and social status reported the object as feeling physically heavier.[24] The wealthier you are, the more likely you are to feel cheery, positive, and satisfied with your life.[25] You feel, quite literally, less weight and burden.

While having an optimistic mindset and being more resilient are both associated with better health, many researchers and scientists admit they don't know the degree to which good health and good health care encourage optimism instead of the other way round. Others are more certain of the trajectory and note that systems and status consistently inform a person's ability to "make the choice to embrace optimism."

So, while it's beneficial to notice and to try to reduce negative self-talk and feelings of helplessness, it's also critical to understand that circumstances are often out of our control entirely. Circumstances are *why* some of us struggle more than others with being positive and use pessimism and pragmatism to move forward.

Enhancing our capacity for resilience by learning to be optimistic shouldn't turn us *away* from appreciating the web of human relationships that support us throughout our lives and sustain us during crises. Ask yourself, if the people around you are struggling to survive and spiraling into poverty and sickness, but you are working, healthier, and wealthier, are you optimistic and resilient, or are you a hardy, cheerful, entitled asshole who has the resources to justify a way of life sustained through denial, exploitation, and injustice?

We all live within a system that implicates us in harm to others, but resilience takes thinking about those parts of life and of society that aren't going well and don't make us feel good. Interrogating ourselves, and the relationships we are part of, is essential to our learning to adapt in ways that don't hurt or exploit others.

Toxic Optimism

Being unrealistically optimistic and resisting uncomfortable and difficult truths doesn't cultivate resilience but instead can easily lead to self-destructive behaviors, shame, and despair.

Let's return for a moment to escalating suicide rates in the United States, particularly among white working-class Americans. Remember that a key operating mechanism in learned optimism is the perception of control. Believing that you have control over your future can help reduce the ill effects of stress. There are real consequences, however, to overemphasizing control, one of which is that feeling a lack of control leads to a greater likelihood of depression. A second is that it can lead to our attributing far more power to our choices and actions than is realistic, what's called illusory control. When the reality sets in that some aspects of life are legitimately out of our control, the result often heightens stress and disorientation.

Economists link these suicides to the hopelessness caused in large part by a psychological gap between the optimistic promise that hard work yields prosperity and status, and the reality that this is, for most families, not true. White men, the historical beneficiaries of our social and political entitlement systems, have, as their alarming rates of suicide show, particularly fallen down this rabbit hole as economic inequality has grown. A combination of cruel optimism and aggrieved entitlement propels these tragedies. Older African Americans, with different life experiences and expectations, are more resilient to vicissitudes.[26]

There are also ill effects for others. When you encourage a person to be optimistic instead of validating their suffering or hearing their needs, you risk actively degrading their ability to be resilient in healthy ways. Optimism that swamps reality isn't, for example, doing America's girls any favors.

In February of 2022, the Centers for Disease Control and Prevention reported "never-before-seen levels of hopelessness and suicidal thoughts among high school students in the U.S.," especially young girls. Nearly three in five teen girls (57 percent) surveyed reported being "persistently sad or hopeless." Almost a third, 30 percent, had seriously considered suicide, a rise of 60 percent since 2013. The report said that teen girls are living with "an overwhelming wave of violence and trauma."[27]

Parents and pundits alike speculated as to why girls, in particular, are feeling this much despair. Most analyses in media homed in on the harms of social media. Op-eds about the problem also frequently referenced climate trauma, school shootings, and general increases in violence. What most *did not do*, in spectacularly gaslighting fashion, was consider what girls experience *as girls* or explore how adult minimization of inequality, in the face of ample evidence, might be contributing to their distress.

Toxic positivity is baked into many relationships by cultural default, but girls and women especially are expected to maintain optimistic attitudes and "good feelings" for the sake of appearances, and of men. We expect girls, more than boys, to be cheerful, optimistic, and grateful, to forgive and forget in order to put the people around them at ease. Girls learn, through endless childhood interactions, that certain expressions of need are, among other things, *rude*,[28] a message that leads to emotional repression and self-harmfully displaced emotions.

Additionally, generalized reasons such as the spread of social media are no doubt contributors to the problem, but during the ten-year coming-of-age period covered by the study, American girls' identities and lives have been shaped by political and social backlash.

Online and off, girls experience and witness pervasive bullying—an anodyne word for often violent and soul-crushing misogyny, racism, homophobia, and more. This bullying operates at a scale that is more intense than was ever possible in earlier generations. Girls also have to contend with rising rates of surveillance and sexual violence. They've grown up watching highly politicized and public debates over what constitutes sexual harassment and what the legal expiration date on rape is, and listening to high-profile women credibly describe their assaults in ways that girls recognize from personal experience. Their access to birth control is threatened, and their rights to bodily autonomy and privacy have been taken away in entire swathes of the country.

In the meantime, they sit at dinner tables, on buses, in classrooms, with boys and men—their brothers, fathers, uncles, teachers—most of whom believe sexism is over and that feminism has gone "too far," and the boys they know frequently act in toxic ways and revere public figures who freely spout hateful gibberish.[29]

Girls are experiencing distress and skyrocketing rates of trauma for complex reasons, including that their emotional states and rates of suicide align with those of the adults in their communities. However, it is worth considering how gaslighting them and urging them to be optimistic, grateful for what they have, and gritty in the face of existential threats might be making matters worse.

Women in violent relationships are often similarly expected to think positively, put on a smiling face, and do the emotional work of helping others. For instance, a woman who reveals that her spouse is abusive and that she is considering leaving him might be encouraged by friends, family members, or religious leaders to be patient and reconsider in the belief that she can improve the situation. She might feel pessimistic about the future in a moment of crisis, but if only she can embrace a more positive attitude, she might be able to save her marriage. Optimism bias and positivity intensify abuse and exacerbate women's risks.

"Empathy, hope, acceptance and resilience," researchers of a 2020 meta-analysis of the relationship between positive psychology and domestic violence concluded, "are associated with refraining to leave abusive relationships; and forgiveness increases the likelihood of further transgressions."[30]

These gendered expectations of optimism, sacrifice, and forgiveness, often normalized in religious communities, are now fueling a right-wing push to bring a legal end to no-fault divorces, a legal reform that resulted in massive declines in rates of suicide among women, intimate-partner violence, and spousal homicide.[31]

Optimism Bias at Scale

Optimism bias has other names: personal fable, the illusion of invulnerability, and false hope syndrome.[32]

An influential study of people who were in or near the World Trade Center on September 11 looked at the relationship between optimism and self-enhancement—the kind of positivity that confirms identity and makes you feel good about yourself—and resilience. The researchers relied on self-reporting surveys to gather their findings, but they supplemented these by gathering information from subjects' friends and relatives. Self-enhancing subjects described themselves as adapting well to what happened on 9/11, but friends and family often disagreed with them, describing them as dishonest and increasingly socially maladjusted.[33] Subjects' positive outlooks and confidence didn't align with their actual behaviors, and their optimism taxed their relationships, making them less resilient overall.

Unchecked, positivity and self-enhancement lead people to see themselves as more compassionate, talented, and capable than they actually are. They also tend to believe they have more influence and control over outcomes than is actually the case.[34]

Donald Trump's tenure as president was bookended by two spectacular episodes of this effect at scale. Despite ample, verifiable evidence to the contrary, he began his presidency insisting that millions of people flocked to his inauguration. While he'd traded in self-enhancing narratives and lies for decades, this blatant disinformation from a sitting president should have raised red flags for anyone who wasn't already waving them. Instead, this was an optimistic, self-enhancing fantasy that millions were willing to indulge. His presidency ended with the Big Lie, his denial that Joe Biden had legitimately won the 2020 election. In between these bookends, Trump's optimism took its toll on the nation in other ways. Many Americans suffered in ways that could have been reduced or entirely avoided. In a 2021 congressional report, the beleaguered leadership of the Centers for Disease Control and Prevention described being bullied by White House staff, who threatened to fire them unless they depicted what was happening in line with "the more optimistic view of the pandemic espoused by Donald Trump."[35]

In many ways, the relationship between the American public and Donald Trump mirrors the well-studied dynamics of intimate abuse. Aided by a media rife with distorting false equivalences, minimizing language, and the optimism of American exceptionalism, Trump was an upbeat, gaslighting machine of false hope, self-enhancing blather, and menacing denialism and misinformation.[36]

Choosing Pessimism and Accepting Sadness

Time to reset: We know that positive thinking is a stress-buffering mechanism, and that resilient people use optimism, positive affect, and humor to achieve equilibrium and build strong social relationships. But resilience depends on knowing *when not to be optimistic*. Being pragmatically pessimistic is essential to adapting to adversity.

Psychotherapist and holocaust survivor Viktor Frankl, whose pessimism enabled him to remain hopeful even during the darkest of times, called this adaptability "tragic optimism."

No one says, "Maybe you should look on the dark side of things," but pessimism allows you to assess your situation, navigate obstacles, and strategize for the future in ways that optimism generally doesn't. Pessimistic thinkers are better at recognizing and assessing risks. Because they envision challenges ahead of time, they can pursue options that avoid threats. This defensive pessimism also helps people manage anxiety and expectations so that they are motivated to pursue goals.

Pessimism also often involves acceptance of sadness, which not only encourages us to be self-reflective but more compassionate. People who are sad are kinder toward and more generous with others, which helps forge relationships. Prolonged sadness is a problem deserving attention, but in specific sadness we gain insight and perspective.

So do others. When we urge people to be positive, grateful, and optimistic, it often results in their repressing their more negative imaginings, causing cognitive dissonance, shame, and even depression.[37] It also comes off as gaslighting and is alienating, both of which undermine care and adaptability.

In moments of dire crisis, repressing fear or sadness *is* essential to coping, but, as a life habit, repression is maladaptive. When you allow yourself and others to be pessimistic, to grieve or be sad, you build pivotal resilience tools for you and those around you. When you validate a person's pragmatic pessimism, you show that you are listening and care deeply about the person's well-being.

Resilient people use both optimism and pessimism strategically to gain the critical insights and information they need to adjust to change. Again, the key to using optimism to enhance resilience is in rejecting black-and-white, either/or thinking.

5

RESISTING THE LURE OF PRODUCTIVITY

> How are we going to reimagine work, so that it
> enhances our humanity?
>
> —Grace Lee Boggs

The summer of 2020 was staggeringly stressful. We were three months into the lockdown and trying to sort out how to manage virtually every aspect of life in new ways. During those early months of the pandemic, Breonna Taylor, George Floyd, and Ahmaud Arbery were murdered, spurring global protests in defense of Black lives. Like so many others, our family juggled health worries with protesting, self-isolating in rotations. Everyone was tired and on edge as uncertainty filled the air.

And yet, life went on. We studied, ate, saw socially distancing friends. During this period, I was negotiating both a new book and a new job, for a position made possible because of COVID. Moving for work wasn't an option, but now doing the job from home was. By June, I had a start date of July 6.

On the night of July 5, however, my brother called with the news that my father had died. He was at home, my mother nearby. My brothers and sisters were only minutes away, but I couldn't get home because of COVID restrictions on travel. It was profoundly sad to be away from my family during his illness, but if you had told me only months before that it would be impossible to find a way home if he was dying, I wouldn't have believed it.

Just six weeks prior, my father's last remaining sibling, his ninety-three-year-old brother, had passed away, which we never told him. They were two of our family's remaining elders, and the remaining two, my aunts, would also pass away within a year. Like millions of other families, ours couldn't come together to touch one another or share comforting memories and rituals. I didn't know then and couldn't imagine that it would be two years before I would see my immediate family.

The next day, I had to push back the start date for my job, which begged the question of how much time I could take from work to grieve the loss of my father. What was that time for, now that we couldn't mourn with one another? How were we meant to grieve in a dangerous world turned upside down? I was fortunate not to have had to consider these questions before.

For some people, being productive, working, and "keeping busy" is a way to cope with stress and loss, but for others it's a shattering burden. But, the *choice* of whether or not to work in times of family crisis is a privilege. There is no choice when you can't take time off because your family depends on your hourly wage to survive. If you can't take the time or travel relatively freely, which most people can't, your sadness and supportive connections are consequently constrained.

We have, as a society, ceded our lives to corporate interests, ceded ourselves and our loved ones, regardless of circumstances, to productivity and profitability. As always, the internet is a mirror of our mores. A quick online search reveals a plethora of sources that promise to help you "work your best while grieving" and learn, while grieving, how to "increase your productivity and happiness." Resilience today is frequently defined in this trajectory from grief to happiness with productivity snuggly nestled in the middle.

As I went to sleep on the night of the sixth, I was mourning but also had swirling worries. I again found that I was struggling to distinguish between distress over my father's passing and the grief I felt about climate change. Earlier that day, I'd read about yet another troubling though not unexpected discovery: over the prior five years, the sea ice in the Weddell Sea, a large swath of Antarctica, had decreased by a million square kilometers—roughly, as they put it, twice the size of Spain.

In my late-night anxiety, I lay there thinking about my father, how I might get home to be with my family, the demands of a new job, and fears over COVID, growing political unrest, and rapidly rising seas.

As I fought to sleep, I found myself cursing the cult of Ernest Shackleton.

The Shackleton Effect

If resilience were a person, the dashing and charismatic Anglo-Irish Antarctic explorer Sir Ernest Shackleton would be your man. You may not be enthralled by early twentieth-century nation-building polar quests, but Shackleton's spirit has surely left an indelible mark on your thoughts about resilience and productivity. He is an enduring emblem of grit, optimism, and determination.

On a fateful December 5, 1914, as World War I's Battle of Ypres raged, Shackleton and his handpicked crew of twenty-seven largely inexperienced men set out for the South Pole aboard the appropriately named HMS *Endurance*. With a stowaway, sixty-nine dogs, and a brave cat named Mrs. Chippy on board, they aimed to claim the uncharted continent for Great Britain.

For weeks, the *Endurance* braved treacherous seas and thick ice sheets until, on January 18, 1915, it was locked in place by the Weddell Sea's massive ice floes. Trapped, Shackleton and his crew constructed a settlement around the ship. They built igloo-like shelters nicknamed dogloos for their dogs and accessed the ship when needed.

For more than ten grueling months they battled the drifting ice that was slowly crushing their vessel. Despite the harshness of their situation, Shackleton "did not rage at all, or show outwardly the slightest sign of disappointment," wrote Alexander Macklin, the ship's surgeon. "He told us simply and calmly that we must winter in the Pack; explained its dangers and possibilities; never lost his optimism and prepared for winter."[1]

Ghostly black-and-white photographs taken by the expedition's photographer, Frank Hurley, tell a striking story of intrepid survival. He showed men going about work routines, cooking, cleaning, and playing soccer. They often smile and laugh, finding fellowship and solace in effort and humor. The crew survived the winter through hard work, trust, and sacrifice—attributed to Shackleton's leadership.

Finally, in April 1916, the ice relented sufficiently for them to set off in three lifeboats for the uninhabited Elephant Island. There they created a new base while Shackleton and a smaller party of five men made the more-than-eight-hundred-mile trip back to a whaling station on South Georgia Island to find a rescue ship. They made it to the island, but disaster struck once again. For twenty-four hours, they rowed against hurricane-force winds to make landfall, realizing, once they did, that they were on the opposite side of the island from the settlement they were aiming for. Shackleton and two of his crew then traveled by foot over mountains and glaciers, eventually making it to the station.

Shackleton still needed to save his crew, which he did by convincing the country of Chile to provide a ship. On August 30, 1916, after repeated failed attempts to land on Elephant Island, he succeeded. Within the hour of the ship's arrival, every crew member was heading home, twenty months after their doomed expedition began. The journey is considered one of history's most epic feats of survival.[2]

In the hundred-plus years since, Shackleton has repeatedly been evoked as a model par excellence of resilience, leadership, and survival in the face of risk and obstacles. He's admired for his never giving up, optimism, sense of humor, and faith. Mentally and physically fit,

Shackleton demonstrated a whole constellation of resilient habits of mind: grit, optimism, a sense of control, and belief that a good outcome would result.

This one man is such a shining example of resilience as we appreciate it today that social scientists explicitly included dimensions of his personality—faith and optimism—in the CD-RISC. Shackleton also demonstrated hardiness, commitment, self-discipline, and sangfroid control, characteristics that now define the resilience of workplace success.[3]

Resilience as Workplace Stress Management

Shackleton's resilience—relentlessness, productivity, and performance in the harshest and most extreme circumstances—is featured in materials ranging from recreational sports pamphlets and Outward Bound guides to military training materials and congressional reports. Resilience training and leadership programs, now rote in schools, at retreats, in locker rooms, and at conferences across the globe, routinely use his example as inspiration for how to lead, persevere, and succeed despite obstacles.

Military leaders, professors, coaches, and inspirational speakers admire Shackleton for many reasons, but what exactly makes him so attractive to people and corporations? Overall, it would seem to be his capacity to withstand immense stress and get the job done.

In 1979, researcher Suzanne C. Kobasa wanted to understand why, in the face of stress, some workers persisted and were successful in their jobs while others dropped out of the workforce. Her groundbreaking study of business managers at the Illinois Bell Company identified a cohort of men who progressed up the corporate ladder and remained healthy even as their peers quit. She described their stick-to-itiveness as hardiness, a psychological trait characterized by a sense of control in the face of stress and hardship.

Kobasa and her partner, researcher Salvatore Maddi, initially identified what they called the "BIG 3" personality traits that make a person hardy: commitment (rather than alienation from an undertaking), control (a counter to feeling powerless), and a challenge orientation (instead of a threat orientation). Confidence was later added to the list, becoming the fourth C.

People who aren't hardy, explained Kobasa, were more likely to feel powerless and "were nihilistic, and low in motivation for achievement." The 4 C's, she concluded, help a person positively adapt to stress and, as Maddi asserted, even thrive. The researchers went on to develop techniques to better manage workplace stress.

The four C's match up well with optimism as a resilient asset. Hardy individuals feel they have control over what happens to them, perceive obstacles as challenges to be overcome, and are highly committed. These characteristics mean they engage in self-advocacy, good health practices, and develop good social support. This set of attributes is now considered so vital to personal resilience that *hardiness*, like *strength*, is used interchangeably with *resilience*.

Do you believe resilience should be so seamlessly entangled with being a good worker? In its earliest and defining stages, hardiness was based on the traits of a particular category of people who shared gender, ethnicity, class, and sexual preferences: married, heterosexual, white men working in white-collar jobs. These men, the standard for an ideal worker, could dedicate themselves to work continuously, with little or no responsibility for housework or childcare. They were married to women who were almost all stay-at-home wives, responsible for managing stresses related to life outside their husbands' wage earning. Wives were, in effect, an unnamed hardiness resource.

Over the next few decades, studies in hardiness expanded to include more diverse pools of people in different contexts: patients dealing with chronic or terminal illness, nurses struggling with burnout, and teachers grappling with stress. However, while the concept developed, the baseline foundations of hardiness as a cognitive and psychological advantage that enabled a person to effectively weather stress to persist at work remained intact. Resilience as a key component of productivity becomes confused, in this way, with productivity being a necessary component of resilience.

You may feel that resilience is being engaged, motivated, and that achieving goals—being productive—brings a sense of personal satisfaction and even happiness. But is that about productivity or validation, belonging, and approval? Is it about self-efficacy or capitalist subjectivity? What are the costs? Hardiness tightly weaves together workplace productivity, resilience, social approval, and self-worth.

The pressure we feel in times of stress and crisis is not only a matter of being more resilient by better managing our time, but of returning to work as quickly as possible without interruption.

Productivity as a value and a goal is embedded in the heart of the type of resilience standard that Shackleton and hardy men represent. Americans work more hours than people in similar countries. We have less leisure, vacation, and parental and family-leave time. We have, for instance, no legal bereavement leave, but rely on individuals and corporate interests to do what they must or see fit. This, too, is an approach overly steeped in individualism since it erases the reality and benefits of collective need, rest, and grief. Even if an individual is coping well with grief and is hardy and capable of working, that person might be a vital support to others in need. The stress that this resilience recognizes is individual stress that might intrude on work. It's not relational outside the bounds of workplace efficiency, profitability, and success.

As a concept, hardiness was a way to shift how "stress," specifically the workplace stress men experienced, was perceived toward late in the twentieth century. In the years before Kobasa's research, public awareness of the negative impacts of stress was high as media delved into the reality that stress made the overworked "type A man" of the sixties heart-attack-prone. Those men shared a great deal with the hardy worker of the 1980s, but instead of being sick, a hardy man had a better relationship to stress: he was professionally committed, productive, and healthy.[4]

Today's corporate resilience programs are supposed to achieve similar goals, teaching us to "optimize ourselves" as a form of resilience that meets performance and profitability needs while not necessarily making us sick. Burnout and stress are at record levels across work sectors today, however. This "productivity as resilience" model even frames exhaustion and burnout in the interest of more productivity: if you are tired and discouraged, if you experience burnout and depression, how can you be as productive as you should, need to, and maybe want to be? The ideals of hardiness make for a perverse grind-culture resilience, another way that capitalism makes its way through our bodies, self-conceptions, and relationships.

Confidence Men

Feeling in control and having confidence in yourself, often regardless of ability, drives productivity resilience. Like a resilience of strength and self-sufficiency, this resilience is disproportionately grounded in narrow-banded masculinity and related roles.

Lessons in how to be a provider and protector, a good soldier and potential leader, start early and make their way into our imaginations with wry humor and warm paternalism. Like the 2021 *New York Times* article about a boy hiking with his father, resilience parables socialize us to think in these terms. Another example appeared in a 2015 *Time* magazine interview with renowned resilience expert Dr. Dennis Charney, dean of the Icahn School of Medicine at Mount Sinai in New York City and coauthor of *Resilience: The Science of Mastering Life's Greatest Challenges*.

Charney explained that his efforts to teach his five children how to persevere meant each of them had "hated him at some point or another," particularly after "'semidangerous' adventure trips." He regaled the reporter with his thirteen-year-old daughter's response to having to tromp through terrible conditions in the wilds. "When she said she despised me, it came, like, from her soul," said Charney gleefully. On another expedition in Patagonia, his son told him that he "never wanted to speak to him again." Charney is both an expert in, and, after being shot by a disgruntled employee in 2016, a subject of the topic of resilience.[5]

It's hard not to see the full array of Shackletonesque ideals built into neat and theoretically value-neutral lessons such as these. Both the 2015 and 2021 stories feature personal-adventure narratives involving risk and exploration. "Leaders" guide less experienced and knowledgeable "crews," who must trust their leaders' judgment and authority and endure a grueling gauntlet. The crews learn to subjugate their bodies, ignore their emotions, and dominate their environments. There are painful obstacles, hard goals, productive outcomes, and eventual triumph. The resulting resilience comes from withstanding the stress and committing to the task, successfully achieved through self-discipline, determination, and persistence.

Stories such as these may say one thing—resilience, character development, grit—but they do another, namely, transmit information about what our society values: the mental toughness, self-sufficiency, mastery, control, and hard work it takes to succeed and win. The list doesn't stop there. These tales also signal patriarchal governance, the superiority of masculine rationality, and the demonstration of physical strength, even when girls are involved. Both stories, for example, implicitly center the importance of allegiance to a father figure's authority and the cultural inheritance that it conveys.

Have you ever read a story published by a national media outlet that features a mother forcing unwilling children through brush, mud, and rain to instill character in them and teach resilience? Or, better yet, a story whose resilience lessons center around teaching a child how to make a delicate pastry, a binary gender alternative?

I've never seen one. Instead, like Charney's daughter, women are expected to meet established standards, not create or demand new ones. More than forty years after Kobasa's influential study, most American corporate and public leadership is composed of straight, white, heterosexual men, disproportionately married to stay-at-home wives. Is this because they are more capable and committed? Because they are more resilient to stress? More "naturally" able to work hard and lead? Women continue to make great strides in income and economic parity, and the American workforce grows more diverse every day, but workplace systems in the United States remain woefully structured around the ideal worker of the 1950s.

Elastigirls to the Rescue

So what about girls and women? Since control, physical demands, and sacrificial dedication to work are associated with a virtuous and productive manly resilience—even when women promote and perform them—what is our virtue?

It's elasticity and a limitless capacity to absorb other people's stress: being stretched as thinly as possible is the kind of resilience expected of women. As sociologist Sarah Bracke has wryly pointed out, this expectation is perhaps best illustrated by insightful caricature.[6] In 2004, three years after 9/11, the popular animated children's movie *The Incredibles*, about an American superhero family with world-saving skills, was released. Mr. Incredible's superhuman strength and powerful protective bulk come with overconfidence, military bluster, and the drive to never say die. Mrs. Incredible, on the other hand, is called Elastigirl and is known for mind-boggling feats of being overextended in every direction. She has no physical limits.

A woman who gave up her professional ambitions to raise exceptional children, she struggles through the tensions of returning to a job she excels at while still being a happy homemaker. Her cheery disposition and infinitely malleable body go hand in hand.

Her tensile powers and shock-absorber capacities never cease to amaze those around her. Unlike her husband, she doesn't have a best friend that helps in a pinch, but rather, when she acts, she's almost always alone. Her one physical weakness, her Achilles' heel, is that she might get cold, an interesting subliminal play on having to be eternally hot.

The idea of a woman who effortlessly stretches and shouldn't be frigid is familiar to most American women. This magical being is supposed to do whatever is necessary and flexibly meet the changing needs of the people around her. She's the working assumption—the resilience resource—behind the ideal male worker.

That may have worked for a subset of the population in the mid-twentieth century, but even for that subset, it's a system that has been falling apart for decades. It is incompatible with the fact that women are primary wage earners in our families, making up more than 40 percent of breadwinners.

American women today are expected to prioritize work, often juggling multiple jobs and paying off student loans, while maintaining responsibility for domestic life, children, aging parents, and an extended community. They do this while working around wage and wealth gaps, shrinking social safety nets, escalating sexual and domestic violence, and eroding citizenship rights.

For these reasons and more, while the pandemic was a stress factory for everyone, it was especially burdensome for girls and women, especially those who were struggling before COVID. By late 2021, media covered #MomScream events featuring hundreds of women gathering to yell in collective rage and helplessness. While the screaming may have provided a fleeting relief and a sense of community, it did nothing to change their circumstances—a breathtaking lack of care and social, political, and institutional support. By January 2022, nearly 2 million fewer American women were in the paid workforce, while all male COVID-related job losses had been regained.

Fun times.

Is What Counts as Work Changing?

If standards for adapting to stress and change are tied to productivity and performance of work, the question of what *counts as work* is important in thinking about resilience.

Caring for others, for instance, is low status and financially impoverishing. It isn't even considered "real work" and certainly not widely understood as an infrastructure need. Gross national product, for example, continues to exclude intimate, domestic, healthcare, and other forms of care work. If you cook for your family, breastfeed, do laundry, go food shopping, or tend to your ailing parents, you are officially *unproductive*.

These roles continue to fall to women in huge disproportion. While men are taking on more unpaid work at home, they are still far less likely to be default parents or primary caretakers in their own families and routinely overestimate the time they dedicate to this role. Throughout the lockdown period of the pandemic, for example, almost 50 percent of fathers felt that they spent more time attending to their children's homeschooling needs than their spouses did. Only 3 percent of women agreed, with 80 percent saying they did more work.[7]

Statistics such as these can seem mystifying because everyone feels stress, and the sense is that gender equality movements have closed gaps such as these. Additionally, we often assume younger generations are more progressive, but that is not automatically the case. Since the mid-nineties, gender-egalitarian attitudes, particularly among boys and men, have been dropping, not rising. Among millennials, for example, support for more egalitarian domestic arrangements is lower than two decades before in the same age cohort. Among Gen Y and Z, a gendered liberal/conservative split between women and men is widening, not shrinking. At best, most young men seem conflicted about the shifting balances of power that come with equality and democracy.

Women as Resilience and Productivity Resources

Productivity resilience is complicated for women in ways that metrics based on how most men move through the world don't reflect. It's still the case that women's roles, like those of subaltern people in a society more diffusely, make them collective resilience resources to the people around them. The work we do is mainly designed to reduce stress for others around us.

How women learn to be resilient to this reality hasn't been the concern of many researchers over the past century. Coping with the stresses of nurturing roles isn't built into our standards, nor does it resonate with the resilience values reflected in visions of productivity, exploration, domination, and glory. In fact, we're more likely to encounter humiliation and contempt for our work and ways of working.

One of the most searing memories I will always have of how gendered expectations distort our lives occurred in late 2021. The prior year had made unparalleled demands on teachers, health-care workers, mothers, and people doing body and care-intensive work. The nation faced crisis levels of burnout and shortages in education and health care. Like mothers, teachers, doctors, and nurses were at saturation point.

That December, a South Dakota mortgage company thought they would help their local schools by sponsoring a "Dash for Cash" fundraiser during halftime at a local hockey game. When the buzzer rang, ten people, almost all women, ran out onto the ice and frantically scrambled on their hands and knees, competing to grab $5,000 worth of one-dollar bills. The sponsoring organization thought the event would be "a positive and fun experience for teachers" and a terrific way to fund school supplies.[8]

In the months following this event, teachers' unions across the country fought for more money, better safety measures, and resources for teachers as they taught through the impacts of COVID, ongoing threats of mass shootings, and worsening student engagement and mental health. Their demands were often met with contempt.

"Teachers' unions," said Greg Gutfeld, cohost of a nationally popular cable TV news show, "have managed to take one of the most beloved occupations and redefine it as selfish and lazy."[9] He was put out by the suggestion that teachers want more, need more, and deserve more of everything: time, money, respect, safety, and care. All in chronic short supply.

"I don't want to be resilient," explained teacher and education policy expert Dr. Tracy Edwards in March 2022. She was attending a seminar on self-care techniques and increasing teacher resilience. "I want school systems designed with humans in mind that don't demand my resilience. I want educators to experience community care, support, and compensation."[10]

Demeaning cash grabs for people's casual entertainment don't count.

Every one of us requires care at different points in our lives, and caring is an exhausting business. Securing and preparing food, ensuring it's safe to eat, being emotionally supportive, being considerate of other people's complex needs, transporting people, being patient, and finding ways to laugh, be affectionate, have desire, cry, hug, and hold all take immense time and effort. So does navigating the information, bureaucracies, institutions, laws, and rules that regulate our bodies, relationships, and health.

Too many men with influence and power are willfully ignorant about what it takes to keep people alive and well, from the cradle to the grave. They know so little about the intense attention, emotional labor, mental load, and physical demands required to tend to other people, to bodies and their sustenance and well-being.

Because men buffered from intense care demands still make up the vast majority of our political leaders, senior corporate executives, and economists, care demands are chronically undervalued and misunderstood in resilience agendas. Instead, by unspoken and exploitative consensus, mothers, nurses, teachers, health aides, and other people who quietly do the messy work of caring are supposed to do it selflessly, ideally without complaining. At least half of the country genuinely believes women should sacrifice themselves to this crackpot scheme. Worse, as countless internet armchair experts are keen on perpetually and ridiculously pointing out, if women pay a personal price, so be it, because *men go to war.*

A powerful undercurrent of resilience today is a cultural hostility that maintains that if clamorous women want equality, then we must earn it on preexisting terms and by the standards men have always been held to. Women should sacrifice and be dedicated and ruthless if they intend to compete with men for jobs, money, and influence. Instead of protesting stubborn norms and resisting systemic inequalities, women—in the conventional mold of hardy and resilient men—are supposed to work hard, all the time, and be optimistic, gritty, and grateful.

In the face of obstacles, successful women and good girls know how to take control and turn challenges into opportunities; transform themselves and take a seat at the table. Resilience here is a therapeutic and decidedly capitalist self-management, which would include demonstrating the strength to recognize, for example, sexism as a problem, but to persevere, nonetheless.[11] The Lean In, Confidence Code, and Girl Boss movements of the past ten years aren't feminist as much as they are expressions of resilience along these lines. Their claims aren't entirely wrong, but they also do little to alter the circumstances causing concern and crisis for so many. They focus on individuals and their choices, not on structural change for the greater good.

Individualistic performance as resilience exacerbates class and racial divides between women because the most privileged can execute as expected while the least are pushed further into crisis, poverty, and chronic exhaustion. For low-income people who lack money, status, or cultural capital, being hardy and productive necessarily takes a second seat to the exhaustion of surviving. For those in more privileged circumstances, overcoming obstacles as an individual can turn into a badge of honor, further reducing any reward for or incentive to fight for structural change. So far, few corporate resilience investments have focused on structural changes that would reverse the trajectory of these realities.

In effect, we are supposed to lean in to burnout.

Resilience and Future-Proofing the Workforce

During the past fifteen years, "building a resilient workforce" has become the self-described core tenet of a $90 billion corporate training industry in the United States.[12] Having a resilient staff—one primed with lessons about personal hardiness, optimism, and growth—is considered a strategic advantage, the key to profitably, even an existential necessity. In situations of chronic pressure or episodic crisis, striving for "normal" as a resilience goal often translates into being as productive as possible. In this context, it's increasingly common to hear that stress can be good for you. And when we do, we can sign up for resilience training designed to improve our wellness and productivity both.

Already prevalent before COVID, corporate resilience training became the go-to response to the health sector's escalating rates of resignation, exhaustion, and suicides. In 2022, one in ten physicians reported considering or attempting suicide. One-third of nurses planned to leave their jobs and the nursing field entirely due to high-stress conditions, burnout, and moral injury.[13] That year, one of New York's largest medical facilities, Mount Sinai Health System (MSHS), launched a Stress, Resilience and Personal Growth center to mitigate the impacts of COVID-19 and "future-proof" their workforce.[14]

Other industries are taking similar approaches, launching programs in which employees can learn to improve their self-image, develop more positive attitudes, manage their impulses and emotions, and set personal and professional goals.[15]

Do you know what future-proofs a workforce? Food. Sleep. Making sure people are paid enough to lead safe, healthy lives.

In March 2020, Kroger, the largest mass-market food-store chain in the United States, spent more than $1.5 billion on a Pandemic Preparedness and Business Resilience Plan to "protect front-line associates while staying open to serve customers and communities."[16] They provided protective equipment, awarded workers with appreciation pay, store credits, fuel points, and other incentives to do high-risk jobs that might expose them and their families to the deadly virus.

In 2021, the company topped $132 billion in sales and more than $2.5 billion in net income as workers' hourly wages declined 3–5 percent in value. The year before, 14 percent of Kroger's workforce reported homelessness, and their CEO made $22 million.[17] In 2023, the company's annual report asserted their dedication to "collectively create more resilient, equitable and sustainable systems."[18] This was just after a survey of thirty-seven thousand Kroger workers found that more than three-quarters had uncertain access to food.[19] Workers in the sector also make up a disproportionate number of the 20 percent of Americans who can't afford to pay their energy and heating bills.[20]

Privatized resilience is personally expensive. Even the hardiest and most flexible individual cannot overcome the limitations of stacked economies, dysfunctional workplaces, and cruel systems. That's always been truest for low-wage service and health-care workers. Today, however, workers at the higher end of wage and status scales are feeling the strain of a system that works for fewer and fewer people.

One of the unexpected consequences of COVID lockdowns was that they *alleviated* workplace and economic stresses. Having to work from home highlighted the many ways that workplace norms are out of sync with contemporary life, social equality, family care, and personal health. The unplanned hiatus that many experienced has been short-lived, however. By mid-2022, business leaders, government offices, and economists began calling for workers to return full-time to in-office schedules, a change that primarily cisgendered white men pushed for and that, surreally, once again, ignored care needs and the impacts of hostile environments on workers.

Nonwhite workers uniformly, disproportionately opt for hybrid or entirely remote work arrangements.[21] Twenty-one percent of white knowledge workers wanted to return to work full-time, only 3 percent of Black knowledge workers did. For Black women the stresses of returning to work were most acute. Overall, women were 50 percent more likely to want to work from home, and not only because it gave them more flexibility.[22] It is still the case that women are frequently forced out of their professions not because they don't want to work, but because the pressures brought to bear by the terms of their working are so depleting.

Who incurs the costs of a resilience agenda that refuses to acknowledge these problems? Workers can certainly work hard to personally develop resilience habits, but these habits will never suffice in a context of corporate and political austerity and a "return" to "best business practices" based on an idealized Golden Age of Ideal Male Workers. If companies really cared about resilience, then hundreds of millions of dollars would be spent to support care-based corporate and political policies such as funding for community centers for the elderly and people with disabilities, childcare programs, and paid family and medical leave.

It's not by chance that women and low-wage workers are at the forefront of movements rejecting unfair working practices and corporate resilience cultures. The past decade has been tumultuous for everyone, whether you consider social, economic, technological, or political life. During that period, women—even in that group's enormous diversity—reported skyrocketing levels of stress and, an ongoing trend, increasing levels of unhappiness, sadness, and anger.[23]

Needing ways to manage health, time, and financial demands is leading people to push back against obdurate, uncompromising powers, sad girl culture, "quiet quitting," "girl dinner," and "lazy girl jobs." These resistance techniques don't necessarily or automatically name capitalism as the problem. They often even name capitalism, but a softer, more humane version. At their core, though, is awareness of a paradox: that in a capitalist order women are an externality, more "productive" when they don't have to be paid. We may think of capitalism as the cause of our escalating Crisis of Care but, really, it is *itself* the Crisis of Care.

Pushback isn't only superficial fodder for viral content. In 2021, widespread labor strikes emerged across the country, challenging unfair labor practices and brutalizing workplace conditions. Popular approval for these actions is the highest it's been since 1965.[24] A resurging labor movement, made up of a more diverse workforce and reflecting its changing needs, reflects popular discontent. In August of 2023, several of the nation's largest labor unions announced they were backing the Care Can't Wait campaign, which planned to spend $50 million in anticipation of the 2024 election cycle to demand that policymakers prioritize care provisions that were forced out of President Joe Biden's Build Back Better program. The plan includes provisions for universal childcare, medical leave, paid family leave, and billions dedicated to supporting child and elder care.[25] Among the most prominent of the unions backing the policy initiative is the American Federation of Teachers, 75 percent of whom are women, led by Randi Weingarten.

When former CIA director and secretary of state Mike Pompeo called Weingarten "the most dangerous person in the world," what he really meant was "the most dangerous person in *my* world."[26] There are others worth fighting for.

Resilience and Nurturing Intelligence

Productivity resilience exacts personal costs, but it also ignores the interpersonal and collective essence of resilience and sidelines the role of nurturing intelligence. Shackleton's legend, so steeped in his individual attributes and glorification, in fact, illustrates the strength of both.

An out-of-scale fixation on Shackleton's qualities and behaviors drowns out the critical role of almost everyone else who survived the disaster. Despite hardship and friction, his men suffered and survived as a team. The ethereal quality of Hurley's photographs camouflages the grievous mental and physical hardships that the crew of the *Endurance* experienced. They remained productive to survive, sacrifice, and maintain discipline, but the precarity of their camp required them to constantly move and rebuild it as ice advanced. The men were perpetually sick and wet, living in freezing temperatures and blinding gale-force winds. Wracked by exhaustion, dysentery, and seasickness and continuously facing starvation, they eventually ate their beloved dogs. The youngest crew member, a twenty-three-year-old, had toes amputated in a brutal and primitive surgery.

Shackleton organized his men into teams that improved their chances of success because he had emotional intelligence. He used humor, feelings, intimacy, and genuinely caring for his charges to encourage esprit de corps and cultivate adaptability as the emergent quality of the group.

Perhaps the greatest irony of Shackleton as the twentieth-century face of masculine leadership and resilience is that so many of his most effective attributes were so spectacularly feminine. Despite his conventionally handsome mien and physical bulk, Shackleton was a skilled *nurturer*, a word we rarely use in tandem with *resilience* and *strength*. Despite his sometimes-harsh governance, he built strong social trust and community bonds. He was a committed and caring authority figure who sussed out emotional needs and provided stability and structure that offset chaos and anxiety. His understanding of personalities enabled him to arrange teams to reduce friction, dissent, and possible violence. He could, for instance, afford to be optimistic because he effectively outsourced negative thinking to his notoriously pessimistic first officer. Shackleton was highly skilled in managing people living in intimate settings, creating systems of mutual care and respect, perhaps due to having eight younger sisters and a brother.

Even prior to this voyage, he consistently used his relationships and connections to achieve his goals. He could stage his expedition because his independently wealthy wife, Emily Mary Dorman, used her money and connections to fund his ambitions. She also cared for their family during his many uncertain and prolonged absences. Together, they convinced merchant-class businessmen with social desires to donate enormous sums to his enterprise. He also had relationships with other wealthier and more prominent women who were enlisted to support his ambitions.

Shackleton's legendary good humor also gives us insight into the social nature of his resilience. Using humor is about relating to other people, showing you know what they are like and care about what engages them. It signals intelligence and generates trust. Funny people, especially amusing men, are more attractive to the people around them. They are also more influential, affecting people's decision-making and opinions, than people who don't use humor.[27]

All in all, Shackleton's resilience looks very much like what, today, is consistently identified with women's more effective leadership qualities:

- Interpersonal skills that inspire the people that work for them
- Habits that motivate creativity and problem-solving
- A propensity to develop collaborative teams
- Actively promoting a culture of openness to learning

Researchers know that skills such as these lead to women leaders being more trusted and effective in crises.[28]

Like these leaders, Shackleton trusted his lieutenants, was decisive, and valued a diversity of experience, skills, and ways of thinking.

Instead of our learning about his more nurturing qualities and characteristics, however, we are left with one more tale of Great Man Glory.

Shackleton could just as easily be a go-to exemplar for exceptional dumb luck and narcissistic folly, considering that his risk-taking constantly endangered his life and the lives of the people around him. In his own times, this much-admired avatar of resilience and leadership was commonly depicted as a fame-obsessed, deluded, albeit charismatic, failure, who was remarkably skilled at media manipulation.

His oversize sense of control and stubborn denial of circumstances may have contributed to his saving his crew, but first he led that crew into crisis after crisis, as he ignored warnings at every stage of his undertaking. Shackleton's poor budgeting and planning, questionable hires, and scattershot equipping all led to dangerous failures. More experienced people repeatedly advised him to delay his expedition to avoid catastrophe, but he grittily proceeded. In 1921, Shackleton ignored his doctor's warnings and his wife's concerns about a known heart condition to return to Antarctica, where he died, a year later, of a heart attack on the island of South Georgia at the age of forty-seven.[29]

Given that he never reached the South Pole, consistently endangered the lives of his crews, left his children fatherless and his wife with, in today's dollars, more than $1.5 million in debt, and risked death repeatedly, his story is more a testament to pernicious individualism, delusional fantasy, and the enduring ability of a certain kind of white man to fail upward.

It's notable that throughout the twentieth century, popular lionizations of Shackleton—in film, news, or educational systems—have spiked during periods when traditional masculinity and white supremacy were being challenged by shifting migration patterns, women's political gains, labor disruptions, or terroristic threats.[30] As I type, a Shackleton biopic starring British actor Tom Hardy is slated for upcoming release.[31]

New Models and Metrics

In the fall of 2023, the *Washington Post* published an extensive story about how AI photo generators see, and so represent, the world we live in. Along with search prompts such as "Toys in Iraq" and "Attractive People," journalists asked AI generators to share images of "a productive person" alongside those of "a person at social services." The ten images provided for "productive" were all white men, most in suits, sitting at desks. Those representing "social services" were all people of color, 80 percent of whom were haggard-looking women.[32]

Do you associate the idea of rest and restoration with resilience? Not "rest so you can be more productive later" but rest for its own delicious sake?

Because we all need rest and sleep, it would be easy to believe everyone struggles equally with disruptions and deprivation. Like leisure and health, sleep—which is easy to think of in individual and universal terms—is also a collective and political issue related to the ability to adapt positively to hardship. While 31 percent of white adults report sleeping less than seven hours a night, more than 43 percent of Black adults do the same.[33] For parents with multiple children, there are also substantive gender gaps in duration and quality of sleep.[34]

"This culture," explains Tricia Hersey, the founder of the Nap Ministry, "doesn't allow us a moment to grieve collectively, to have space, to just be, to have leisure, to really be a human being."[35] Sleep and dreaming aren't luxuries. They heal us, enable us to process information, solve problems, engage in exploration. They enrich our bodies and waking hours, restoring our cognition, memory, emotional balance, and health. Instead of building a society and an economy that appreciates all of this, we have done the opposite and turned sleep into an advantage for those who can afford it. It's a nifty trick, actually, turning resting and sleeping into "doing nothing" and "wasting time," or, conversely, into paths to greater productivity. We learn to feel guilty or inefficient if we rest, as though we aren't engaging in activities that will lead us to grow—into wealthier people, more productive workers, more capable parents. In any case, "normal" today means accepting that rest, restoration, and sleep have to be earned and so are a function of wealth, and—in the renunciation of "laziness"—morality.

In 2013, Hersey, now a theologian with a public-health degree, was in seminary at Emory University, raising a young child and working two jobs. She found herself falling asleep in libraries, on sofas, and on park benches. Eventually, she realized that time that she "should" have spent being productive—working, studying, parenting—was better spent on quiet, peaceful, bodily restorative sleep. Rest, she insists, is necessary in an environment of nonstop work and growth that deprives us of quiet repair. In explaining why, she reveals how white supremacy, Black-enslavement plantation economics, and perpetual labor are connected and endure. She started a movement that urges people to resist productivity culture.[36]

Resting is a necessary individual response to a collective crisis that we culturally resist acknowledging.[37]

We can redefine "productive," "work," and "normal," as a matter of policy and economics, social norms, and desires. Continuing to tout productivity as an inherent moral good while ignoring the life-reproducing labor that makes work possible is damaging to all of us and, ultimately, not only depleting but delusional.

Resilience isn't resilience if its parameters are profit and productivity. It's just a form of adaptation calibrated to sustain exploitive power. Real adaptation takes envisioning new worlds—systems, relationships, values, and new normals. It requires us to create alternative approaches to care, to reconsider time, to accept our needy bodies, and to cultivate healthy shared spaces. We can reject approaches to resilience that demand we discipline ourselves with urgency and without demands.

We need new metrics and models. We haven't, for example,

standardized resilience norms around the beliefs, experiences, objectives, and personalities of radical anticolonialist feminists proposing alternatives to the twenty-four-hour workday and exploitative heteropatriarchal systems. Our culture currently doesn't, with rare exceptions, make blockbuster movies about Black women heroically managing multigenerational community survival or Indigenous leaders defending lands and natural resources against powerful multinational corporations. We have to create new standards that are consciously developed to create compassionate societies, instead of predatory ones.

Movements such as Hersey's, for instance, push back against harsh and distorting status quo norms in unexpected ways. What would our resilience ideals look like if we broadened our examples and lauded alternative approaches such as hers? What would resilience resemble today if the fifty-year standard-setting sample pool for studies was primarily made up of teachers, nurses, single working mothers, or queer couples managing two jobs, school debt, children, and caring for aging parents? What would the standards be if resilience was defined by trans people living in hostile states and by people with disabilities adapting in a culture that regularly puts them in danger? How would the four C's of "hardiness" change?

They might look like community thriving and political compassion. Instead of control we might center care; instead of an internal confidence, bridge-building creativity. They might include rest and pleasure and be designed around meeting our needs as people instead of denying them in favor of using people as fungible, disposable, profit-generating machines. Instead of wondering how we can help restore our productivity after a shock or a loss, we can ask instead, how can we lead value-sensitive lives?

As it is, however, we'd rather ensure that we are our own worst enemies.

6

THE PARADOXES OF SOLDIERING ON

An abnormal reaction to an abnormal situation is normal behavior.

—Viktor Frankl

Naomi Osaka was twenty-three when, in July of 2021, she refused to attend a press conference and withdrew from the French Open. She was the world's second-highest-rated woman tennis player.

"The truth is I have suffered long bouts of depression since the U.S. Open in 2018, and I have had a really hard time coping with that," Osaka wrote in a social media post. "Anyone that knows me knows I am introverted, and anyone that has seen me at tournaments will notice that I'm often wearing headphones as that helps dull my social anxiety. Though the tennis press has always been kind to me . . . I am not a natural public speaker and get huge waves of anxiety before I speak to the world's media."

After she withdrew, officials rebuked her and fined her $15,000 for not attending the mandatory press conference. While this decision was later revoked, many pundits and opinion writers continued to point out that since Osaka's fame and success were due to public attention, she owed it to her fans, future potential athletes, and the media to speak to them.[1] Many pointed out that since Osaka materially benefits from media attention, allowing her to achieve "tremendous wealth and privilege," she owed it to the media to speak to them.[2] She prioritized her health and was willing to pay the fine if she had to.

Less than a month later, gold-medal gymnast Simone Biles similarly opted out of the women's all-around final at the 2021 Tokyo Olympics and publicly shared her struggles with mental stress. While her teammates supported her, Biles, like Osaka, faced a barrage of public insults and disparagement.

Institutional and public response to both women's decisions revealed shifting and polarizing public opinion. Disgruntled audiences proclaimed that the women were weak and not mentally tough, that they were elitist and selfish, letting down their teams and fans. It was part of their jobs, critics effectively argued, to sacrifice personal needs and to suffer pain for the good of others. At the same time, however, the public and many of the athletes' peers showed high levels of support for both women, signaling an evolution in public attitudes toward mental health and the demands placed on athletes.

Professional sports are physically, emotionally, and cognitively demanding. More than a third of high-performing athletes report anxiety, depression, or other kinds of emotional and mental distress. However, most don't seek out help for fear that they'll be stigmatized for being weak.[3] They aren't wrong to be concerned. As the industry's response to Osaka showed, a lot of lip service is paid to prioritizing the needs of athletes, but when push comes to shove, physical prowess, sacrifice, and profitable performance win.

Like explorers, military heroes, and even highly successful business leaders, athletes are among our most common resilience role models. Resilience goals follow accordingly.

Performance, Profit, and Patriotism

Both Osaka and Biles were addressing a pervasive issue in sports: how to be resilient to the pressure put on professional athletes to be "strong"—which means putting aside emotional needs and mental distress—and to perform at the highest levels. To sacrifice for others. Like warriors. Their commitment-at-all-costs resilience glorifies the best of us.

Whether they want to be or not, athletes are expected to function as proxy soldiers and are subject to martial ideals and pressures. They are symbols not only of exceptional athleticism but American *exceptionalism*. And that exceptionalism is structured around elitism, honor, performance, and dominance orientation drawn from militarism.

Our athletes are Spartans, warriors, and commanders, throwing missiles, conquering foes, bombing, and blitzing opponents into oblivion. Coaches style themselves as generals, leading armies organized in military structures, executing strategies, and running boot camps. They frequently rely on military analogies, military role models, and war scenarios to teach and inspire athletes.

War framing is common in our lives even beyond sports. CEOs read military-strategy books and adopt the posture of leading their troops to victory. It's standard business practice for companies to launch kick-ass products, target customers, and engage in price wars. At work, people close ranks, bite the bullet, and annihilate opponents with preemptive strikes, guerrilla tactics, and strategic alliances. Most of us will never be soldiers, yet military ideals of sacrifice and domination shape how we think every day.

In sports, however, these associations aren't only matters of metaphor, but the mixing and merging of material cultures. Sports teams, especially football teams, run boot camps, including those where military personnel and players occasionally train together. Service members and veterans are recognized before games and on scoreboards. Flags fly, unfurled by fans wearing team-emblazoned camo. The military additionally spends millions sponsoring teams and advertising on sports platforms to raise visibility, build their brand, and recruit service members.

Performance and human-optimization psychologists also deliberately work across the two sectors to create models of resilience for an elite corps of high-performance human beings. Beings whose sacrifice and exceptionality are inseparable from American identity and patriotism. These ideals and ideas have seeped across every sector of the economy.

Conformity and Resilience

The kind of resilience that Biles and Osaka were criticized for not having comes from a fundamental idea: that athletes, like soldiers, are supposed *to do what is expected of them without questioning authority.* Even if athletic systems reward the most talented, creative, and hardworking, those same systems require obedience and conformity, in the same way martial cultures do. When athletes deviate from these expectations, they almost inevitably find themselves at the center of a cultural storm, one that frequently includes discussions of patriotism.

It was notable, for instance, that two Black women, the highest performers in their respective sports, spurred a global conversation about mental health and professional sacrifice. The criticisms leveled against them were a nasty swirl of racist and sexist stereotypes conflated with profit-and-patriotism resilience ideals. They combined outrage over Osaka's and Biles's rejection of Strong Black Women expectations with the recurring plaint that they were selfish, unpatriotic, and degrading professional standards and were not worthy of their prominence.

A Texas deputy attorney general compared Simone Biles to 1996

Olympics gymnast Kerri Strug—"a national hero for her grit"—who won a gold medal while dangerously vaulting on two torn ligaments. Biles's decision not to vault, he maintained, before bowing to public pressure and apologizing, made her a "national embarrassment" who betrayed "all Americans."[4] Over and over, we see this pattern of using an alleged lack of resilience, tied to a betrayal of national identity, as a bludgeon.

The same norms resulted in Colin Kaepernick's professional blackballing after he kneeled in protest against systemic racism and police brutality. From the minute he took the knee, Kaepernick was lambasted for being unpatriotic and insulting members of the U.S. military, even though he decided his form of protest out of respect for them. Years after, football fans and politicians still criticize his "politicization" of the national sport, as though their commentary isn't an ironic demonstration of the same.

In 2019, soccer champion Megan Rapinoe was also the target of vicious attacks. The former U.S. women's soccer team captain is a well-known liberal activist. That year, she led her team in stunning and highly visible victories. After scoring two goals against France to propel the U.S. into the World Cup finals, she celebrated like a conquering queen—or a male superstar soccer player. Feet planted on the ground, a smirk on her face, she raised her arms to screaming fans in a brazenly iconic pose . . . that enraged many people. Critics called her a "self-aggrandizing attention whore," famous only for being an "outspoken lesbian" who happens to be good at soccer. Her "bad sport" display would "mar or spoil or tar what could have been this great unifying victory." After Rapinoe knelt in solidarity with Kaepernick during a National Women's Soccer League game and subsequently declined to sing the national anthem before other matches, she was attacked as treasonous.[5]

Osaka, Biles, Kaepernick, and Rapinoe regularly demonstrate the characteristics that typify resilient leadership: mental toughness, strength, optimism, grit, and elite performance. But all four used these qualities to subvert status quo systems and discrimination. They represent a threat because they upend a core belief of mainstream resilience: "soldiering on" without question. They refuse to conform and be quiet.

In the United States, we pride ourselves on autonomy, freedom, and independent thinking, but these beliefs operate within a much-deeper investment in hierarchy, fraternity, and the conventions of order and discipline that reach their acme in military culture, a model for how our corporations, athletic teams, medical facilities, and other institutions operate.

Resilience and the Call to Sacrifice

So, what about the rest of us? Athletes aren't soldiers, after all. And life isn't war. Or is it? The beliefs that life is war, sacrifice is necessary, and pain is good for you are hard to avoid.

"Resilience is the virtue that enables people to move through hardship and become better," explains former Rhodes Scholar, Navy SEAL, and Missouri governor Eric Greitens in his 2015 book, *Resilience: Hard-Won Wisdom for Living a Better Life*. Greitens was paraphrasing philosopher Friedrich Nietzsche's 1888 aphorism, a go-to resilience quote: "What does not destroy me, makes me stronger."

Nietzsche's quote was, fully, "Out of life's school of war—what does not destroy me, makes me stronger."[6]

Greitens's education, career, beliefs, and ideology well illustrate resilience as a matter of elite performance, mastery, and status. In his book, he relies on the language of antiquity and philosophy to associate resilience with becoming a better person through pain and suffering. It's resilience as nobility, moral character, and a fraternal badge of honor. This brand of resilience is one of the most powerful mechanisms for generalizing military ideals, principles, and culture to life broadly.

It's no doubt that war metaphors *are* useful, especially when we encounter societal threats. They rally people, uniting us against a common enemy, and establishing a difficult-to-challenge rationale for superhuman effort and sacrifice. We've declared wars on drugs, obesity, terror, and Mother Nature. Even in the realm of climate change, media pit "climate hawks" against "eco-warriors," repeating a framework that insists we see every problem in terms of either/or conflict and domination.

When the threat of COVID became undeniable, many governments responded in a traditional way—by "going to war" and declaring the virus an "enemy." "We are at war with a virus," said UN secretary general António Guterres. "We must act like any wartime government," intoned United Kingdom prime minister Boris Johnson. "We are at war. . . . Nothing can divert us," claimed France's president, Emmanuel Macron.

Not to be outdone, Trump declared himself "a wartime president," referring to the virus as a "foe" and to policy decisions as "fighting" and "battles." Instead of instituting commonsense public health guidance, he mobilized with military resources at the Pentagon. He wouldn't wear a mask, only reluctantly supported vaccines, and made fun of doctors and public health officials, but he *did* invoke the Defense Production Act and send military ships to viral hot spots in an attempt to tap into an aura of military heroism.

Applying wartime resilience framing required more visible enemies than a microscopic virus. Despite World Health Organization guidelines, many people insisted on calling COVID-19 "the Chinese virus" and the "foreign virus." As president and leader of U.S. armed services, Trump actively demonized specific ethnic groups, spurring a wave of violent anti-Asian bigotry and Islamophobia. Blaming the "invasion" on people of Asian descent led to a sharp spike in terroristic hate crimes across the United States. Between 2019 and 2020, the Federal Bureau of Investigation saw a 77 percent increase in anti-Asian hate crimes; more than nine thousand hate incidents were registered with hate-monitoring groups.[7]

Depicting viral threats and resilience to them in terms of war also established sacrifice expectations that made abandoning entire classes of people more acceptable. So that the rest of us could fight the good fight, in warlike cost-benefit equations governments decided who would die first: the elderly, the homeless, the incarcerated, people with disabilities, and those in communities at high risk due to racialized health and economic inequities.

Going to work was portrayed as the heroism of the everyman—be brave, face the enemy, save your family, community, economy, and the nation, but these "essential workers," those who couldn't work from home or afford to decline employment, were put at the highest risk with few protections. Professor Shan-Estelle Brown and researcher Zoe Pearson, both anthropologists, described this course as "involuntary human sacrifice, made to look voluntary."[8]

The well-intentioned and widespread habit of calling nurses and doctors "health care heroes" and describing them as "fighting frontline battles" also normalized demands of superhuman performance.[9] As hospitals were overrun, medical professionals were forced to make personal sacrifices and soul-crushing decisions that directly stemmed from failures in our care infrastructures. Already high, rates of moral injury and suicide among health-care workers skyrocketed.[10]

Part of the mythology is that sacrifices are always worth making, a belief strangely and unintentionally buttressed by the theory of post-traumatic growth (PTG). In a1998 study of six hundred people who'd had traumatic experiences, Richard Tedeschi and Lawrence Calhoun, both psychology professors at University of North Carolina, found that many of the participants felt they'd experienced positive changes after their suffering. They described having greater purpose, better relationships, and improved well-being. In the years since, as studies have elaborated PTG, there has been ardent debate about the validity of the idea. Some argue that the positive changes result from our natural tendency to forget negative experiences over time. Others believe that PTG is simply a coping mechanism and doesn't represent an actual change in a person's personality. Additionally, what constitutes "growth" can be highly variable, subjective, and difficult to measure. It's also culturally contingent: what constitutes growth in one context might be considered regression in another. The theory also begs the question, What happens when a person suffers chronic traumatic stress or multiple episodes?

Studies show that while adversity can impart important life lessons, over time each additional trauma *reduces* coping and resilience. Exposure to new hardships and painful experiences tends to evoke the harmful effects of earlier ones, resulting in a greater, not lesser, likelihood of suffering and reducing adaptability over time.[11]

Nonetheless, our cultural faith in the power of transformational suffering is stubborn.

Well, I wondered, how is it working out for soldiers who embrace these ideals, such as Greitens?

The year his book came out, a woman known only as K.S. credibly testified in front of a majority-Republican state legislative committee that Greitens "hit, groped, and coerced" her into unwanted sexual contact and then threatened to publicly share photos depicting her partially naked if she talked about what happened.[12] She acquiesced to his demand of oral sex, she explained, because she felt that she had to in order to safely escape. The following year, 2016, he was elected governor of Missouri.

In 2018, Greitens was forced to resign as governor following claims of financial improprieties and after he separated from his wife, Sheena. She similarly testified to coercive behavior and physical abuse. Fearful for her and her children's safety, she left their home and publicly disclosed details of their marriage, after which her husband called her "hateful and disgusting," "nasty," and a "lying bitch."[13]

Life is only war if we allow it to be.

How Does Military-Resilience Programming Work?

Many veterans struggle to adapt to civilian life, where the emotional and psychological skills that served them well as warriors become sources of frustration and pain. Loneliness, sexual assault, and family violence are unfortunately common in soldiers' lives, and especially for veterans. Additionally, soldiers who experienced childhood adversity or traumatic events prior to joining the military are more, not less, likely to respond to the traumatic stresses of war with distress.

So why are we so fixated on promoting military-resilience attitudes, values, and ideals in everyday life?

Military training emphasizes excellence, strength, honor, and resilience, but life as a soldier is also defined by anxiety, loss of control, mental exhaustion, near-complete reliance on others, and a constant awareness of physical danger and the possibility of death.

No one knows this better than military leaders. The development of theories of trauma and resilience over the twentieth century is indivisible from the military's desire and need to build effective fighting forces.

Every war of the past 150 years has had its unique language to describe soldiers' debilitating stress and fear: railway spine, shell shock, battle fatigue, soldier's heart, psychological collapse, and post-traumatic stress disorder, to name a few. In war after war, men were treated for their war-born emotional suffering with cruelty and condescension. Accused of cowardice and malingering, soldiers who could not or would not fight were considered unmanly for their weakness of mind. They were often subjected to harsh techniques, ranging from prolonged solitary confinement and public shaming to primitive electroshock treatments. Over time, however, as psychology, public awareness, and trauma studies expanded, the treatment of soldiers' deep anguish and distress became more compassionate.

A significant step in better treatment was the 1980 creation of a new diagnostic category: post-traumatic stress disorder (PTSD). PTSD, the first official trauma diagnosis to be included in the *Diagnostic and Statistical Manual of Mental Disorders (DSM)*, was a direct response to the plight of Vietnam veterans, who suffered high rates of suicide, substance abuse, and intimate-partner violence.

While the new malady legitimately attempted to address concerns about soldiers, it was also controversial because it was considered more a political tool than a mental health diagnosis. It was unique because it was the only diagnosis that tied a disorder to exposure to a traumatic event. It also has a temporal dimension in that a person had to have defined symptoms over a specific period of time. Importantly, PTSD was tied to benefits—insurance, Social Security Disability Insurance, or Supplemental Security Income. These were available to active military and veterans, so were a meaningful form of political entitlement.

This history still shapes public and even medical understanding of PTSD. Because the original diagnosis associated PTSD with men and war, it sidelined women's experiences of rape, intimate abuse, and exposure to threats of violence and discrimination.

In 1992, psychiatrist Judith Herman, who had for years worked with women suffering from the effects of childhood sexual abuse, intimate violence, and rape, proposed a more nuanced diagnosis, which she called Complex PTSD (C-PTSD), a syndrome resulting from sustained and repeated trauma. Herman included somatic symptoms, the prevalence of unstable relationships, and persistent cognitive, emotional, and behavioral difficulties. Whereas PTSD focused on individuals and their capacity and willingness to change, Herman's framework was more relational and suggested a sequence of treatment with more relational components—establishing safety, remembering, mourning, and connection. Despite diffuse uses of her techniques, her more expansive version is still not included in the *DSM*.[14]

Today, the primary reason people experience PTSD is rape, *followed* by combat experiences, but public awareness remains low, and even clinicians report being perplexed that more women than men exhibit symptoms.[15] It is difficult for people to contemplate what it means that women's "regular" lives can result in the kind of vigilance and distress that soldiers develop in war.

In the two decades after the PTSD diagnosis, the toll of war on soldiers became an even more urgent and expensive concern for the U.S. military as substance abuse, intimate violence, and rates of suicide steadily and sometimes precipitously increased. The situation was compounded post-9/11 by wartime engagements that deployed troops continuously.

In 2009, to stem this tide and as part of a push to move from after-the-fact trauma treatment to prevention and intervention, the U.S. Army launched the Comprehensive Soldier Fitness (CSF) resilience program. CSF was the brainchild of Martin Seligman and Army chief of staff General George Casey Jr., who had discussed how positive psychology could be used to improve troop morale and build psychological resilience in service members.[16] Service members' personal resilience would augment the military's ability to manage what now seem like ceaseless wars and unpredictable humanitarian and militarized crises. One of the program's overall goals, as Seligman (who had in the past compared positive psychology to the Manhattan Project) put it, was to create "an indomitable army."[17]

Every officer, enlisted soldier, and reservist was automatically enrolled in CSF, which was designed to "increase psychological strength and positive performance and to reduce the incidence of maladaptive responses of the entire U.S. Army."[18] Training was organized around five areas of resilient "fitness": physical, social, spiritual, emotional, and family. CSF was eventually extended to spouses and children and recast as the Comprehensive Soldier and Family Fitness (CSF2) program.

Through this and other resilience programs, soldiers learn to be more adaptable, optimistic, productive, creative, and goal oriented.

In resilience-skills-training modules soldiers are encouraged to use gratitude journals and not indulge in negative thoughts. In addition, participants learn "problem-solving and how to think optimistically" so they can develop lifelong skills that "maximize one's potential." The programs also, controversially, suggest that soldiers pursue spiritual practices, a policy that has resulted in the military being sued for, among other things, discriminating against secularists and atheists.[19]

In essence, as critics claimed, CSF was an experiment conducted on military members. Among the more startling aspects of the program, for example, was that it was largely based on research involving children aged ten to fourteen, a cohort whose lives are stunningly different from those of adults who, on average, are twenty-nine-year-old men and women facing situations of extreme violence. Over the years, CSF has been called out for a lack of scientific process, rigor, replicability, and for ethical ambiguity. It remains the largest-ever longitudinal social study—in return for designing it, Seligman's Penn Resiliency Program gained access to the CSF data.[20]

There are also real concerns about the impacts of applying a resilience of individual optimization and positivity in an environment that is so persistently demanding and uniquely stressful. Service members who undergo CSF training might assume they are more resilient to being traumatized and act recklessly. Those who go through the program, but continue to struggle, might feel like failures for not making themselves resilient enough. Shame at feeling distress might make soldiers and veterans *less* likely to seek out and get the help they need.

CSF and its iterations are multifaceted interventions that are difficult to assess, however. Scant reports regarding the program's evolution or success, or what even constitutes success, have yielded conflicting conclusions. Department of Defense analysts have, for instance, concluded that "a large proportion" of CSF-related programs are "unable to document evidence of program outcomes," nor do they track expenses.[21]

What we do know is distress and social dysfunction among soldiers and veterans have risen steadily in the years since the program's inception. Five years after CSF was launched, more than 50 percent of an estimated 770,000 soldiers surveyed reported high levels of pessimism, agreeing with such statements as "I rarely count on good things happening to me." Forty-eight percent reported pessimism as well as low satisfaction in, or commitment to, their work.

The program's positive-psychology spin, explained David Rudd, who served on a scientific panel that reviewed the program, did "not have much impact in terms of overall health."[22] By 2019, the Army's suicide rate was 29.8 per 100,000, higher than any other service's rates and higher than the rate of 20 per 100,000 in 2009. Substance abuse, family dissolution, intimate violence, and military sexual assault among active members and veterans have not declined but instead gone in the opposite direction.[23]

Given the scope and complexity of the task, and an absence of detailed findings, it's reductionist to conclude that CSF training doesn't work, but it would also be a gross overstatement to say that it's having beneficial results.

In some ways, overwhelming evidence of negative trends may attest to a curious success.

What after all is a resilient response to militarism and war? What is "normal" and how are we pathologizing healthy responses to devastating actions? Soldier's suffering, emotional distress, and trauma are characterized as *maladjustments*. But what if individualized resilience training based on optimism, spirituality, personal happiness, and cognitive flexibility leads soldiers to question the nature of war and their role in it?

Dress the ideals of war in any uniforms you choose, sprinkle them with as much gratitude and happiness dust as you can amass, but resilience training is designed to do one thing—make the soul-, body-, and relationship-crushing work of war more psychologically palatable. Arguably, being resilient, whether based on individual happiness or collective well-being, would make us all pacifists.

Fear and anxiety are reasonable responses to the evisceration of war. Painful responses and distress are ways that we initially defend ourselves against overwhelming threats. We ask soldiers to sacrifice their health, safety, well-being, relationships, futures, and families for the greater good, and when they do, what they experience often isn't post-traumatic stress but moral injury. Moral injury results when a person has made choices and behaved in ways that violate their core values and sense of themselves.

This dilemma isn't limited to military life. During the first years of COVID, rates of moral injury among medical care workers sky-rocketed as doctors and nurses made life-and-death decisions that violated their values, social codes, and medical ethics.

Part of the challenge of helping people suffering from moral injury is that their anguish *confirms the core beliefs and ideals* they were forced to abandon in the line of duty. Training soldiers to develop resilience through positive psychology or cognitive behavioral therapy can therefore be *harmful and counterproductive*. The preferred treatment isn't to learn optimism or to be thankful, but adaptive disclosure therapy, a trauma-processing approach based on Judith Herman's trauma-recovery work.[24]

Soldier Civilians and the *Resilience Paradox*

It's easy to think that a collection of resilient individuals adds up to resilient collectives, be they fighting units, sports teams, corporations, communities, or countries. Studies show, however, that this is not the case, a counterintuitive problem known as the resilience paradox. Being blindly optimistic and overconfident deepens the disconnect.

Anyone who has lived through a hurricane knows what this looks like. In every hurricane there are people, not because they can't but because they won't, who refuse to leave their homes even under evacuation orders. These people are the most confident in their expertise and abilities. They cope with risks by repressing negative emotions and increasing positive ones: optimism, competence, and a sense of being in control. But by staying in place, these people endanger themselves and others when they then have to be rescued under lethal conditions. They are also the least likely to take the steps necessary to lower risks or to generate more positive outcomes in the future. Individual confidence in one's abilities—the kind that CSF training, for example, might cultivate—heightens feelings of invulnerability.[25]

The Resilience of an Authoritarian Right

So what happens when resilience ideals calibrated to build an "indominable" force are explained as "life skills"? What happens when people exposed to positive psychology, rigorous fitness programming, and honor bound ideals of resilience leave the military and enter an increasingly politically polarized civilian life?

CSF teaches soldiers and their families to understand resilience as a resource for "everyday" life, a valuable skill in any context, not only military ones. This training was also designed to help soldiers be more effective in unorthodox wars and less predictable military settings. In nontraditional, volatile environments, resilience is critical to responding dynamically to fast-changing, potentially hostile environments with no clear enemy. These environments include potentially hostile neighborhoods, refugee and migrant camps, and chaotic post-climate-disaster relief zones.

Or the U.S. Capitol on January 6, 2021.

Fourteen of the first 150 people arrested for their involvement in the January 6, 2021, insurrection were current or former members of the armed services, more than twice their proportion in the adult American population.[26] To the alarm of political analysts, insurrectionists were not basement-dwelling fringe conspiracists of popular imagination, but law enforcement officials, lawyers, judges, doctors, corporate executives, real estate agents, and older professionals. They were 95 percent white, 85 percent male, and disproportionately had ties to the military.[27]

Veterans and military personnel are also more highly represented in extremist movements. In 2020, at least 25 percent of members of extremist American paramilitary forces, somewhere between fifteen thousand and twenty thousand, had served in the U.S. armed forces.[28]

Most veterans and members of the military *do not* join violent extremist movements, but engaging veterans, border patrol officers, and police officers is a core strategy for those movements. Recruiting veterans and members of the military is, for instance, explicit in the stated mission of the Oath Keepers. Hundreds of Oath Keepers are either current or former employees of the U.S. Coast Guard, Immigration and Customs Enforcement, DHS's Border Patrol, and the Secret Service, people honor bound to protect the nation against *invasion*. That word is operative, considering that another predictor of January 6 involvement was the rate of nonwhite migration into a participant's residential neighborhood.

The browning of America is an inevitable demographic shift represented in conservative media as an invasion of foreign forces poised to destroy the "real American" way of life.[29] Many of the participants on that day believe that they are a resilient line of defense to threats against America, a motivating factor for the political right generally.

If you think of problems in terms of war and of the nation as a body that needs protection, resilience is how you justify containing and eliminating invading forces—namely, people different from you. You treat those people the way you would a disease or an enemy you want to eradicate. You cage their children, hunt them down with animals, terrorize them in their places of worship, and incarcerate them. You support vertical laws that punish undesirable groups, pass laws that criminalize abortion, pursue transphobic policies, and close borders to specific populations. You elect and support strongmen, politicians

who invest in surveillance and policing and control women's repro-
duction. Men who, as failed GOP candidate for Arizona governor
Kari Lake said in admiration, have "big-dick energy." Lake is almost
certainly one of the 42 percent of American voters who, in 2022, revealed that they thought "having a strong leader for America is more
important than having a democracy."[30]

A series of 2023 televised Republican Party presidential candidate debates put the prevalence of this thinking, language, and
posturing on dystopian display. Candidates used dog whistles for
a rhetoric of violent self-defense against invasion, infection, and
potential contamination—from other people. At the same time,
Donald Trump was publicly decrying immigrants' "poisoning the
blood of our country," an assertion that made 42 percent of the
GOP Iowa caucuses *more* likely to support him.[31] Body politic dem-
agoguery like this has fueled centuries of racist violence and political injustice, from anti-miscegenation laws to internment camps and
eugenics designed to eradicate people with disabilities and sterilize
"inferior" communities.[32] It follows and builds a logic of fascism and
genocide.

Strongmen don't make people safer, a baseline for resilience at any
scale. Rather, they maintain power by making people more afraid. They
use language, images, and metaphors that increase contempt, anxiety,
and disgust, and when they do, they can count on mainstream resilience
as a recruitment tool. In the post 9/11 years that led to the election of
Donald Trump, pathology and war metaphors undeniably informed
an increasingly violent reactionary white supremacist moment that
understood resilience as *resistance*, a synonym, after all, for *immunity*.

A 2019 text analysis of conservative pundit dialog and online communities revealed how resilience has been used repeatedly to justify
violence. *Informational resilience* is resistance to "fake news." *Episte-
mological resilience* drives rejection of liberal norms: gender fluidity,
trans people's existences, women's equality, and interethnic and racial
marriage. *Free speech absolutism* is also a resilient defense against being

told "how to think." Asking people to use empathetic language that is mindful of other people's safety, dignity, or experiences, is perceived as *cognitive oppression*. January 6 was supposed to demonstrate *heroic resilience* because the ultimate response to the threat felt by these communities is militarized resistance against liberal democracy. This adoption and promotion of resilience ideas is part of the flow of what Jeff Sharlet calls "the undertow of fascism."[33]

The researchers also found that references to resilience justified a specific condition of success: the availability of guns.[34]

During the 2017 Unite the Right rally in Charlottesville, Virginia, a mob composed almost solely of white men chanted, "You will not replace us!," "The South will rise again!," and "Blood and soil!," a pernicious translation of a Nazi chant. Marchers came from groups with such names as Proud Boys, Independent Men, and Men Going Their Own Way. The purpose of the rally was to further "the resilience of our men and our ideas." In this worldview, ethno-cultural masculine pride is a vital and positive adaptation that rationalizes virtuous violence.[35] Ultimately, these movements are channels of white rage and palingenetic ultranationalism, not resilience in the sense of positive adaptation.

That so many boys and men gravitate toward hostile—to women, to Jews, to ethnic and religious minorities, and LGBTQ people— communities and extremist movements is a serious threat to our political stability. Boys and men can turn to alternative organizations and role models that explore healthier and more egalitarian ways to think about themselves, relationships, and masculinity. The problem is that their exposure to these alternatives has to start earlier than most parents and educators want to contemplate. Charismatic internet personalities are engaging children at younger and younger ages. A second issue is that faced with this growing concern, many parents and educators are actively doubling down on traditional norms of masculinity that violent ethno-cultural masculine pride ultimately depends on.

The relationship between the military's resilience programming and the growth of movements that threaten democratic safety and pluralistic values is perhaps a resilience paradox worthy of further study and discussion.

Life Is Not War

It's hard to resist a culture of military glory and the resilience that goes with it. "Soldiering on" seeps into everything: our identities, language, habits of mind, and institutions. It happens in ways we never consider.

For instance, as I wrote this chapter, I looked up popular children's names, always an interesting cultural bellwether. The number one name for boys in the United States between 2020 and 2022 was Liam, and the number one name for girls was Olivia. Liam is a short form of William, which means "resolute protector" or "strong-willed warrior." Olivia? It means "peace." An entire generation of children has been named, via zeitgeist, according to a gendered ideology of war and peace, suffering and solace, resilience and vulnerability. Some things you can't make up.

Life-is-war resilience easily becomes war-is-life resilience, but it's not inevitable. We can do better than a resilience of borders and belligerence, superiority and triumphing over others.

As a society, we don't have to speak and think in warlike metaphors. Using martial suffering, hierarchy, and conformity as broad resilience norms limits our ability to understand and solve problems creatively, peacefully, and radically.

There are many ways to be honorable and strong, to strive for excellence, to be faithful, dutiful, and vigilant. Approaching every challenge, threat, or conflict using adversarial thinking does nothing to help us forge deeper connection, trust, understanding, or meaning. It certainly doesn't help counteract the effects of violent backlash against social change, equality, and democratic norms. That requires a different kind of resilience, one that operates through healthy and stable relationships between political communities, diverse cultural institutions, and leaders and citizens defining evolving shared values.[36]

Most of us will never have to bear the costs of being soldiers or members of military families. But, if we accept and use military metaphors, language, and values to define resilience, we have to also accept their corrosive associations and unintended outcomes.

When war frameworks dominate, you end up with a culture, ours, where resilience requires children to wear bulletproof clothes to walk to school and know more about ballistics and evasive maneuvers than they do about tying their shoelaces. You end up with scared, armed, hypervigilant men shooting strangers—a sixteen-year-old boy; a twenty-year-old woman; a four-year-old girl looking for a ball in the wrong garden—out of a distorted sense of strength, honor, protective masculinity, and personal responsibility. In a status-anxiety fever dream, resilience has been distorted beyond any recognition, a feature in the machinery of perpetual war.

We can collectively restore a resilience that resists this understanding of the world. We can use different words and language, promote ideals and values that make new meanings, create different ways of belonging, and generate alternative visions of the future, ones that don't assume violence and war.

Our ability and desire to do this already exists. While I was appalled by the baby naming preferences indicated, I was happy to see the second and third most popular girls' and boys' names. They were Emma and Charlotte, Noah and Oliver.

"Whole" and "free." "Rest" and "peace."

7

THE FANTASY OF BOUNCING BACK

> Time is a river that sweeps me along, but I am
> the river; it is a tiger that mangles me, but I am
> the tiger; it is a fire that consumes me, but I am
> the fire.
>
> —Jorge Luis Borges

After a crisis or hardship, most of us think about how to "bounce back
to normal." If you think back on your life, you might recognize such
moments. We rely on the comforting idea of bouncing back in situations ranging from losing a job to surviving a tornado. Even when it's
clear there is no turning back, we long for the seeming innocence of
a time before.

But what do we want from "bouncing back"? Do we really mean
returning to an idealized past way of life? Or an amorphous sense
of stability and predictability? Often there are markers to what it
means: restoring schedules, economic metrics, recognizable relationships.

After Hurricane Dorian, Bahamians bounced back in this way.
The country's post-disaster path followed our resilience script—life
was normal, the storm came, there was terrible loss and suffering,

the storm left, there was a period of disruption, and then order was restored.

Once the storm had passed, government aid, relief efforts, and recovery programs eventually created some stability and safety for the over seventy thousand people left homeless. The government prioritized getting children back to school, providing order and continuity to their lives. The country invited the international community to support the recovery by visiting the parts of the country unaffected by the storm.

The starting point of the cycle, the moment to bounce back to, everyone seemed to agree, was the time *just before* the storm hit. Before the catastrophe happened. But catastrophes, as Walter Benjamin wrote, aren't disruptions, but rather "that things 'just go on.'"

As a *hurricane,* Dorian was set in motion by thunderstorms over warm seas in the central Atlantic Ocean on August 24, 2019, but as a *disaster,* Dorian began in 1492, when Christopher Columbus set sail from "the old world" to find a new route to China and India, a source of riches for the Spanish crown.

Despite the furor that Columbus's standing causes in the United States, he never set foot on the North American mainland. Instead, after a two-month journey from Spain he and his crew of ninety men made landfall on a small island in what Columbus described as Baja Mar, Spanish for "shallow water," The Bahamas. He then traveled farther and farther south.

Upon their first landfall, the sailors encountered Lucayans, a people who called themselves the Lukku-Cairi and their home Guanahani. Between 500 and 800 CE, this offshoot of the Arawak-speaking Taíno traveled from larger islands farther south up to the Bahamian archipelago. Over more than eight hundred years, the two groups continued trading and sharing language and cultural norms. By the time Columbus arrived, more than forty thousand Lucayans lived across a swath of "shallow water" islands.

Columbus was immediately struck by the Lukku-Cairi's openness and generosity. Peaceful and matrilineal, they lived in multihousehold dwellings, fished, grew root vegetables, and wore few clothes. They were curious and offered the men food and hospitality. His takeaway? "With 50 men they can all be subjugated," he wrote in his logs. His crew promptly kidnapped several of the inhabitants and sailed to the island later known as Hispaniola—now known as Haiti and the Dominican Republic—where a much larger community of Taíno lived. Columbus observed that the Taíno also "never refuse anything that is asked for . . . and show so much love that they would give their very hearts," noting that it would make it easier to seize the enormous island and enslave its people.

Columbus's crews raped with impunity and forcibly took Indigenous girls as young as nine and ten years old as slaves for European men, establishing a linchpin of settler-colonial domination and warfare that lingers today as Indigenous women across the North American continent are sexually assaulted and killed at higher rates than women in other demographic groups. Native women today are the *only* women assaulted more often by men *outside* their own communities than within them.[1]

As egregious as Columbus's actions were, they were sanctioned and encouraged by political and religious authorities. In 1493, within a year of Columbus making landfall, Pope Alexander VI issued a papal bull in which he consolidated earlier dictates to create what came to be called the Doctrine of Discovery, providing a sanctioned foundation for European colonialism, Indigenous genocide, and the African slave trade. The bull built on earlier decrees that gave Portugal the right "to invade, search out, capture, vanquish, and subdue all Saracens (Muslims) and pagans" and "reduce their persons to perpetual slavery."[2] Alexander VI confirmed this policy and went on to declare that as non-Christians, "barbarians" and "savages" had no legitimate claims to land, rights, or governing power. For centuries the Doctrine of Discovery justified mass enslavement, land grabs, colonization, and genocide as it made its way into international relations and law. The U.S. Supreme Court cited it to establish legal claims and precedent.[3] In April 2023, the Vatican repudiated the doctrine but in a way that many Indigenous leaders found problematic.[4]

"This goes beyond land," explains Michelle Schenandoah, when we talked about the effects of the Doctrine in the summer of 2023. "It created an illegitimate assumption of superiority and authority impacting all of the Americas." A member of the Oneida Nation, Schenandoah is a professor of Indigenous law and founder of the story-telling platform Rematriation. "It really has created generation upon generation of genocidal policies directed towards Indigenous peoples. It resulted in the loss of millions and millions of Indigenous lives, forced assimilation, the continued issue of missing and murdered Indigenous women, and the end of Indigenous nations, languages, and cultural ways of life. It's time," she explained, "for colonizing governments to take full accountability for their actions."

Like class-quakes—earthquakes that lay bare the political nature of disasters—hurricanes paint a stark picture of the relationship between power, resilience, and the ideal of bouncing back.

When Dorian hit The Bahamas, the country had no Indigenous people, and the poorest and most vulnerable residents were the descendants of those enslaved in Haiti centuries before. Those who could afford to leave, find safety, and rebuild tended to be lighter-skinned Bahamians, Americans, and Europeans. History is nothing if not inscribed on all of our bodies.

Hurricane Katrina, which hit New Orleans in 2005, illustrated similar dynamics. The storm hit the city on a day when many were planning to mark the fiftieth anniversary of Emmett Till's murder. Instead, the city's almost half million people braced for the megastorm. Within hours of its making landfall, the levies that were supposed to hold back rising waters failed, and upward of 80 percent of the city was flooded, driving more than half of the population into streets and chaotic, ill-prepared public shelters. In the wider Gulf, more than a million people were forced to leave their homes. The federal government's failure to respond quickly and compassionately to the catastrophe extended residents' suffering.

With losses of more than $135 billion, Katrina ranks as one of the costliest disasters in U.S. history and, also, as one of the most searing examples of how systemic racism continues to influence Black lives and communities. After the storm, African American communities endured the greatest displacements, personal and commercial losses, and sustained rates of illness and unemployment. In general, white communities fared better, reporting less psychological distress or disruption—economic, educational, social, or professional. Ten years later, the white population of New Orleans had rebounded and rebuilt, but the Black population had shrunk by almost one hundred thousand.[5]

From the minute the first post-hurricane images surfaced, it was clear that poorer Black neighborhoods were the most hurt. It was also clear that many Americans were willing to blame the victims for not being clever, capable, or resilient enough to have saved themselves. This theme, of some communities being more resilient, capable, adaptable, and worthy, is consistent.

When Hurricane Maria ripped through Puerto Rico in 2017, a media circus ensued in the wake of then-president Donald Trump tossing paper towel rolls into a dispirited and angry crowd of survivors. The hurricane killed more than three thousand people and laid waste to forests, buildings, and infrastructure. Puerto Ricans were plunged into the longest electrical blackout in U.S. history, more than seven months. A 2021 investigation found that federal government officials blocked Puerto Rico from receiving hurricane aid and that the Trump administration obstructed probes into why federally approved funds were not being distributed.[6]

After acting U.S. Homeland Security secretary Elaine Duke described chronically inadequate federal relief efforts as "a good news story," San Juan's Mayor Carmen Yulín Cruz countered with "This is a people-are-dying story." The year that Maria hit, only 54 percent of Americans surveyed knew that Puerto Ricans are U.S. citizens.[7]

Puerto Ricans organized their lives, adapting every system and support to survive. Through mutual aid societies, grassroots activism, and makeshift schools and medical clinics, volunteers rebuilt communities and designed newer, more adaptive systems. "In Puerto Rico," wrote Professor Juan Giusti-Cordero, alluding to a long history of imperialism and its enduring ill effects, "we invented resilience."[8]

Island Time Matters

The effects and inadequacies of "bouncing back to normal" are directly linked to how we learn to think about time and our place in it. It assumes short-term parameters calibrated to individual perceptions and experiences. The idea pivots around personal lifetimes and discrete events. "Bouncing back" requires a linear concept of time that makes clear distinctions between the past, present, and future. It's also a "progressive" notion because even though we say bouncing *back*, what we are actually focusing on is a *better future*.

"Bouncing back" reflects modernity and its temporal requirements. As a result, our perceptions of risk, stress, loss, and trauma are limited, lack context, and are compartmentalized. These assumptions make it difficult to fathom the cumulative effects of history, change, and stress and all but impossible to invest in the long-term systemic change we need to adapt positively to so many of the crises we face.

By way of comparison, let's contemplate "island time."

As a person from a small island, I am used to people thinking that the place I come from is slow and somehow not part of the "real" world. To many non-islanders, "second-" and "third-world" islands are not serious places where serious people live. If people give The Bahamas any thought beyond a possible quick vacation, it's usually to confuse it with Barbados, Bermuda, or some other tropical country of fleeting pleasures and anonymous freedoms. One of the sillier questions I've ever been asked about The Bahamas, or anything, is "People *live* there?"

For almost half a million of us, The Bahamas is a home with a rich and complex past. Comprising hundreds of islands and hidden shoals and known for aquamarine temperate seas, it has always been a haven for enterprising risk-takers: intrepid Lucayans, Puritan seekers of religious liberty, dispossessed Seminoles, free and enslaved Blacks, Pirate Republicans, British Loyalists, entrepreneurial Greek spongers, avaricious drug lords, revolution-fleeing Cuban elites, and, today, desperate but hopeful migrant Haitians. The Bahamas has sustained them all and at a pace perennially depicted as out of sync with the modern world: island time.

Island time denotes a slower cadence of life, generally a positive quality in a stressful, accelerating world. Its slower sensibility and detachment from the demands of the industrial clock time that governs our non-island lives is one of the reasons tropical islands are sought-after destinations. They *feel* like refuges from "real life," meaning one that is chronically and stressfully time pressured and relentless feeling.

Regardless of its positive connotations, however, *island time* contains within it a belief not only in difference but in inferiority. Its most salient characteristic is slowness, which, in modernity, is a disadvantage and a *disability*. In many circles, it's still acceptable, overtly or implicitly, to disparage and discriminate against "retarded" people as "thick," "slow," and less capable. People who aren't doing something quickly enough, for instance, are "dragging their feet." They cannot keep up with what is necessary. The same is suggested by "underdeveloped" and "developing" countries.

The slow island time of indolent "natives" and "local cultures" marks us as eternally *premodern*—at best, quaintly backward and at worst, perenially behind and corrupt.

Speed is a way to maximize opportunity and to optimize yourself. High-income people have more money, but what they really have, a source of power, is time at their disposal. Middle-class people want as much of it as possible, so schedule and scramble to amass it. The poor utterly lack it. As a competitive advantage, faster speeds and more time enable a person to *accumulate*, including accumulating more time. This, in turn, gives people more control over their bodies, relationships, other people, and environments. Speed also moves you toward the future, a resilience asset because, in theory, you can apply yourself, learn valuable skills, work hard, and grow.

These time beliefs, implicitly disdainful and discriminatory, are critical to our culture's possessive individualism, technological advancement, and quest for dominance. This has enormous implications for resilience and how we pursue it.

Just as we are supposed to, as individuals, own, trade, and amass property, we are meant to own, trade, and amass time, with scant regard for collective interests or values. When you are patient, for example, you might say, "Take your time." When you are exasperated, "You're taking your sweet time." To make time for one thing, we take it from something—and someone—else. What is your time versus mine?

When we "take time" whom are we taking it *from* anyway?

Few intellectual pivots have been as consequential as the Enlightenment era's attachment of identity to time, in the shape of progress. In the same way that different people were organized into levels of rationality, intelligence, and capacity for self-governance, they were also defined by their relationships to time and progress.

In theory, all people could evolve beyond their state—they could progress—toward a higher state of personhood and rationality. So, for instance, if Black and Brown men, and it was mainly men, worked hard enough, they could progress as individuals into an improved condition.

But even as this happened, European men would *also* be progressing, so others couldn't *really* ever catch up. Everyone else existed in the past, a purportedly permanent temporal rear guard. In this way, as philosopher John Harfouch succinctly puts it, speed and progress became properties of whiteness.[9] They also became properties of masculinity. This organization of time and progress produced a worldview in which whiteness and maleness defined both the acme and the avant-garde of human existence, an idea that lives on today.[10]

What characterized the white supremacy of European colonialism therefore wasn't only racial constructs or "Culture," but this relationship to time and progress. That colonized people—like women—lacked rational foresight and were not future thinking was part of the paternalistic rationalization for why they needed—and, for many, still need—to be ruled over. This eternal belatedness is inherent in the suggestion of the "slowness" of island people today.

So, when we talk about resilience as moving forward as fast as possible, when we refuse to contemplate the long tail of history and the time it takes to adapt, grieve, and imagine alternatives, we trade in these foundations.

Ambiguous Grief and Bouncing Back

Resilience *takes* time when we are all expected to *make* time, mainly for other people. Because most of us work to survive and take care of others, our time is not our own. For most people, taking time to adequately nurture the people we love and ourselves to stay well is exceedingly difficult. Because we are socialized to think of time as linear and in individualistic, competitive terms, it is difficult to understand its social and political uses and to adapt in ways that emphasize community well-being and ecological adaptability.

Closure is also implied in bounce-back resilience promises, but our traumas and trials rarely comply. We often experience grief and loss as diffuse and ambiguous, the grief that comes from living in situations that lack definitive resolution. This grief of loss rarely has no recognition or rituals. People living with substance abuse, addiction, and terminal illness, or like my family, navigating diagnoses of degenerative memory losses, dementia, or Alzheimer's, are familiar with this kind of loss.

"Ambiguous loss," explains Pauline Boss, the psychologist who developed the theory, "is a relational disorder caused by the lack of facts surrounding the loss of a loved one." Because the problems emerge from connections, outside and apart from ourselves or anything we can control, individual mindset or attitudes can't bring resolution.[11]

Boss developed the concept of ambiguous loss and unresolved grief during thirty years of working as a family therapist, and her approach assumes the primary role social connections play in our adaptability. As her work revealed, families, sometimes factories of trauma, are also reservoirs of resilience. Without realizing it, those in close families support one another in ways that never appear in most of our resilience narratives.[12]

Most of us experience events or prolonged life circumstances that involve this type of grief. It's the looming sensation of sustained sadness and stress that comes with situations ranging from having incarcerated family members to living in refugee camps. You might feel it when a child leaves home or when home no longer exists or is inaccessible.

The anticipatory mourning of climate change that millions of people are experiencing is also a form of ambiguous loss. Our experiences of climate disruption aren't only a matter of experiencing physical risks but of anticipatory grief for the places and memories we cherish. We mourn ourselves and the feelings of affirmation, belonging, and nurture we derive from our damaged and threatened environments.

The Necessity of Rethinking Time

Bouncing back is a metaphor that doesn't only describe but, like all metaphors, also shapes how we think. Whether pursued through therapy, self-help, or politics, this approach overlooks the nature of adaptability and makes important aspects of our time and history invisible. It's fundamentally conservative because it focuses on individual control and benefits and divorces resilience from both socially constructed vulnerability and strengths.

In addition, resilience is increasingly defined as "the strength *and speed* of our response to adversity."[13] Wrapping speed and urgency into a recovery formula makes for a heavy burden. Like stages of development or stages of grief, which in fact aren't fixed or lockstep, resilience now has a prescribed path—trauma, resilience, growth—that individuals often feel they should follow, and as quickly as possible.

Adapting to adversity takes its own time and doesn't usually happen quickly or in a straight line. Resilience doesn't care about clock time, speed, or faux emotional closures. In fact, the expectation of quick improvement after a setback or crisis usually *heightens* stress, encourages unhealthy habits, and leads us to fall back on short-term Band-Aids instead of sustained well-being.

Even if we want to think time is linear and progressive, our healing is not. After a crisis, a person or community might experience well-being for a time, only to then fall into disruption and despair again, then again into improvement. Trauma makes us feel as though we are out of the "normal" flow of time, and the desire to restore that sense is powerful. Keeping busy and having schedules can bring a sense of relief and predictability, but speed itself has no place in the alleviation of sorrow or the manifestation of grief. When we impose a standard of speed, usually out of a sense of urgency and necessity, we struggle. Failing to go through a linear progression of grief to happiness or trauma to growth can make you feel like a resilience failure.

If you lose a spouse and don't recover in a timely fashion, what's wrong with you? If you miscarry and don't immediately try again to get pregnant, then buck up and do so. If you are angry for your losses and don't feel like a "better person" who has learned valuable lessons, do you feel shame? Speed and urgency foreclose self-compassion and empathy, easily contributing to unhealthy tactics and short-term Band-Aids instead of sustained and healthier outcomes.

Most of us are powerfully drawn to this focus on speed and the future. Future resilience is the goal of parents, educators, CEOs, military leaders, and sports teams. Nations are focused on "building resiliency" to events to come even as legacies of events gone by wreak havoc.

But even while we prepare for the future, what most people and societies need is resilience to the past. They need to develop ways to positively adapt not to outlier events but pervasive and enduring harms.

The Anthropocene and Slow Violence

One of the ways we adapt is by creating new concepts and words that enable us to rethink what we know. *Solastalgia*, for example, is a word that was created to describe eco-anxiety and the fears brought on by climate destruction and change. It captures the melancholy dread and displacement that come with loved places being made inaccessible and unrecognizable by climate change.[14] It also describes the feeling of homesickness or nostalgia that you can have while you are still at home.

Another useful expression in the exploration of resilience is *slow violence*, a term coined by environmentalist Rob Nixon in his 2011 book, *Slow Violence and the Environmentalism of the Poor*. Nixon describes creeping, delayed destruction that happens over time and that is frequently impossible to see. This damage, he explains, "is typically not viewed as violence at all."

Nixon, an English professor at Princeton, was writing about environmental toxicity—nuclear waste, oil spills, food deserts, toxic chemicals, and climate change. He described harms of duration, juxtaposing them to the kind of time-condensed frenzied violence the media likes to turn into spectacles. The phrase has been widely taken up by legal theorists, political activists, and scholars, who've applied it to a wide range of problems.

In the 1980s, atmospheric chemist Paul Crutzen and ecologist Eugene Stoermer first began using the word *Anthropocene* to describe a new geological epoch defined by planetary-level changes resulting from human activity, changes that lead to our greater vulnerability and exposure to risk. The word was envisioned as a wake-up call for human societies to address possible existential threats.[15] Climate disasters, coral reef destruction, extinctions, increased risks of pandemics, are all slow-moving and hard to see, but they are no less and arguably far more destructive than forms of violence that we traditionally recognize by virtue of their individual harms. The Anthropocene also has grossly disproportionate impacts on the poor and most vulnerable people in communities the world over.

During the past three decades, building resilience to Anthropocene crises has become a standard practice in areas as diverse as urban planning, supply chain logistics, disaster response, health care, community sustainability, biodiversity efforts, education, and military preparedness. Acknowledging the problems we've created as a species and naming them with new words and thinking suggests that we are moving in the right direction, that to adapt and survive we are willing to engage in self-reflection, recognize our intellectual and economic sins, and consider formerly unfathomable options.

But is *Anthropocene* itself, to paraphrase Audre Lorde, a master's tool?

Anthropocene, many argue, will fail us because it suffers structurally from the same broken worldview that led us to our crises. Its defining *anthropos* (Greek for "human") sets us apart from "nature" in a traditional way that strongly suggests humans as the central, dominant, and theoretically controlling agents of what is to come. As a result, Anthropocene resilience agendas largely still prioritize human-centered and human-driven growth, including incremental deck-chair-on-the-

Titanic modifications, "Conscious Capitalism," and dubious high-risk technologies that might accelerate our collapse.[16]

"As a Métis scholar," explains Zoe Todd, an anthropologist and scholar of Indigenous philosophy, science, law, and the Anthropocene, "I have an inherent distrust of this term, the *Anthropocene*." The concept, she notes, came from the Euro-Western academy with little openness to alternative worldviews and conceptions. This is a space where we are taught to think of science as "objective," "neutral," and superior to other approaches to understanding time, nature, and our relationship to the world.[17]

While "Mankind" did indeed propel us to our current crisis point, *humankind* did not collectively decide to pursue technologies, social structures, and economic systems that destabilized our environment, generated cataclysmic climate risks, escalated global inequality, and fueled pervasive political violence and war.

We may, as individuals, adopt climate-friendly personal habits, but these habits are pyrrhic in the face of the challenges we face. Despite increases in China's emissions, consumers in the United States still produce twice the emissions, per person, than those in China and twenty times the rate, per person, of sub-Saharan Africans.[18] Ongoing wars are an utter calamity for the climate and climate negotiations. If it were a nation-state, the U.S. military would be the forty-seventh-largest greenhouse emitter in the world, exceeding the production of other industrialized nations such as Sweden, Finland, and Switzerland.[19] Across eighty-six countries, the richest 10 percent of people consume around twenty times more energy than the poorest 10 percent.[20] We can't individually solve our systemic problems.

Even the most ardent recyclers aren't shutting down the economy to protest a global economic system in which one hundred companies generate 70 percent of the planet's greenhouse gases. In fact, the people who do are lambasted as unhinged teenage girls, oversensitive vegans, and anti-American traitors, by critics sustaining a perverse form of capitalism as patriotism to the death.

Anthropocene urges us to understand our role in generating catastrophe and the "world's end," but, again, which world are we talking about? In 2016, the Anthropocene Working Group, an expert global panel of scientists, designated the year 1950 as the turning point for this new epoch, a time that marked the start of population explosions, skyrocketing energy consumption, and nuclear weapons development. It also coincides with the start of what's known as the Great Acceleration.[21]

But, world-threatening and world-ending human activities have happened before. The date to count from, many suggest, is more appropriately 1600, at the end of an era known as the Great Dying. Between 1492 and 1600 an estimated 56 million people were killed—90 percent of the Indigenous population of the Americas or roughly 10 percent of the global population. So many people died, scientists believe, that their absence led to the rapid and widespread reforestation of the Americas, which, in turn, contributed significantly to a highly consequential cooling of the planet.[22]

Debates such as these have generated a host of thoughtful and deliberately provocative alternatives to *Anthropocene*. Ecologist Theodore Grudin uses *Petrolocene*, to highlight consumerism and fuel sources.[23] Taking racial and gendered capitalism into account, philosophers and theorists of science Anna Tsing and Donna Haraway use *Plantationocene* to viscerally evoke the concrete relationships and corrosive structural legacies inherent in the damage we humans are doing.[24] Historian Salar Mameni uses *Terracene* to describe a planetary age defined by the convergence of climate and environmental destruction and unhinged militarism.[25] Political economist Jason Moore argues for *Capitalocene*, a term that focuses on capitalism's exploitation of nature to explain our plight in ways that *Anthropocene* does not.[26]

The scope and complexity of these possibilities make them feel overwhelming, but together they achieve one goal: they creatively and intellectually refuse the worldview that generated the problems at hand.

Resonance as Resilience

Time thinking illuminates the way that climate crises are environmental crises are epidemiological crises are economic crises are reproductive and social justice crises.

It also helps shed light on the way many of us feel in our daily lives.

Do you ever, for instance, have the feeling that you are racing all the time, but going nowhere? Or maybe have amplified feelings of looming surprise and impending crisis?

If so, you're having experiences that your great-grandparents might have found familiar. The twentieth-century history of trauma is also a history of modern-European time. Then, as now, our relationships to and experience of time are altered by new technologies and their impacts. The schedules and standardizations made possible and necessary by trains, steam, electricity, and factories caused radical changes in the rhythms of daily life.

These technologies also brought industrial accidents and train disasters, causing injuries that often involved many people and witnesses, as well as horrifying injuries. Doctors began seeing patients, people who had either been in or witnessed crashes or accidents, who exhibited new and unique symptoms: disruptive memories, headaches, nervous tics, an inability to sleep, personality changes, and interpersonal conflicts. Populations also began reporting more diffuse and greater malaise due to time-based disruptions to daily life. Stark differences between personal time, circadian time, work time, and even the global time required for transportation, communication, and war systems strained people and societies.

In our era, the stress we feel often results not only from speed and its effects but from the *acceleration* of technical and social change. In the nineteenth and early-twentieth centuries, technologies such as electricity and steam power, for example, took between sixty and one hundred years to achieve saturation in any given nation, but wholesale adoption of the internet by a nation today takes, on average, only sixteen years.[27]

As individuals, we may experience acceleration as exciting or exhausting, hopeful or harrowing, but, regardless, we have to adhere to time standards not of our own making. It's not only that we feel life moving faster, but that our biological and subjective time are subsumed by standardized time and its regulations. All you have to do is look at the phone in your hand to see the schedules, calendars, alert systems, and data processes that shape your day and track your body and govern your emotions.

Acceleration affects our relationships (consider dating's gamification) and the exporting of workplace efficiency standards into our biometrics (such as wristbands worn by Amazon workers to measure their movements and productivity). It also affects our political systems. Many of the fault lines in our democracies stem from the tension between our accelerated lives and the slowness required for deliberative processes to be effective. One result of this tension has been that executive branches and strongmen, capable of quick decision-making, are growing more powerful, especially in crises (which they have the ability to generate).[28]

In times of crisis, time is elastic, a sensation we experience as "unnatural." Time slows down, speeds up, or even stops. Our sense of self and stability, as we've seen, creates what we think of as "normal life." One of the ways we become aware that something is "wrong" with us or the world around us is when we experience time differently. Losses, shocks, and crises often highlight how densely our perceptions of time and our sense of "normal" are entwined. Intrusive memories are distressing not only because they cause us pain but because of the way that they collapse the past into the present and, in a fearful apprehension, the past and present into the future. It's also hard, when you are anxious or stressed, to look forward to a time when you won't feel the same way, because negative feelings can feel permanent. Under stress and in crises, you are more likely to respond to empty urgencies, seek immediate rewards, and minimize future risks, a cognitive habit known as temporal discounting.

Part of the excess stress women feel comes from our not even having awareness or understanding of temporal frictions in our day-to-day lives. As a working mother of three young children, I experienced more time-based conflicts than my spouse did. On any given day, he had to work primarily around two types of time: the demands of a full-time job based on billable hours and his personal time for meals and parenting when home. As default parent, I had to integrate the clock time of work life, the care time of tending to children according to their individual needs, my reproductive and circadian cycles, and the strictly imposed rules of my older child's school and schedules. This is pretty typical in heterosexual marriage, where women generally also have to be more alert or responsive to their spouse's time needs. Being optimistic, self-sufficient, grateful, strong, productive, and knowing how to turn obstacles into challenges can't really help with time-order stresses such as these. What does help is collective support and temporal flexibility.

People who adapt to change more easily manipulate time. Specifically, they treat time with less rigidity than others and shift expectations more readily and fluidly.[29] For example, they easily move from the clock time of their jobs, to the subjective time of their body's needs and rhythms, and shared time with friends and family. Integrating time, known as temporal work, enhances cognitive flexibility and problem-solving.[30] From war refugees to entrepreneurs to survivors of earthquakes, this way of using time as a resilience resource helps people reduce stress and cope with change.[31] As an orientation, it is also more prevalent in other cultures, such as island cultures, where people don't identify as powerfully with standards of Western modernity.

Arguably, acceleration is itself the source of stress so many feel and contributes to the chances of traumatic outcomes because we didn't evolve to adapt to change at the pace in which it is happening. Even as this is happening, however, we turn to more time-based habits, measuring our sleep, calories, units of mindfulness, and exercise to gain control where little exists. Our reliance on measuring everything according to clock time contributes to an implicit catastrophizing of change itself because we learn to equate change with a lack of control, anxious uncertainty, and powerlessness. Metrics and clocks aren't regulating our nutrition, sleep, or time but regulating *us* through the illusory promise of predictability and stability.

Often, the full force of accelerations only hits when a crisis does. But, between "normal" and "crisis," we are constantly experiencing disconnections, including time-based disconnections, from ourselves and the world. Amid this relentless and constant change, our awareness of having to resiliently adapt is blunter. Our adaptive responses can be both negative and positive, but, in either case, because of the pace of life we often have amplified feelings of looming surprise and disruption. We don't necessarily think of resilience as the effort to resist the temporal orders or technological and cultural shifts that we have no individual choice in, but we should.

The resilience we need can't be the resilience of bouncing back or even bouncing forward. Instead, we can rethink resilience by considering how we *make time* for others by redistributing power, money, and other vital resources. Including how we relate to the world.

Ultimately, what "bouncing back quickly" usually means is returning to preexisting and highly undesirable alienation. Alienation, sociologist Hartmut Rosa believes, is the human response to acceleration.[32] Acceleration generates stark tensions between our needs, biology, and cognition and the time forced on us by dominant institutions, technologies, and culture makers. As a result, we are continuously acting in ways we don't want to and don't choose ourselves. None of us can slow down the world. We can take breaks and pace ourselves, but most of us have to work to live. So, what do we do? Rosa suggests the answer is to seek out and experience harmonious relationships with others and the world, what he labels experiences of resonance. Resonance is a sensation of a deep connection to . . . everything.

Rosa's theory is in many ways remarkably like Indigenous world-views that make relatedness, instead of separateness, foundational to our understanding of the world. This relatedness is also a function of time, understood as cyclical, fluid, and tied to the natural world. Indigenous origin stories, science practices, language, and philosophy are structured deeply around concepts now being given names such as "resonance." Indigenous people, already postapocalyptic, have found ways to adapt.

Over centuries, different cultures have creatively confronted, undermined, and challenged power working through time and making claims to bodies and the future. Indigenous communities protect language, culture, and traditions essential to their ongoing fights for sovereignty. Caribbean islanders, for centuries, defiantly "kept time" with forbidden drums and frenetic musical genres, rhythmic ripostes to oppression and charges of stupidity and slowness. The descendants of enslaved Black people created Afrofuturism, a global movement claiming and producing radically liberated futures.

Resonance works well with the understanding that resilience is a process over time and that it is, first and foremost, relational. Conforming to bouncing-back urgency does the opposite, foreclosing our ability to understand history, find creative solutions to problems, and be compassionate with others and ourselves.

8

RISK AND THE BURDEN OF RESILIENCE

Let's by all means grieve together, but let's not
be stupid together.

—Susan Sontag

No one who watched Dorian spin over the northern Bahamas can
deny the prodigious energy and force of water. Anxiously watching
from afar, I was thrown back to memories not of other hurricanes, but
of the Boxing Day Tsunami.

On the morning of December 27, 2004, I opened my front door
to grab the morning newspaper and immediately knew something
terrible had happened. The above-the-fold headline, a now-obsolete
visual clue to the scale of an issue, was oversize. What I read was difficult to fathom: a 9.0-magnitude undersea earthquake in Indonesia
had generated a massive tsunami that, over seven hours, killed "thousands," a number later revised to a quarter of a million people.

The tsunami wasn't just one, but a series of giant waves, some
up to a hundred feet high. The total energy generated is estimated
to have been double that of all of World War II's explosive power,
including the two atomic bombs. The earthquake lasted eight to ten
minutes and made the entire planet vibrate. Customarily, Indonesian

authorities would have sent a regional alert, but lightning had shut down the country's sensor and communication systems, so there was no warning.[1]

As I watched videos of Dorian showing newly created rivers sweep over Bahamian people, buildings, and towns, this is what I thought of. Rapidly moving water is an unstoppable force that turns once-familiar landscapes into deadly obstacle courses. Less than seven inches of fast-flowing water can sweep you off your feet, and a flash flood can result in waters thirty feet high.

We don't have to imagine the risks of climate change, we know them. How well we adapt to crises is not a matter of risk, however, but of how we *perceive* risk and make decisions about what we will do about it.

Being Resilient Means Anticipating Risks

We tend to think about resilience in reactive ways—how do we respond after adversity—but in practical terms resilience includes the steps we take to avoid adversity to begin with.

As individuals, we are constantly assessing our environments for threats and calculating the likelihood of risks, but we do it so quickly we aren't even conscious of what goes into our thinking. Until we conflict with another person we are not usually aware of how differently each of us thinks about risk.

Have you ever gone for a lovely stroll alone at night? Through quiet city streets or alongside a river? Will there be people around who are hostile? Is the path lit or not? Are there people around if you need help? Every time I do, I go through this rough risk assessment. I'm navigating the possibility of being followed or being photographed by strange men or of sexual harassment and rape. As a woman, thinking this way is a necessity. Most of us plan ahead, often at great psychic and financial cost, to avoid danger and threat. Each of us has our own levels of risk awareness and adaptation, and our planning is a resilient adaptation. While we culturally believe men are more inclined to take risks, the definition of risk used to reach this conclusion rarely includes the risks that women take to normalized male violence.

At larger scales, every industry sector and government agency has designed elaborate and expensive risk and resilience systems to identify threats and reduce harms. From health care and disaster preparedness to banking and technology, risk avoidance and resilience are ever-expanding fields with massive investments in technology, information, and human expertise. The emphasis is on threat awareness, risk management, and harm reduction.

Despite the resilience expectations resting on our shoulders as individuals, each of us has to trust experts and leaders to make decisions, hopefully better informed, on our behalf. But even authoritative people and experts fall back on cognitive shortcuts and personal experiences.

Take my nighttime walks. My risk-assessment practices are universal for women, most of whom feel less safe in public spaces and while using public transportation, especially at night. We are taught that safety is our personal responsibility, and so, as girls we learn to adapt, primarily by self-restricting our speech and curtailing our freedom of movement. The same is true for people who refuse to conform to conventional gender and sexual norms.

Our greater vulnerability isn't a function of biology but of who decides what threats and risks are worthy of attention. With few exceptions, cities aren't designed for women or people with disabilities. Ignorance and careless risk assessment by people tasked with building and managing shared space continues to make this true.[2] The great majority of city planners continue to be able-bodied men with vastly different experiences of risk and threat. We are left to contend with inadequate conceptions of what a "good city" looks like. Their risk perceptions have historically *produced* risk for women and other marginalized people, who, as a result, have to be more resilient in daily life than they might otherwise.

Or take deregulation as a political goal and a policy initiative. Deregulation might be profitable, but those profits almost always come at the expense of people not involved in risk decision-making.

On February 3, 2023, a train carrying vinyl chloride, a known carcinogen, derailed near East Palestine, Ohio. Eleven of the train's thirty-eight cars contained hazardous materials, which spilled into the environment, forcing rescue workers to start a controlled burn to reduce the danger of the train's exploding and spreading even more toxins. More than one hundred thousand gallons of chemicals were ultimately released into the air and waterways.

Five thousand frightened residents, many of whom were already experiencing breathing difficulties, nausea, skin irritation, burning eyes, and headaches, immediately evacuated. What happened here was a compressed, high-speed version of the Flint, Michigan, water crisis in which carelessness, poor decision-making, and environmental injustice have led to years of lead poisoning and environmental contamination that continue to sicken people.

A chain of decisions turned East Palestine into a place where residents can also no longer trust that they are safe when they drink water, send their children to play outside, swim in the lake, or even breathe. At every step leading to this disaster, experts, industry leaders, regulators, and professional risk managers weighed the risks associated with transporting a large quantity of a deadly and volatile substance and decided they were acceptable. The train company didn't violate any regulations because decisions about risk thresholds related to wheel bearings, among other things, reside with railroad companies, not the federal government. How did the train derail anyway? A railcar wheel bearing, a small device that ensures wheels run smoothly, overheated and was damaged. It takes all of ten minutes to replace a faulty one.[3]

Little stands in the way of a repeat incident. A 2016 U.S. Department of Transportation report found "little deterrent effect" to similar events because regulatory structures are weak, criminal penalties languish with no consequences, and little can be done about train cargoes getting more and more dangerous.[4] During the four years of Trump's presidency, his administration was committed to extremes of deregulation, almost one hundred environmental protection rules were revoked, and dozens more removals were in progress when his term ended.[5]

We choose leaders who confirm our values and beliefs and share our visions of what makes a good society. What are the parameters of "good"? Whose communities will be sacrificed? Who will get sick? Whose homes will be destroyed by accidents or disasters? Whose families will suffer? *Who will have to be the most resilient?* It's rare that "learning to be resilient" includes civics and the influence of voting on our lives, but elections are risk calculations tied to resilience expectations.

Weeks after the derailment, the Department of Health and Human Services (HHS) provided emergency-response grants to the state of Ohio "to support community wellness and resilience."[6] This is as good an example as any of how, as Naomi Klein put it, disaster capitalism works.[7]

We're schooled to think of resilience in highly individualized ways, but the degree to which we can and have to be resilient depends on people we empower to make *risk decisions* for us. We give others the authority to impose *their* risk perceptions and resilience understandings on the rest of us.

Business leaders, economists, politicians, technologists, and scientists have the power to determine the quality and safety of our food, the nature of our communications, the energy we rely on, and the shape, look, and feel of the many technologies that impact our lives. While we can each do our best to prepare ourselves, our families, and maybe even our neighborhoods from possible dangers, most of us have little ability to prepare in a meaningful way—by assessing risks and acting to reduce their likelihood *at scale*.

Who Decides What a Risk Is?

It's fair to call the past 150 years an Age of Toxicity. Our water, soil, air, oceans, food, and bodies have been poisoned because the risks of new substances, foods, and technologies have been routinely underestimated, minimized, or ignored. Even as resilience, like stress, has been privatized—intently funneled into our individual responsibility—technological, economic, scientific, and political forces have steadily eroded our power to address risk. We rely on risk decision-makers, at scales we can't control.[8]

The real power that risk decision-makers have, though, isn't just in defining what constitutes a risk, but defining what constitutes *an acceptable risk.* Acceptable to whom? For how long? At what cost?

What informs our perceptions, and why can they differ so drastically?

Questions such as these keep Paul Slovic up at night. He's been asking them professionally for more than fifty years. A pioneering decision-science researcher, Slovic has spent his life studying how humans make risk-related decisions.[9] He and his collaborators investigate the vital connections between the human need to protect our identities and values, how we perceive risk, and our political choices.

One of Slovic's more influential studies was conducted in 1994, when he and his team asked fifteen hundred people across the United States to evaluate environmental risks that were at the center of political debate. The researchers found that white men tended to assess risks as far less likely to happen and as more acceptable than other demographic groups. White women perceived risks as more consequential than white men did, but as less threatening than non-white women and men, who scored risk at roughly the same degree. The study revealed a subset of the white men to be the most risk-prone, approximately 30 percent, who had greater-than-average trust in authority and technology. These men tended to be conservative, hierarchical thinkers, and hypercommitted to individualism.[10]

"Perhaps," the researchers concluded, "white males see less risk in the world because they create, manage, control, and benefit from so much of it. Perhaps women and non-white men see the world as more dangerous because in many ways they are more vulnerable, because they benefit less from many of its technologies and institutions, and because they have less power and control."[11]

Slovic and his team called this finding "the white male effect." In the decades since, further studies revealed that status, inequality, and social capital, not race or gender per se, are the operative factors. In the United States, for example, white men as a class generally have higher status and more influence and political power than other groups of citizens, but in Sweden, where gender gaps in equality and status are narrower, white men and women have roughly the same risk-tolerance levels compared to minorities and immigrants.[12]

The effect that Slovic and his colleagues discovered has led to theories of cultural cognition that explain how we make judgments to protect our identities, confirm our beliefs, and reinforce our specific visions of what makes a good society.[13] In other words, our world-views inform how we think about risk, influencing everything from whether we will eat genetically modified foods and what we think about gun control to if AI is an existential threat and how disaster-response systems are built.

Resilience Means Embracing Other Ways of Knowing

Immediately after the Boxing Day Tsunami, humanitarian aid poured into the affected region. Rescue efforts focused on possible losses of life in already-stressed aboriginal communities in the Indian Ocean basin. Anthropologists were worried that an entire tribe, the Onge, had been wiped out.

Contrary to these fears, however, once rescuers located the tribe, they found *fewer* deaths and injuries among the Onge and other aboriginal communities than in the wider population. Long oral histories of experiences with earthquakes and tsunamis meant that these communities were better prepared than many others. Their storytelling included valuable warnings and preventative strategies that worked. Experts concluded that, among the Onge, folk tales were the key to why all of the one hundred remaining tribe members survived.[14]

These tribes used their stories—not considered by Western experts to be sources of valuable technical expertise—to share and expand their knowledge of ecosystems and the environment. Newer populations and tourists scattered along Indian Ocean shorelines had none of this expertise or knowledge, leaving them unprepared and vulnerable.

During the past two decades, disaster response and resilience programs have expanded to look beyond Western standards of science, measurement, and technology to incorporate Indigenous histories, knowledge, and the influence of social order and political power in the course of "natural disasters."[15]

Take wildfire management. Until Euro-American colonization, many Indigenous cultures effectively used fire to fight fire, modifying their environments to minimize and avoid catastrophes. For more than thirteen thousand years, tribes across California used controlled burns to manage resources, grow food, and reduce the risk of unregulated wildfires.[16] These practices were outlawed for centuries, foreclosing effective disaster management. Not until 2021 did the state pass a law confirming the right to "good fire." Traditional ecological knowledge (TEK) is now being revisited across the globe.[17]

We are just in the earliest stages of doing this, however. In general, Western frameworks tolerate other approaches to ecological risk but are invested in technocratic tools, global cooperation, and open data sharing, all of which, in disasters, can come to a crashing halt.

The combination of overreliance on technical systems and disparagement of alternative knowledge resources is deadly. As I type, Hawaiians are reeling in the aftermath of a wildfire that destroyed Lahaina, Hawaii's historic former capital. Indigenous efforts to manage resources there have been thwarted for decades in favor of tourism, foreign investment, and growth. In the immediate aftermath of the catastrophe and with hundreds still missing, Indigenous Hawaiians implored tourists to stay away. In a surreal echo of *White Lotus*–level entitlement, visitors continued swimming in waters where, only a day previously, rescuers were retrieving bodies. According to news reports, "for some unknown reason" none of the eighty sophisticated warning sirens on Maui alerted the population to what was happening.[18]

Having limited respect for or understanding of different and diverse sources of knowing and managing risk is hardly limited to how we approach natural disasters. Our beliefs and identity-protective cognition can literally make unfamiliar risks, or those that threaten our sense of self and place, invisible to us.

In December 2019, just weeks before the pandemic lockdown, I participated in a conference on the role of media in the rising threat of authoritarianism. For the people in the room—journalists, academics, and researchers who worked at the intersection of media, tech, and politics—the prior five years had been particularly fraught, stressful, and challenging. The 2020 election loomed, and anxiety over risks of violence and disruption cast a worried pall on the room.

The event kicked off with a panel of experts describing global trends in the rise of authoritarian attitudes. One of the panelists said that authoritarian-minded leaders were coming to power with virtually no resistance from either the public or media. He claimed that journalists and political editors hadn't perceived the risks posed by Donald Trump in 2016. Citizens in the United States and around the world seemed complacent, and media hadn't sufficiently raised the alarm.

From my perspective this claim was gobsmacking. Even though a majority of white voters supported Trump, millions of people from every demographic, especially women, well understood the political and social threats he represented. For decades, reproductive-justice advocates pressed media to understand erosions of women's rights in state legislatures. In the years leading up to the 2016 and 2020 elections, women organized and led resistance movements to fight for immigration rights, Black lives, abortion access, environmental safety, ending gun violence, voting rights, disability rights, prison abolition, and more. On the day of Trump's inauguration, millions of people, again mainly women, peacefully participated in the largest global protest in recorded history. Today, women activists, community leaders, and legal advocates are at the vanguard of democracy movements.[19]

This hardly constitutes "no one."

The panelist was referring to an elite class of, as studies have shown, white journalists and editors who underestimated the risks of white supremacy, misogyny, homophobia, anti-Semitism, and xenophobia. Journalists, writers, and activists marginalized by a remarkably homogenous mainstream political media were acutely alert to the risks of tyranny and often frustrated by its whitewashing, false equivalences, and peevish dismissals of concerns about misogynistic ethnoviolence. The problem the panelist identified wasn't that "no one" was resisting or framing the risk, but that because of a lack of power sharing and diversity in newsrooms and political coverage, risk perception was dangerously distorted.[20] As editors and writers, women and journalists from marginalized communities are more likely to cover issues that are otherwise ignored or minimized.[21]

Our resilience, both personal and political, is constantly being tested because our institutional threat assessment is concentrated in the hands of people whose risk perceptions and social values are woefully out of sync with the needs of a diverse and pluralistic society. Across all major institutions, a lack of diversity in our decision-making bodies *is a risk* that we can't afford.[22] No amount of personal resilience skills building or dedicated individual good intentions will generate the adaptability and resolve that we need collectively.

Are there any limits? To the power? To the risk? To the mandates of resilience we are subject to?

Resilience and the American Culture of Limitlessness

Social beliefs within a society vary wildly, and no one dominant vision of the good life exists, but it's fair to say that freedom is uniformly valued in American culture. Americans pride themselves on a commitment to having limited or no constraints on their individual desires and on not being subject to coercion.

Perhaps more than freedom, however, there is another idea that shapes our identities and history: *limitlessness*. Limitlessness also means the absence of boundaries or constraints, external or internal, but *it goes further* to suggest infinite potential and possibilities. It is central to progress and humanism, to the belief that we can transcend the finitude of our bodies and death to find a better world. It is critical to the idea that "Man" dominates "Nature." Limitlessness transforms freedom into an infinite expanse of growth, autonomy, and power; the essence, in fact, of frontier mentalities.

From Manifest Destiny and the Agrarian Ideal to today's reanimated fascination with escaping to the American West, our cultural myths are filled with free movement, free speech, free land, and free people, ideally unencumbered by the limits that come with government, borders, and other people. The limits that come with social care and collective moralities. Limits that are, historically, also associated with the tamed and muted natures of women.

Being a "real" man takes freedom as essential, but limitlessness is what animates the belief that you can be all that you can be, strive to take or make all that you can imagine. Needless to say, not all men can lay claim to this right as a marker of adult manhood. The more limits placed on people, the weaker and more vulnerable they are.

Black men, for instance, have historically been denied the basics of American masculine rights—unfettered access to work, guns, paid labor, white women, voting, freedom of speech and movement, as well as monopolies on state violence.

On the other hand, moving from boyhood to manhood, most likely as a young white boy, is an invitation to expand yourself into the world, exploring where you will, pursuing your potential, and dominating your environment. "God only knows what the limit is of you!" explains a typically anguished-looking Jordan Peterson in a 2018 talk titled "How Resilient Are You?"[23] Jordon specializes in telling his fan base, overwhelmingly young men, to get their acts together and reclaim the promise and power of this ideal.

Late-stage capitalist oligarchs are likewise putting on an exemplary show. Their transhuman, cryogenic dreams and actual penis-shaped-rocket races allow them to manspread through the ultimate frontiers: time and space. In his 2023 Techo-Optimist Manifesto, Silicon Valley billionaire Marc Andreessen identified "the limits of growth" as part of a six-decade "mass demoralization."[24]

One of the more disturbing aspects of girlhood, conversely, is learning to fold limits *into yourself*. Even for women privileged by class and race, the passage to adulthood means having to accept checks on your freedom, speech, authority, and ambitions. It means understanding that there are hard and punishing social and political limits on your ability to control what happens to and in your own body.

In frontier cultures such as the American West, a survival and competition mentality rooted in limitlessness may have provided real advantages to men who set out to find their fortunes, but it's spectacularly ill-suited to the contemporary world. A brute-force resilience of individual survival in hostile, low-population-density hinterlands undermines our collective realities. As a cultural norm, the rugged individualism of frontier mentalities disdains investing in communal well-being and revolts against the investments in mutual care necessary to healthily sustain a diverse, crowded, and connected world.[25]

How, then, are men, not only those who amass unprecedented power and resources, supposed to reconcile their identities with a society that has begun to impose limits—on privileges, power, and perhaps, even more importantly, potential? Much of today's right-wing pursuit of freedom and hatred of progressive causes appears as aggrieved entitlement. In this environment, any attempt to enact reasonable limits, in regulations or empathetic adjustment, becomes a threat to honor.

Take efforts to address gun violence. As is the case with acknowledging climate change and environmental toxicity, conservative white men with outlier risk perceptions are the most resistant to efforts at "gun control."[26] However, change the language of the debate and resistance declines. The word *control* in *gun control* elicits a defensive response from gun owners because it threatens their self-image as strong, independent American men capable of protecting their families and property. *Violence prevention*, on the other hand, doesn't have the same effect. It taps into moral values that make sense to gun owners—protection and safety, without threatening freedom.[27]

The same is true in regards to protecting the environment. When Trump stood in front of a Michigan crowd of women voters in 2020 and promised to "get your husbands back to work,"[28] he harkened back to the golden age of American oil and gas, a time when nuclear families were led by male wage earners who were, particularly if white, beneficiaries of postwar affirmative action programs.[29] It was an era represented by cars, symbolizing freedom and limitless horizons. We might make faster strides toward addressing the risks of planet warming if we analyzed the debate in terms of a global retrenchment of *petro-masculinity* instead of *petroleum dependency*.[30]

None of this is to say that all men feel limitless and powerful, because they don't and aren't. But the *idea* of freedom from control, combined with unlimited potential and, in modernity, limitless progress, is an ideal of manhood and masculinity that undermines collective adaptability. To regain a sense of joyful possibility and trust in the world, in place of the pall of pervasive anxieties and despair, the feelings of loss and longing that so many seem to feel, we have to rene-gotiate these words and ideas as well as the nature of the relationships they sustain and deny.

Killjoy Resilience

Compared to men, women are often described as risk averse and inher-ently vulnerable. We are hovering mothers, anxious girlfriends, igno-rant shrews, and worrying scolds bent on stopping boys and men from having fun and taking risks that might, in the end, bring them glory, wealth, or power. Tasked with managing resilience—care, connection, nurturing, resources, healing—we are considered the ultimate killjoys.

Rachel Carson would have understood this well. Sixty years ago, in 1963, she was invited by the U.S. Congress to answer questions about her landmark book, *Silent Spring,* a blazing critique of America's use of chemical pesticides.

Carson, a marine biologist and writer, argued that human attempts to control and dominate nature hurt the environment and humans. She had grown up with an early love of nature and an awareness of the impacts of chemical waste on plants, waterways, and wildlife. Using growing public anxiety about nuclear radiation as a point of comparison, she urged the government to be skeptical of the chem-ical industry's risk assessments and its promises. She insisted that regulations—limits—were critical.

Carson's research and conclusions were unimpugnable, but chem-ical company adversaries, politicians, and journalists questioned her rigor with contempt. She and her book, wrote *Time* magazine, were "hysterically overemphatic." Others dismissed her as a Communist spinster, simultaneously scaremongering and silly. "If Man were to follow the teachings of Miss Carson, we would return to the Dark

Ages," warned biochemist Robert White-Stevens, who said she was "a fanatic defender of the cult of the balance of nature."

The risks and costs of dangerous chemicals seemed clear to Carson, who had, throughout her life, witnessed the impacts of pollution. When she testified, she was wearing a wig to hide the effects of radiation treatment for breast cancer.

Carson valued healthy life over healthy profits. She knew the stresses and traumas that pollution brought to people, their families, and their communities. Her expertise was enhanced by life experience. Her thresholds for what counted as acceptable risks to bodies, relationships, homes, animals, plants, trees, and water were higher than those of the men she had to appeal to. For her, resilience meant mitigating risks and future pain and suffering.

Despite pushback, Carson's work ignited a global environmental movement and compelled the passage of landmark legislation, including, in the years immediately after she testified, the Clean Air Act (1963), the Wilderness Act (1964), and the National Environmental Policy Act (1969). Just eight years after the publication of *Silent Spring*, the Environmental Protection Agency was formed. But despite Carson's efforts and growing environmental-justice movements, chemical pollution and toxic human-made substances continue to have even more severe consequences for biodiversity, the climate, and life.

When Trump's appointee to head the EPA, Scott Pruitt, restricted scientific inquiry into environmental harms, he did it in a room named after Carson.[31] Despite her influence, babies today are born with plastic *in their bodies*. Every week, each of us consumes up to a credit card's worth of microplastics, and we have no idea what their effects on us are.[32]

Carson's findings challenged market mandates, but the real threat she posed was to the ascendance of America's post–World War II establishment and its technocratic belief in unending scientific progress.[33] That same scientific establishment was, at the time, developing the nuclear power and weapons industries that would compel researchers such as Paul Slovic to delve deeply into the immense gaps between experts' risk perceptions and those of the public.

In the summer of 1987, only a few years after the 1979 Three Mile Island nuclear disaster—which had an enormous effect on the nuclear power industry in America[34]—Carol Cohn, the founding director of the Consortium on Gender, Security and Human Rights, was attending a conference on nuclear weapons and war. She was one of ten women in a program led by some of the country's top defense strategists and intellectuals. Cohn was immediately taken aback by how the experts talked about risk and threats to life.

Among a group of men she described as "unusually endowed with charm, humor, intelligence, concern, and decency," there was "no horror, urgency, or moral outrage" about the possibility of holocausts. Language such as "clean bombs" and "collateral damage" sanitized risk into nonrisk. She also noted how profusely the men used the language of sexual domination to describe the destructive power of their technologies. Missiles were "penetration aids." Nuclear defense was "irresistible because you get more bang for the buck." There were "vertical erector launchers," "thrust-to-weight ratios," "soft lay downs," "deep penetration" tactics, and discussions over the advantages of protracted versus spasmodic attacks. One military adviser called for "releasing seventy to eighty percent of our megatonnage in one orgasmic whump."[35]

This might feel outdated, but it's still casually familiar. Oil and gas extraction, terraforming, and geoengineering are filled with "hard" and "soft" technologies, "stratospheric injections," and "cloud seeding," strategies for penetrating the atmosphere and inseminating the earth. In 2018, Cohn was still warning about the "perils of mixing masculinity and missiles."

Carson and Cohn were risk outliers in their milieus, but as white women they were at least able to gain entrée into the rooms and conversations of the powerful. For decades, minority activists such as Hazel Johnson, Peggy Shepard, and Robert Bullard led grassroots organizations and protest movements that repeatedly ran afoul of white male technocratic political power. Members of environmental-justice movements still grapple with climate and green movements that historically ignored the impacts of pollution and climate change on people of color.[36]

Today's boosters of AI technology have frequently similarly dismissed women as excessively catastrophizing. In March 2022, industry experts published two open letters calling for a stop to the development of advanced AI models because of the future risks the technology poses to humanity. Among those who signed were Elon Musk, Bill Gates, Sam Altman, Demis Hassabis, Geoffrey Hinton, Yoshua Bengio, Stuart Russell, and Nick Bostrom—some of the most influential people, overwhelmingly men, involved in thinking about, creating, and releasing the technology. Geniuses and luminaries all, they spoke out publicly, loudly, and in unison, only *after* products were released and in a way that didn't emphasize current harms but potential future risks.

Three months later, *Wired* magazine ran a detailed story titled "Meet the Humans Trying to Keep Us Safe from AI." *Rolling Stone* followed up with "These Women Tried to Warn Us about AI." Both pieces featured women technologists, ethicists, and activists urging more thorough and diverse risk assessment and a slowing of the pace of development. Individually and in tandem, the women had been pressing for more rigorous threat and risk assessment for years, some paying high personal and professional prices. At least two of them, Ifeoma Ozoma and Timnit Gebru, lost their jobs for speaking out publicly.[37]

If you can't perceive a threat, you cannot possibly prepare to mitigate its harms or adapt positively if they come to pass. To be resilient to threats and vulnerability, particularly those that affect us at large scales, you have to understand that they exist in the first place. You have to be willing to listen to people whose lives and experiences are unlike yours. To listen and, even more importantly, to *trust*.

When Women Make Risk and Resilience Decisions

The women at the forefront of public and professional debates about the risks posed by artificial intelligence and other new technologies are frequently experts at the top of their fields. Their thinking and knowledge, however, aren't readily converted into authority and influence.

Diversifying decision-making is essential to building resilient societies. Global studies show that women assess risk differently from men, including as experts. We know that people with disabilities can recognize harms in ways that others may not. Racialized minorities who might bear the brunt of social harms have firsthand knowledge of risks that dominant majorities don't.

Regardless of country, as voters, corporate-board members, and politicians, for instance, women are more likely to embrace policies and be involved in local activism that safeguard health, the climate, forests, waterways, and clean air.[38] The presence of women legislators leads countries to adopt more far-reaching environmental and climate-change protections.[39] People in countries led by women reported higher rates of happiness and life satisfaction.[40] It isn't that women leaders are somehow "naturally" better. They might have ways of relating that affect their governance, but societies that elect women leaders tend to be healthier, safer, happier, and more inclusive to begin with. In other words, they enjoy high levels of social trust, a key to resilience overall.

Public roles come with pronounced risks for women, for example. When they advocate for risk reductions, regulations, care economies, racial equity, reductions in gun violence, and increases to social safety nets, women—cast as humorless nags and buzzkill *limiters*—are constantly on the receiving end of a maelstrom of threats and violence.[41]

In the U.S. Congress, environmental and climate protections are acutely partisan issues, which means they are also gendered issues.[42] One hundred and thirty-nine members of Congress, practically all white and overwhelmingly male, are climate-change deniers. Representative Alexandria Ocasio-Cortez, on the other hand, is the face of Green New Deal legislation.

Online and off, Ocasio-Cortez is routinely harassed and threatened, a situation she manages with graceful aplomb. In June 2020, fellow legislator Florida Republican Ted Yoho accosted her as she walked into the Capitol, calling her "disgusting," "crazy," "dangerous," and out of her mind. Witnesses heard him call her a "fucking bitch," which he later denied.[43] Three years later, in the summer of 2023, the hottest in recorded history, the Republican Party announced Project 2025, their plan to systematically dismantle regulatory policies designed to protect the environment and reduce climate-change impacts.[44]

Recalibrating Risk Decisions

In 2013, Yoho and now Florida governor and former presidential candidate Ron DeSantis were the only Florida legislators to oppose federal funds for Hurricane Sandy relief efforts. In 2023, the Third Congressional District, which Yoho had represented, was devastated by Hurricane Idalia, forcing DeSantis to seek, for the second year in a row, federal relief funds for his state. With more than 8,400 miles of exposed shores, Florida's recent woes will soon look like child's play. Or, put another way, women's work.

Florida is a less than thirty-minute flight to the northernmost Bahamian islands. As part of a significant and separate resilience effort, The Bahamas is now part of a global initiative known as SIDS, which stands for Small Island Developing States. Member states are island nations that face heightened risks of environmental catastrophe. The aggregate population across these countries is 65 million, a small percentage of the number of people who are, by 2050, estimated to be displaced by climate disaster: 1.2 billion. It's difficult to imagine that a body of women would launch an initiative designed to ensure survival and call it SIDS, an acronym already in use to describe the unexplained deaths of babies in their sleep.

It makes sense to consider climate impacts collectively, but that is not the way of the world. Our risk and resilience regimes remain firmly lodged in another era, and so we are left with perverse acronyms and the increasingly high costs of the stubborn lag.

We can resist resilience rhetoric that makes us more vulnerable, that generates unfathomable risks, and that is sustained primarily through exploitation and quests for glory.

Our ability to positively adapt and cope with the inevitable large-scale crises coming our way will depend on if and how we reconcile our competing visions for what makes a good life.

Like risk perceptions, resilience comes from collective negotiations of meaning, belonging, and power. However, even as technology's dire threats loom, as a species we have never before been as hyperconnected as we are today. We don't yet know what it means that so many people can speak, that we can hear so many perspectives, learn from people we will never meet, and gather in spaces that are nowhere and everywhere all at once. We can't be sure we haven't created a network of knowledge and activity that will generate a consciousness we can't control and that might, despite real concerns, be less of a threat to us then we are to ourselves. That is also an alternative vision of the future.

9

MEANING, BELONGING, AND THE STORIES WE TELL

Human beings are magical. Bios and Logos.
Words made flesh, muscle and bone animated by
hope and desire.

—Sylvia Wynter

If you're like me, you can probably recall the stories you heard in childhood in vivid detail. Stories like those my father told. Do you hold these tales dear or recount them to others? Have they become your own?

Our first stories are the ones our families tell us. They build our relationships and identities, becoming the basis, if we are fortunate enough, for a sense of safety, confidence, and empathy. Through stories, we learn to understand the personal attributes and behaviors important to those we love, establishing and sometimes redefining collective norms and values. Because these stories often get passed on from older family members to younger ones, we tend to categorize them as nostalgic.

The word *nostalgia* is a portmanteau of two Greek words, *nóstos* and *álgos*, which mean "homecoming" and "pain." If you have ever left a home, lost a person, or yearned for another time or place, you understand the feeling of nostalgia in your bones.

In its first uses, *nostalgia* described a troubling mental illness during the seventeenth century. Swiss medical student Johannes Hofer was tasked with repairing the ill effects of homesickness in Swiss soldiers fighting in the Thirty Years' War. Initially, military leaders and doctors thought that soldiers' debilitating malaise and maudlin memories were the result of brain and ear damage caused by cowbells. Hofer believed that men's intensive and ruminative feelings were an unrelated sickness.[1] The men who suffered were isolated from their peers, struggled to have positive relationships with others, and had frequently suffered shocking and painful experiences that filled them with longing for loving bonds and familiar places.

Nostalgia is no longer considered a disorder, but a beneficial emotion. According to philosopher and psychiatrist Dr. Neel Burton, recalling warm memories allows us to travel "beyond the suffocating confines of time and space." We now know that being nostalgic is an important dimension of physiological resilience that involves our reward pathways and memory systems. Being nostalgic boosts creativity, encourages openness to new ideas, and is a healthy coping mechanism for people who otherwise feel socially isolated.[2]

As a storytelling tool, it is also a practice of "change your narrative, change your life" resilience advice. Resilience programs often encourage us to reframe hardships so that they are less emotionally overwhelming and in ways that predispose us to act. We see examples all the time. "Become the hero of your own story!" blares a typical *Forbes* headline. "Want to Change Your Life? Change Your Narrative," urges another.

There is good reason to use this approach, also, more formally known as narrative therapy. Ample evidence shows that shifting how you think about adversity and obstacles positively affects your coping with their impacts. Focusing on redemptive aspects of what you've experienced can reduce despair. When we keep diaries, we engage in similar processing. By writing and rewriting, we project ourselves into alternative outcomes with more deliberation. Narrative therapy helps individuals explore troubling experiences in ways that reduce their relevance and emotional resonance. A 2023 study of veterans suffering from PTSD found that having patients write down what they were thinking and feeling during a traumatic event, known as written exposure therapy (WET), was as effective a treatment as more time-intensive prolonged exposure therapy and had the added benefit of higher retention rates for those in treatment.[3]

Stories are the building blocks of our most important relationships, sustaining them even after deaths. Widowed people, for example, who tell themselves stories of their lost ones or, sometimes, continue to talk to them, find meaning and solace. These narrative rituals confirm our identities and extend relationships in new forms, changing how we process loss. In 2010, for instance, after the death of his beloved cousin, Japanese garden designer Itaru Sasaki created the wind phone, an unconnected telephone booth where visitors could have one-way conversations with lost and missing loved ones. In the wake of the 2011 Great East Japan earthquake and tsunami, which killed more than fifteen thousand people, more than thirty thousand people have used the phone booth to speak stories and reduce their feelings of grief.

A singular focus on "taking control and being the author of your life" barely skims the surface of the true power of storytelling, though. Our ability to tell stories evolved as a cognitive advantage for our species. Stories ripple out from each of us as individuals into our families, communities, and societies and then back in again, weaving themselves into our being.

As we've seen, sharing our personal stories helps to diffuse anxiety, stress, and fear because we aren't bearing the burden of hardship alone. But the purpose of personal narratives isn't simply to make us feel good about ourselves. It's also to communicate with others, form strong bonds, and, ultimately, cultivate empathy, cooperation, a shared knowledge. When we listen to or watch sympathetic stories, oxytocin, the hormone of love, compassion, and empathy, surges in us.[4]

Reading fiction has similar effects. Fiction requires us to put ourselves in imaginary scenarios. When we do that, we stimulate the section of our brains responsible for interpreting other people's feelings and thoughts. Fiction readers are more empathetic, socially aware, and situationally alert. They are more open to new experiences and more accepting of people and cultures that differ from their own; both factors of adaptability under stressful conditions and components of building social networks.[5] After all, the purpose of our personal narratives isn't simply to make us feel good about ourselves, but to communicate with others, form strong bonds, and, ultimately, cultivate empathy.

Family Stories Are Foundational, for Better and Worse

My father's nostalgia didn't only help him by reaffirming his beliefs and values. In telling his stories he bequeathed those beliefs and values to the rest of us, helping us build strong bonds and enhance our family's adaptability. Through his happy childhood memories, we learned to envision our own futures. His nostalgic storytelling provided scaffolding for our intergenerational resilience.

But there are also stories that we don't tell children. They are the ones we can't bear to put into words. Stories about our fears and anxieties, but sometimes, these are the memories that matter the most.

On Christmas night in 2018, my extended family, ranging in age from nine to seventy-three, gathered to celebrate in a raucous and lengthy dinner. As the night progressed, we fell into a joyful recounting of family lore. I heard my mother talking about a night when I was fourteen. I remembered the evening well, and we had never discussed it. I had no idea what prompted her to talk about it.

That night my father brought someone home for dinner. Throughout my childhood, our house was a revolving door of people, so this wasn't out of the ordinary. On that night, however, the man arrived with a bodyguard, a first. My parents expected me to be gracious, present, and helpful when we had guests. When they walked in, I greeted them politely but withdrew as quickly as possible because the man made me uncomfortable. His eyes lingered too long, and his friendliness toward me veered on salacious. It didn't help that his bodyguard, sitting at a distance, was armed. I had no idea what they were doing in our house.

After the man left, my father scolded me for being rude and absent. Who was he? I asked. Why was he here, and why did he need a bodyguard? I was told, years later, that the man was one of Anastasio Somoza Debayle's sons. The Somoza family, which ruled Nicaragua from the mid-1930s to 1979, were figureheads of twentieth-century American imperialism. In 1979, after decades of exploitative rule, the family was overthrown and escaped Nicaragua with hundreds of millions of dollars.[6] The following year, Anastasio "Tachito" Somoza, a graduate of West Point known as "the last Marine" in Nicaragua, was assassinated in Paraguay.

Somehow, during this time, one of his sons had drinks with my father, in our living room.

"Remember that night?" my mother, an inveterate recaster of memories, asked me from across the table. "That man flirted shamelessly with you." I looked around at my daughters, nieces, and nephews and balked at this representation of what had happened. I was, I said, a child at the time and he was at least twice my age; his demeanor was menacing and predatory. He had an armed bodyguard. There was no flirting involved.

"You know," my mother said, "you're right." And we moved on without much fanfare.

My mother remembered the event in a harmless and even positive light. In her coping she reappraised a stressful situation to effectively reduce her discomfort and anxiety. For her, resilience—comfort in her skin, safety, social acceptance, trust, access to resources, and survival—may have meant looking away from constant reminders of predatory sexual violence and her relative powerlessness. For me, a generation later, the opposite was true.

Reappraisal is the subjective reinterpretation of events that are emotionally distressing so that we see them in a new light. Reprocessing threatening, adverse, or stressful circumstances so that we can see them in more benign or beneficial ways helps us regulate our emotions and cognition. This reappraisal is the basis, for instance, of developing a challenge orientation toward obstacles. It's also at the heart of trying to be more optimistic or embracing a growth mindset. Looking for things to be grateful for, even in the most tragic circumstances, is also reappraisal. So, too, is believing that your pain serves a higher purpose toward personal growth.

The exchange my mother and I had wasn't only a matter of our reappraisal or different memories of the situation. We engaged in a public conversation of a fraught topic that families rarely name openly—how differently mothers and daughters negotiate experiences of patriarchal violence. We passed valuable information to younger family members. It was personal and interpersonal, a family story and a cultural story. Our evolving depictions of the threat of sexual predation shifted further. It was a story we told at the dinner table that night, but it took forty years to tell it.

During the early years of the COVID pandemic, psychologists recommended parents use family storytelling to help young children manage social isolation and anxiety. The richer a family's stories, the higher a child's self-esteem, social adaptability, and propensity to form close connections with peers. Children who hear stories about family members benefit from stronger emotional ties, a sense of belonging, and a shared knowledge base. They are better able to manage stress and less likely to develop anxiety or depression in uncertain times.[7] After 9/11, ten- to twelve-year-old children in families that told frank stories about prior family adversities coped better than those in families that didn't.

Sometimes, storytelling, reappraisal, and negotiation have adverse collective outcomes. Take the way white supremacy, anti-Blackness, and colorism—all of which can protect an *individual's* self-image and access to resources—work through family lore in insidious ways.

The story of my great-uncle's young death was rarely told by my family, but when it was, its tellings were always filled with friction. One night in February of 1944, my grandfather Fred and his younger brother Roy went pigeon hunting, something they loved doing together, in a remote part of New Providence Island called Adelaide. Within a few hours of tromping through scrubby pine, they realized they'd forgotten some essentials, so my grandfather left to get supplies. When he returned several hours later, his brother, twenty-six, was nowhere to be found. It took over a day and a half before Fred found him, dead of a gunshot wound to the face.

When my grandfather told this story, he would say Roy died when his gun accidently went off. He always made a point to describe his brother as kind, closing by telling us to be careful with guns. His sister, however, had a different interpretation of what had happened. It was unflinching. She had no doubt that he died by suicide.

Roy had traveled to Florida just months before for a swim meet. He was a powerful swimmer, a lifelong athlete, and excited to go. When the team arrived in Florida, however, the men were segregated by race, and he was housed as a "colored" man. She didn't know what happened to Roy that night in Florida, but when he returned home, he wasn't the same person who'd left.

The Bahamas and the United States construct race differently. This doesn't mean there's no racism in The Bahamas, only that it takes different forms. It is also a majority Black nation, which alters power dynamics and relationships among citizens. In one country, Roy was "dark" or "colored," and in another, he was white or at least whiter enough not to be Black.

Roy's death was a family tragedy, but it was also part of the complex, intergenerational, and collective trauma of colonialism, white supremacy, and the violence required to maintain systems of imperial power. His trauma and death shaped my grandfather's actions until the day he died. They also contributed to decades of my family denying our African ancestry, despite our clear mixed ethnic heritage.

In this sense, whiteness may have conferred advantages, but it also made us less resilient as a family. We didn't have the words, education, perspective, or emotional wherewithal to understand how history, culture, and collective trauma affected us as individuals or shaped us as a family. As a result, we were poorly equipped to absorb, generation after generation, the toll that these crosscurrents took on us. Rarely talked about, the lesson of Roy's life and death left colorism, anti-Blackness, and white supremacy corrosively intact.

But all of us live haunted lives. All of us are part of larger stories than our own.

One such story is the murder of Emmett Till. In 1955, the fourteen-year-old boy, visiting relatives in Greenwood, Mississippi, was lynched by white supremacists because a white woman lied and said he'd whistled at her. Her husband and half brother abducted the child, torturing and shooting him before throwing his body into the Tallahatchie River, where it was found three days later. The men were acquitted of the murder by an all-white jury later that year. The following year, knowing they could not be tried again, they openly admitted to the killing. The woman later said her claim that he'd touched and sexually propositioned her was a lie.[8]

After her child's body was returned to Chicago, Mamie Till-Mobley insisted on a public, open-casket funeral. Even as she grieved, she had the clarity of mind to challenge the complicity of the white-dominated media narratives, which included ignoring the brutality and horror of white supremacist violence and corruption. Thousands of people attended Till's funeral, and news outlets, beginning with Black-owned media and then expanding globally to others, published photographs of his battered body.

Mamie Till-Mobley's resoluteness is part of the collective resilience of people who came after her, evident, for example, in the genesis of today's Black Lives Matter movement.[9]

The public consumption of broken Black bodies is no longer shocking the way it was when Emmett Till's body was photographed. In fact, a firehose of images risks our psychic numbing to the persistent reality of violence and its traumatic effects.

"Black bodies in pain for public consumption," writes poet and scholar Elizabeth Alexander, "have been an American national spectacle for centuries. . . . [B]lack people also have been looking, forging a traumatized collective historical memory," which is reactivated every time another person is brutalized. Regardless of how difficult a trauma process is, she writes, it "allows collectivities to define new forms of moral responsibility and to redirect the course of political action." Alexander was writing, in 1994, about the videotaped coverage of four L.A. police officers beating motorist Rodney King.[10]

Twenty-six years later, in 2020, she was compelled to revisit the same themes in an essay simply titled "The Trayvon Generation." Vivid stories of anti-Black violence, she patiently explained again, "instruct young African-Americans about their embodiment and their vulnerability. . . . These stories instructed them that anti-black hatred and violence were never far."[11]

Racism and dehumanizing violence are built—through narrative—into the fabric of our national identity. It's why white Americans cheerily celebrated lynchings with family picnics and lighthearted postcards. It's why eighteen-year-old Michael Brown's body was left face down on his Ferguson, Missouri, neighborhood's street for four hours after he was shot by a police officer. And it's why, in the spring of 2021, two Ivy League colleges were forced to publicly apologize for using the bones of Black children killed during a 1985 police raid as teaching tools. One course, taught as late as 2019, was titled "Real Bones: Adventures in Forensic Anthropology."

There is no respite. In fact, just the opposite. The August 2023 celebration of the sixtieth anniversary of Martin Luther King's March on

Washington, attended by thousands, was marred by the targeting of a historically Black college by a twenty-one-year old white supremacist gunman who, turned away at the school, killed three Black patrons of a Jacksonville, Florida, market. The gunman left not one but several manifestos detailing his hateful ideologies.[12]

The Many Shapes of Stories

On March 29, 2022, the year Emmett Till would have turned eighty-one, the Emmett Till Antilynching Act, making lynching a federal hate crime, was finally passed. Seven months later, a larger-than-life-size statue of Till was erected in Greenwood, Mississippi.[13] The statue is made of bronze, a very different material from, say, sugar.

In the spring of 2014, hundreds of people flooded into a derelict building in Brooklyn to contemplate a different statue. The walls of the building, a former Domino sugar-processing plant, were rusty with age, dripping with the runny dark sediment of molasses. Crowds lined up to gape at a giant Sphinx made from hundreds of pounds of glittering white sugar.

The Sphinx's nickname is *A Subtlety*, but its full title was *A Subtlety or the Marvelous Sugar Baby, an Homage to the unpaid and overworked Artisans who have refined our Sweet tastes from the cane fields to the Kitchens of the New World on the Occasion of the demolition of the Domino Sugar Refining Plant.* The installation was the work of Kara Walker, an artist renowned for her wry and striking depictions of slave-era cruelty in the form of black-and-white silhouettes, the type that hung on the parlor walls of the white nineteenth-century bourgeoisie.

The immense sculpture, more than thirty-five feet high and seventy-five feet long, had the face of a Black woman wearing a head-cloth knotted above her forehead. Her serene face greeted viewers as they entered the space, and her full and naked posterior, complete with detailed vulva, bid them goodbye. A dozen small blackamoors, modeled by Walker on eighteenth-century ceramic mannequins depicting Black boys and men, often as servants, were scattered around her. Several of these statues, constructed first from sugar, had fallen apart in the heat of the space and had to be refashioned out of resin and covered in dripping molasses. The Sphinx's left arm was poised in a gesture that alternatively conveys fertility, good fortune, or "Fuck you."

The Domino Sugar Company, in a meta-commentary on the barbarous history of sugar commodification, donated roughly eight tons of processed sugar for the project. Art reviewers referenced the slave-labor history of the sugar industry, historical labor disputes at the factory itself, and the role of the building in the contemporary gentrification of the immediate neighborhood. Many wrote about the relevance of Walker's brazen display of a Black woman's genitalia, noting the cultural relevance of Black women's hypersexualization and exploitation.

Viewers altered the Sphinx from an installation to a performance piece by taking to social media with their impressions, some posting pictures of themselves pretending to hold up or squeeze the Sphinx's massive nipples. Others, poised at her rear, pretended they were engaged in cunnilingus. Others still, offended by female nudity and vivid reminders of sexuality, complained about obscenity and pornography.

Walker turned a raw material of whiteness into the carefully constructed body of a regal Black woman and then put on display hordes of people consuming her for their leisure, pleasure, and mock domination, while others wandered by and watched in silence.

Her brilliance doubly lay in using sugar, a naturally brown substance "cleaned" into whiteness. Like sugar, manufactured, ephemeral, and decaying, whiteness is a fantasy of transcendence and purity, the phantasmagoric heart of anti-Blackness. And it is entirely entangled with disgust for sex, women, femininity, and "monstrous bodies"— the hybrid, the nonconforming, the disabled, and the vulgar. She brilliantly used encaustic art to reveal the enduring impacts of a caustic history.

Walker's artwork was a temporary installation. Public monuments and statues, however, establish permanence and require public resources and collective commitment. They are sites of memory that shape us and our relationships and, with them, contribute to or undermine resilience. Every statue you pass commemorates a history, but even more important, each is a subtle catalyst for sensation, knowledge, and meaning. Even if we aren't consciously paying attention, a statue primes us to understand what our society thinks is vital.

Navigating shared spaces involves reviewing a mental list of events associated with places over time. Studies of children who've survived terrorist attacks, for example, reveal that even years later, environmental reminders such as walking past specific memorials heightened children's anxiety and caused physiological and emotional distress. Decaying urban environments, impoverished "reservations," and even racist sports logos work as proxy monuments in the same way, creating embodied reminders of place and power.

In Washington, DC, where I live, I routinely pass statues of U.S. and foreign military men and revolutionaries, yet there are few prominent statues or monuments to admirable women. In general, with scant exception, you are more likely to find a statue of a mermaid or a Greek goddess in cities around the country than a historical female figure. Similarly, even despite well-publicized efforts to remove troubling statues, you will encounter an enslaver before seeing a public commemoration honoring the enslaved or an abolitionist. The more than fifty thousand public statues across the United States skew overwhelmingly pale and male: the top three subjects for U.S. statues are Abraham Lincoln, George Washington, and Christopher Columbus. If you identify with these men, you benefit psychologically and physically from their presence. If, however, they represent a history of harm, conflict, erasure, and enduring discrimination, you don't.

We don't think of artifacts such as statues as resilience resources, but like other aspects of our built environments, they are. They physically create belonging and exclusion, conveying worth or, conversely, worthlessness. As stories they are sources of refuge, mutual care, and recognition or, just as equally, of carelessness and hostility. By default, most institutional spaces disproportionately provide white people, particularly boys and men, with cognitive, psychological, and physiological advantages by confirming their identities, belonging, and status in the society. They contribute, in other words, to making spaces feel safer for some than for others.

When communities or populations don't have enough social capital or political power to erect statues or build public monuments, they turn other objects into sites of memory: words, books, art, and photographs take on symbolic value.[14] Is the body a monument? Is it a memory site and a story? How does it preserve meaning and enhance resilience?

"I have rape-colored skin," wrote poet Caroline Randall Williams in a 2020 *New York Times* opinion piece published at the height of pearl-clutching over demands that statues of slave owners and rapists be removed from public space. "My light-brown-blackness is a living testament to the rules, the practices, the causes of the Old South. If there are those who want to remember the legacy of the Confederacy, if they want monuments, well, then, my body is a monument. My skin is a monument."[15]

Art like *A Subtlety*—monumental, public, provoking—is important to resilience because it invites us to reckon collectively with complicated ideas through memory, shared experience, and diversely informed understanding. It encourages us to contemplate our relationships to one another and the material world and helps us create new narratives about history and our place in it. Public debate, collective action, and negotiation are how we express a desire for change and demonstrate the resilience required to demand it.[16]

Stories That Weaponize "Safe Spaces"

In recent years, statues and monuments have become a global flash-point for public conflicts over trauma, memory, and history as statues of Confederates in the United States and colonial heroes around the world have been defaced, toppled, or officially removed.[17] People accustomed to the comfort of social recognition can find themselves feeling unexpectedly bereft, despite, in fact, relatively minimal symbolic losses. Perceiving themselves as victimized, they turn to defensive mechanisms and policies. They use their power to resist change as a form of personal resilience *not* invested in negotiating new norms.[18]

In recent years, book bannings in school districts and libraries across the United States have steadily risen as conservative legislators propose hundreds of bills prohibiting teachers and librarians from sharing books or materials that refer to race, sexuality, gender, and gender identity. The premise of many of these bills is that this content, even if accurate and important, might make some students feel "uncomfortable" or "guilty" by gender, racial, or ethnic association. That the proposed bills, dubbed discomfort bills, violate the First Amendment doesn't seem to matter to people otherwise fetishistically committed to the law.

In early 2022, a conservative legislator in Texas, the state that holds the dubious honor of banning more books than any other, produced a list of more than eight hundred books he thought should be barred from libraries. An analysis of his list revealed that of the first one hundred titles listed, ninety-seven were written by women, people of color, or LGBTQ authors. This list supposedly related to a Texas congressional bill mischaracterizing and opposing critical race theory. In Wyoming, library employees face possible fines and criminal charges for stocking books with titles such as *Sex Is a Funny Word* and *This Book Is Gay*. A Tennessee county board of education elected to withdraw the Pulitzer Prize–winning graphic novel *Maus* from a Holocaust curriculum because it contained nudity and "obscene" words. By the summer of 2022, book bans affecting more than five thousand schools and almost 4 million students had taken hold in 138 school districts in thirty-two states adopting "Stop WOKE" agendas.

Predictable absurdity ensued. One Florida school district removed dictionaries and encyclopedias for an "inappropriate content" review. A publisher of educational materials for Florida's K–6 grades revised a lesson about Rosa Parks to remove any mention of race or racial discrimination.[19] Another school demanded its principal resign after a sixth-grade art teacher shared a photograph of Michelangelo's *David*, which some parents objected to as pornographic and in violation of Florida's new guidelines. Legislation in the Florida House today would ban any discussion of human sexuality or menstruation in elementary grades, making talking about periods illegal.

The vast majority of banned materials are written by women, people of color, and nonbinary authors who serve as role models and allow children to see people like them admired by their society. Book banning purports to be in the best interests of children who might be uncomfortable or have difficult questions, but targeted books also bring comfort and belonging, teaching critical skills, empathy, and civics. They provide children with ways to learn about and talk about difference, with compassion. They teach them to treat others with respect. Denying children the protective benefits of social dignity and recognition is an assault on their resilience; a blatant theft of cultural capital and social resources. These efforts clearly recognize that emotional comfort, cultural affirmation, and societal acceptance are assets, only these assets are limited to a chosen subset of students, by political fiat. It's a timeless strategy of abuse and corruption that has long centered on controlling children and what they learn.

Telling Stories of Historical Trauma

For 150 years, the U.S. government operated or supported more than four hundred residential boarding schools for Native American children. At least sixty thousand children, up to 83 percent of Native American school-aged children, were taken from their families and communities and placed in institutions where physical, sexual, and emotional abuse were pervasive. To date, there is no conclusion regarding how many students died as a result.

"Native schools" were designed, as infamously explained by Captain Richard H. Pratt, to "kill the Indian and save the man." Pratt was in charge of the first U.S. government-funded Carlisle Indian Industrial School, founded in 1879. He initially recruited students who were voluntarily sent by tribal leaders in the belief that children who learned English and colonizers' ways could help tribes fight against treaty violations by U.S. settlers. In 1891, however, children were compelled to attend by federal law.

The Bureau of Indian Affairs explicitly created these boarding places for Christian indoctrination and assimilation. Of the 367 schools now identified, at least 84 were Catholic institutions that contracted with the U.S. government.[20] Once at schools, boys were trained in low-wage, low-skill jobs and girls were indoctrinated according to the unfamiliar, sex-segregated norms of Christianity. Administrators, often priests and nuns, used a harsh military model of schedules, uniforms, and cultural indoctrination, including shaving children's hair and inflicting harsh corporal punishments, especially when children used their own languages. Isolated from their families, the children were effectively prisoners of war. They endured ridicule, physical and sexual abuse, and daily cruelties designed to undermine Native American resistance and destroy indigenous languages.[21]

The harms of these schools have reverberated across decades. Among Native Americans, this history continues to cause distress, chronic stress, and family dissolution. Indigenous communities have higher chances of childhood poverty, substance abuse, and negative life outcomes.[22] This separation of children from their families is a repeated strategy of domination, visible today in the separation of families in systems of mass incarceration and of migrant families at the U.S. Southern border.

During the 1980s, Professor Maria Yellow Horse Brave Heart, who is Hunkpapa/Oglala Lakota, recognized the critical need as a resilience and healing strategy to change public understanding of American history. A world-renowned social worker, professor, and mental health expert, she had a unique toolbox of knowledge, skills, and experience. As a psychoanalyst who had studied the intergenerational effects of the Holocaust on individuals and families, she understood that a treatment paradigm based on individuals, divorced from context, culture, and history, could not address the scope of the damage in Native communities.

Brave Heart coined the term *historical trauma* to explain trauma and grief expressed over centuries.[23] She and her collaborator Lemyra M. DeBruyn developed therapies that recognized the importance of collectively addressing history and its impacts. Like many other Indigenous scholars, she continues to challenge dominant therapeutic narratives to develop culturally sensitive and effective alternatives.

Brave Heart and DeBruyn showed how tools used to inflict collective experiences of pain, loss, and threat—stories, meaning, recognition, connection—can be transformed to achieve collective recovery, and stories were at the core of her achievement.[24] Brave Heart's therapeutic approach immerses members of Native American communities in their cultural and social narratives, incorporating rituals and spaces that generate safety, belonging, respect, care, and knowledge. "Treatment" includes parenting curricula, prayers, sacred places, and kinship networks. The first programs based on her work gathered Lakota and Dakota counselors, traditional healers, sun dance leaders, and community members. Traditional customs, including recognizing and respecting relationships between humans, land, plants, ancestors, and the environment, are essential. Because trauma is, at its heart, a pervasive crisis of meaning, recovering is a process of creating and defining new meaning.

These programs don't only try to eliminate grief and strengthen resilience but recast the notion of resilience in countermainstream terms.[25] This trauma-responsive approach recognizes adversity as intergenerational, relational, materially defined, and collective. By comparison, the more typical programming is still focused on individual therapy, cognitive behavioral change, and building resilience for the future, even to the future. It's persistently insensitive to relationships, history, and power.

In the same vein, Dr. Joy DeGruy uses the term *post traumatic slave syndrome* (PTSS) to describe the cumulative impacts of slavery, Jim Crow, mass incarceration, and institutionalized racism on Black Americans. PTSS affects individuals through internalized racism and low self-esteem but extends into relationships and communities. Like Brave Heart, she believes that this collective experience of relationships and place contains the roots of resilience and resistance over time.

Racism also dehumanizes those who embrace it, hardening their humanity, and limiting their ability to feel, learn, change, and grow. White communities, for instance, are also scarred by their histories, but intergenerational trauma is more likely to stay masked by stories of exceptionalism and dominance. Psychotherapist and author Resmaa Menakem, whose practice integrates neuroscience, biology, genetics, and historical trauma to develop anti-racist healing tools, believes that until white historical trauma is also acknowledged and resolved, our collective problems will remain intractable.

"If you study the history of Europe during the Middle Ages," he writes, "you'll see that the same cruelty—dislodging brains, blocking airways, and so forth—was what powerful white bodies did to less powerful white bodies for many hundreds of years. This created deep trauma in many, many white bodies."[26] It also created a model for how to treat others.

We live with the consequences of not reconciling ourselves to hard truths. We have few, if any, formal mechanisms for talking with nuance and complexity about identity, history, meaning, and how we come together to envision and build new futures.

Part of the problem is, simply, shame. Emotional discomfort, shame, and cognitive dissonance often result from contemplating what it means to be a person on the wrong side of an equation, associated by identity or privilege with the perpetration of harm. The traumatizing histories and stories that help some communities heal might threaten your sense of being a good person or call the legitimacy of your abilities, entitlements, and successes into question. Belonging and collective pride also suffer, provoking self-defensiveness and the disorientation that can come with stigmatization.

The point, in terms of trauma and resilience and change, is not to focus on injury and victimhood as ends in themselves. Rather, it is to establish a starting point for broader understanding and the formulation of new social alliances and poiltical configurations.

Instead of listening to people who have alternative views on history and its effects, a common knee-jerk response is to silence their efforts, cast doubt on their intellect, and refuse the legitimacy of their memories and claims. The result is book bans, suppressing speech, and harassing and punishing truth tellers. These actions might allow communities to cope, but they are not resilient behaviors, they are oppressive ones, to everybody.

There are alternatives to withdrawal, denial, discomfort, shame, and aggression, however. Conflicts can be addressed through truth and reconciliation processes that provide some structure for cultivating understanding and generating *intercollective* stories. Group narratives that recognize the past, acknowledge enduring harms, and create new and positive interactions build resilience. Other countries have had similar problems and faced them head-on instead of engaging in the fantasy that historically rooted harms aren't real and enduring.[27]

I'm not saying that discussing difficult subjects and the emotions they elicit is easy, but it is essential.[28]

When we tell stories, especially traumatic ones drawn from the past, we move both our suffering and our knowledge from the realm of individual psychology to the realm of social and political discourse. When we listen to and acknowledge people, we build intergroup understanding, providing a resilience-building resource available to *more* people and communities. The process itself *is* the shared story necessary for building a new society. It can only really work, however, if participants are able to move beyond the stark and oversimplifying binary of "victims" and "perpetrators." While collective trauma can harden intergroup conflict over generations, it can also, research finds, effectively result in the same groups reaching agreement to build more peaceful, safe, and free futures.

New Stories Make Us All More Resilient

What part do you play in the stories we tell? Are you curious or hostile to alternatives to the histories you learned? Can you weigh, and possibly reject, the values that suffuse stubborn traditions and subtly inform denigrating habits?

Shared narratives are a fundamental unit of our resilience. We might give our storytelling different names, for example, *the law, science*, and *coding*, or *history* and *art*, but all serve similar ends: they help us know, relate to, and care for one another. Stories are how we move through time, empathize, and gain perspective. They enable us to negotiate, make meaning, shape social norms, and define our values.

Stories teach us to cooperate and allow us to build the communities and cultures that make our resilience and survival possible. Whether binge-watching a favorite series or obsessing over the news, we consume stories to relate to one another and interpret what is happening around us. They are how we dream worlds, gods, and ourselves into existence.

Look at any list of resilience lessons, however, and chances are that telling stories together—whether as myths or law or science or anthropology or art—doesn't make the cut, when it should be at the top of the list.

To adapt to existing adversities and prepare for anticipated crises, we have to appreciate the role that shared storytelling and story listening plays in our adapting. Believing that your story is the one absolute truth is nihilistic. It forecloses the possibility of communication, compassion, and cooperation and, instead, fosters distance, division, and domination. There is no room for questioning and revising beliefs, for self-reflection, or the introduction of meaningful new evidence. It's a recipe for stagnation, conflict, and political disintegration. The stories we tell ourselves about resilience are hurting us in these ways. Their narrow fixedness limits our ability to live peacefully in the world as we know it to be.

We can't look to precedent to prepare for the unprecedented. Future dystopias, for example, are often grounded, metaphorically, in holding on to solid "mainlands," idyllic and unchanging places we hope to save and sustain. But why not think in terms of waters instead? In our stories, frameworks, and problem-solving for the future, we use the idea of "green" too much and the idea of "blue" too little, or too negatively. Even in our own bodies, we are not of the earth but of the sea. Liquid moves through, in, and from our bodies through, in, and from the world. There is much to gain, as a resilient way of relating and transforming, by thinking *with* the ocean instead.

You may disagree with me, but having come this far, by reading this and thinking about this book, you and I have already collaborated in creating new understanding.

10

WONDROUS BEGINNINGS

Become tender with the Earth and the resources
that it affords us.

—Bernard Ferguson

We've come full circle: What is resilience, and how can we best adapt
to change and adversity?

By now, I hope I've convinced you that the nature, structure, and
quality of our prevailing matters and inspired you to look askance at
how resilience is conventionally conceived. Wrapped up in rugged
individualism, unchecked optimism, hardened masculinity, and depleting productivity, it is an ideal that can ultimately only be achieved
through brutality. Hegemonic. Reactive. Closed-minded. Destructive. It's a "we-them" resilience that doesn't teach us how to survive
adversity but how to survive *the worst of one another.*

Resilience means persevering, but it also means celebrating when
we see each other persevere. What goes by the name resilience today
doesn't recognize this fact. Instead, it easily turns into narcissistic
maladaptation that tacitly relies on carelessness and exploitative behaviors toward others. It unreflectively turns us away from one an-

other, rather than toward one another. Its conceptual framework is inadequate to the challenges of today's world.

The truth: We cope, change, survive, and thrive together, in interdependent, mutual caring relationships.

That an inclusive resilience of care, connection, and kindness might seem naive or impossible stems *directly* from our deepest and most corrosive cultural beliefs: that *some* of us are special and chosen; that you can only rely on yourself; that we must suffer to be saved, must work for our rewards, have to compete to the death to survive. Teaching that love and tenderness must be earned and that we have to continuously prove our worth leads to isolation, competition, and despair—widespread ills we are now all too sadly familiar with.

Our mainstream resilience doesn't make inclusivity, connection, and collective care over lifetimes a priority. You can, for instance, be resilient in conventional ways and still support white supremacy, mock pacifism, harbor contempt for difference, and believe that conscious capitalism will save us from ourselves. If, on the other hand, you reimagine a resilience in which all of these are unacceptable, then you can envision new worlds and how you can move through them.

Toxic individualism, rigid gender ideologies, and global white supremacy have strangleholds on our culture, but they don't have to define us as they do our myths of resilience. They don't have to determine our futures.

We may live individually in moments of time, but we are everything that came before and will come after us. Each of us is a complex mixture of biology, technology, stories, relationships, and meaning making. This complexity, and the caring it depends on, is the real weft of our resilience. We can will a new world into being, tell richer stories, and relate to one another in healthier, more sustaining, nurturing, and joyful ways. We have the capacity. But we need to propel the will.

Does what I describe seem too big a shift? Impossibly idealistic?

It's a dilemma to be of the world even as you seek to change it, but I wouldn't be here typing this paragraph if people who lived long before I was born couldn't imagine a world where I could.

Part of the dilemma for me as a writer is immediately practical: the structure of books reflects the same systems I've critiqued. It pressures me to provide you with a happy, pat conclusion, a set of pithy "rules" or "principles" to live by. Most of the time, however, rules don't prepare us for uncertain futures as much as they comfort us with mores of an always idealized past. They aren't about creativity and problem-solving as much as conformity and obedience. Top-down authority is antithetical to the openness we need to create new worldviews and reimagine resilience.

In compromise, I offer, instead, a summary of observations in the hope that they will free us to pursue *daring* ways of being in the world together, with peace.

No one can go it alone. Resilient people have nurturing relationships and are part of communities of shared belief. The strength, quality, and reach of our social connections are our most effective resilience resource. This doesn't mean learning personal coping and adapting skills isn't worthwhile because, clearly, there are benefits. However, pretending that our resilience is all up to us as individuals is ridiculous, and depoliticizing social realities, and the suffering, trauma, and crises that stem from them, undermines us. Focusing as an individual on traits and skills doesn't build social trust or challenge systemic causes of stress. It doesn't generate safety, dignity, or resources. No one, for instance, can personally resilience themselves out of accelerating climate change. No one can replicate, by themselves, the exuberance of collective joy that comes from reveling in the well-being of others and the persistence of life.

Self-sufficiency is a fantasy that comes at great cost. Our families and societies are dense relational networks. We are physically, emotionally, neurologically, and materially reliant on one another. We are dependent on nature for our sustenance, the air we breathe, the water we drink, the energy we consume. Only in the rarest and most extreme circumstances are people, usually under great duress, forced to meet all of their needs by themselves, to independently solve every problem they encounter, without the help and support of others. So, why are so many of our resilience values and social policies built around this presumption instead of the truth?

Each of us can help shift resilience culture commensurate with our means and capacities. Start with your family, your local community, reconsider your neighborhood, your sidewalks, your public spaces. When you can, find need and help abate it. When people talk, really listen. Give them what they say they need, not what you think they "deserve."

Cognitive flexibility is critical. Resilient individuals are open to difference, receptive and adaptable to change. Cognitive flexibility allows you to shift your understanding of the world, apply your knowledge, and adjust your life strategies in the face of obstacles. It is the key to knowing that difference doesn't mean deficiency, a belief frequently grounded in suspicion and fear, both of which hinder adaptability. Cognitive flexibility also reduces acceptance of harmful stereotypes, including the many binaries and hierarchies that shape our thinking and institutions: mind over matter, Man/Nature, white/Black, men/ women, being/nonbeing. Another way of approaching this challenge is to embrace both/and thinking. Either/or mindsets make our choices oppositional, flattening information and leaving us with a sense of loss and sacrifice. Both/and thinking, though, acknowledges life's complexities and the fact that many things can be true at the same time, allowing for more nuance and possibility. This is a kind of resourcefulness because it frees us to envision alternative ways of thinking and living, sometimes, necessarily, radically different.

Emotional competence is liberating. Resilient people use all their emotions, not only positive ones. They derive insights from their sadness, anxiety, and anger to make sense of experiences and to propel change. Instead of "staying positive" through thick and thin, they are pragmatic about optimism itself, using pessimism thoughtfully and strategically to influence future outcomes. Paradoxically, strategic pessimism is *hopeful*. Optimism and hope are frequently used synonymously, but optimism tends toward vague future states; it's the expectation that "somehow" everything will work out for the best. Strategic pessimism, however, often leads us to be more specific, to establish future goals based on realism, desire, and capacity.

Resilience means looking outward, not primarily inward. Many traits and habits of mind that fall under the rubric of individual resilience—optimism, gratitude, problem-solving, and spiritual practices—help us self-regulate and cope in times of stress and chaos. But resilience over and across lifetimes takes interactions between our interior states, other people, and the external world. It means learning how to *unself*, to become, as Iris Murdoch believed, morally transformed by your awareness of the immense world and your being part of it.

If all you do to be resilient leads you to turn inward, inward, inward, what is left for the world and its people and places? It is impossible, in the society we live in, to avoid complicity in the oppression of others, but we can strive to define our resilience in ways that aren't built on the backs of others. "Adapting positively" in ways that detach you from other people isn't really resilience but an expression of the belief in survival of the fittest. Instead, resilience should rely on the compassionate promise to endure with others, never alone: that in your need and dependence, you can be loved and love others. Even the qualities we think of as internal and individualistic, optimism and gratitude, for example, are effective because they signal to others that we are interested in and capable of social connection and trust— outward-facing values—which are the more meaningful advantage.

Resilience is a dynamic and complex process, not a universal standard to adhere to. There is no model for how to adapt to hardship in all circumstances. If there were, then we would, by now, have the ability to predict who will adapt well and who will struggle, and we can't. We *can* take comfort in formulas that make our lives easier, we can learn habits and behaviors that help us reduce stress and achieve goals, but in different contexts, those same formulas, habits, and behaviors might hurt our adaptability. The only hard-and-fast standard is that positive responses to adversity are infinitely variable. This means thinking *rhizomatically* to see resilience as an expansive capacity with no beginning and no end, complex, culturally sensitive, and often taking form in surprising ways. A resilience that is more possibilistic than probabilistic restores openness to the world instead of closing it off.

We don't adapt to change. We, and our relationships, change. Resilience talk focuses a lot on how we can improve our responses to change, but what is really happening is that *we change*. We can try to more consciously think of ourselves as fluid, of our identities as multiplicities that respond to people, context, and time. We learn to think of our identities as somehow fixed when, in reality, they are anything but. How we relate to others and to our environments is being reconfigured constantly. Being resilient means knowing how to use change, including in yourself, to your advantage. Aging is an excellent example. Most of us understand and acknowledge that we will age. Some embrace this change, while others resist it. Older people tend to be more resilient than younger people because they have the experience of change and have learned to use a wide variety of tools—strategic pessimism, strong friendships, forbearance. They know that adapting to hardships happens not in predictable and logical stages but in fits and starts, two steps forward, one step back.

Reorienting time is a resilience advantage. Rethinking time not only enhances our adaptability to adversity but redefines what counts as adversity to begin with. When we are more conscious about how time works its way through us, we can better resist shortsighted urgency. To be sure, emergencies require immediate responses, but so many of the stresses and crises we encounter take on the urgency of emergencies when, in reality, adapting to them often requires us to stop, step back, and slow down. Rethinking time also makes us more aware that the stress we feel often comes from having to manage multiple and conflicting time orders. It reminds us that what matters to us in one time will be utterly irrelevant in another.

Being deliberately time-aware is critical to thinking about resilience in different meters and scales so that we broaden our understanding of stress, what constitutes crisis, and how we can mitigate the trauma of *duration*.

The Haudenosaunee adhere, for example, to the Seventh Generation Principle, which teaches responsibility, social governance, and resilience for future generations. This ancient philosophy stresses the interconnectedness of generations and weaves future, present, and past together, informing personal and collective identities, choices, beliefs. It changes how concepts such as "happiness," "well-being," and "resilience" are defined and understood. This frame of reference teaches us that we are connected to one another and to our communities and that communities exist over time.

Life is not war unless we make it so. The deeply social, embodied, and cooperative nature of resilience confounds the idea that we evolved to violently compete, a belief that underlies our "soldiering on." Military metaphors turn problems into battlefields of suffering, winning, and losing. War thinking and language force us into thinking in adversarial, sacrificial ways. In the military, this approach to resilience might enhance connections with fellow soldiers or within a unit, or a change of command, but ported into other contexts, "life is war" values turn into competitive individual performance. "Soldiering on" as a way to understand resilience broadly doesn't help us adapt to adversity as much as it requires us to dominate, accept unnecessary sacrifices, and conform to excessive demands.

Limits are real and we need to respect them. Our hardships and adversities are often hard limits—on life, on relationships, on choices, resources, or time. As we've seen, we aren't keen on what limits represent: our finitude. As a result, we don't learn to think with and about limits, which sets us back. Resilience is adapting to the reality of *endings*. It takes creatively responding to the reality of limits and constraints so that we can perceive new ways of being alive. Climate change, for example, doesn't portend the "end to the world," but rather *a* world as we know it. We have the imagination and the capacity to design new worlds and, with them, alternative social, economic, and political relationships. To do this, however, we *have* to accept limits: on endless growth, infinite potential, immediate profits, exhaustible bodies, and continuous consumption. The planet will survive without us, but if we'd like to stay, we have to ask, What does a resilience of *limits* look like—to our identities, relationships, beliefs, economy?

Human exceptionalism is antiresilient. We are wondrous creatures in a wondrous world, but that is different from saying that we are exceptional. Being resilient means refusing the snobbery of believing we're "better than everything else." It means respecting infinite variations of life and consciousness. Our species self-glorification means we deny our connections to vital, more-than-human life. The rigid silos and boundaries we've constructed in our quest for dominance not only isolate us from one another but from life itself. Dethroning ourselves is a formidable task, especially given the continued influence of religious beliefs shaping our politics. Take the idea that certain Christians—exceptional, chosen, and superior—should control everything, from education to government, Christian dominionism. To some, dominionism may seem marginal and cultish, but it holds within it the same mindset that animates a broader cultural belief in supremacy; of Man Ruling over Nature, men over women, white people over non-white, beings over nonbeings. A resilience born of this thinking can only lead to nihilism.

———

Threaded throughout these themes is a persistent truth: resilience depends on our mutual care and interconnectedness, at every scale. Our capacity to adapt positively to hardship is born in the spaces of our entanglements. Our traumas are born in their denial.

We can't simply discard the conceptual foundations of our identities, relationships, economies, and technologies, but we can begin by admitting to their dire impacts as a starting point for creating more just alternatives. All of the crises we face today are crises of *disconnection*: loneliness, suicide, sexual predation, intimate violence, sacrificial people and sacrifice zones, climate disaster, mass migrations, globally worsening mental health, pervasive plastics, growing wealth inequality, and rising authoritarianism, militarism, and fascism. Scratch the surfaces of any or all of these, and you will find failure after failure to prioritize nurturing and mutual care and to value the people and cultures that do.

At the most basic unit, the question of resilience then substantively comes to *who and what we will care for and who and what we will abandon and destroy*. If we don't redefine how we *relate* to one another and the Earth, we will create newer, ever more negative versions of our current polycrises.

Lastly, redefining resilience in these ways requires us, collectively, to be resilient *to our worldviews themselves*. We *have* to deliberately, methodically dismantle a culture of disconnection and domination to joyfully build new ways of *relating*. We can think in terms of a "do good" resilience instead of a "feel good" resilience. Instead of a set of "rules" that drives us to dominate and control, this resilience is a process that assumes dignity and liberation. From this perspective, being resilient means finding new ways of being at home in a world of sprawling possibility, a resilience of reenchantment.

AFTERWORD

Two years after my father passed away, I could finally go home and be with my family. It was the longest I'd ever been away from the people and landscapes that always bring me back to my oldest self, the one on which the world imprinted itself.

I welcomed the familiarity and was gleeful to see everyone I loved, but this time, I also saw the place through the lens of resilience. I looked at my home with new eyes and my extended family with a deeper appreciation.

In Nassau, I'm keenly aware of constant flux. My senses come alive as I bask in the color of the sky, the texture of the heat, and the mood of the ocean. The coastal road is where water meets land in a constant denial of borders. It is a place where I am brought back to knowing that we are mainly water—the "Earth," our bodies, our way of being. The cadence of it all seeps into me—always such a relief.

Being small islanders has always meant living together on what is essentially a constantly shifting rock in an expansive sea. This geographic happenstance makes us more intimate, often more tolerant of difference, more attuned to the spaces we take up. It feels as though people live more comfortably and with a greater affinity to the earth's feedback loops, the rhythms and tides, the clouds, and the humidity.

Over centuries, people from virtually every continent converged in the Caribbean and The Bahamas to live in constrained physical circumstances. Millions were enslaved, indentured, and impoverished in systems built to reward small European minorities. Constrained resources and marginalized living conditions, coupled with an inescapable interdependence and strict limits on growth, expansion, and escape, make for complex identities and relationships. These conditions also led to the emergence of previously unimaginable relationships and unsanctioned hybrid worlds.

Even as colonial systems and capitalist economies rippled out from epicenters such as the Caribbean, the people gathered there built societies that were unrecognizable to "the Old World" and threatening to the "New." The region has for centuries survived human-engineered violence, political chaos, depletion of resources, prolonged inequality, natural disasters, environmental degradation, intergenerational trauma, and political abandonment by more powerful nations. Yet, people adapted over time and in ways far removed from our mainstream ideals and myths. It is a creole resilience, nimble, multifaceted, nuanced, and responsive. A resilience that, even in the face of obdurate powers, has always accepted contradictions, blended traditions, and created new beliefs and meaning. It has made for creative, joyful, self-supporting, and visionary cultures.

To be clear, this isn't my attempt to glorify places still riven by violence and the ongoing and ugly dynamics of colonization. While comparatively wealthy, The Bahamas isn't a utopian haven of equality and peace. Sexual minorities and women have limited citizenship rights and suffer from high rates of gendered violence, for instance. Try as I might, I can't avoid a mental checklist of areas where, throughout my life, I've known children and women who were beaten, assaulted, and killed by men they knew and men they didn't. Homophobia, driven by religious beliefs, is rife and dangerous. Wealth largely continues to be held in the hands of a minority white elite. The fight to safeguard the environment pits local activists against powerful global forces. Yet, the country is peaceful, people report high rates of happiness, and citizens feel great pride in its beauty and culture. Many contradictory things are equally true at once.

You may read this and think, Which country or geography *doesn't* demonstrate resilience? Adapting is inherent to life itself. But islands, like frontiers, make unique demands on us for survival, and as a result, they offer alternative frames of reference and narratives of adaptation. For these reasons, resilience-minded people in fields as far-flung as anthropology, climate studies, and ecology look to islands and archipelagos because they provide examples of complex dynamic systems involving humans, animals, plants, marine life, oceans, and the climate.

Islands or rather *thinking with islands* help us pull apart mainstream ways of resilience thinking and reassemble them in unpredictable and novel ways.[1] Research has found that people who live on smaller islands are notably less invested in modern conceptions of time, autonomy, agency, and the human/nature divide. People living together in close proximity are less likely to think in linear and essentialist ways about one another and their relationships. Navigating one another's differences in appearance, beliefs, and worldviews means learning to listen, accepting the need to change, and being flexible and open to newness.

"Impossible" relationships not only emerge from islands defined by geography but from islands set apart for other reasons, from queer communities, maroon villages, and Indigenous "reservations" to internment facilities, refugee camps, and prisons. As metaphors, ecologies, and societies in stress and flux, island places show us how to pull apart mainstream resilience thinking and reassemble ourselves in innovative and caring ways.

We know now that Earth is an island, not unlike the one I grew up on. Limited space, diverse people, our fortunes entwined. We share histories, are related to one another, bounded and mutually dependent. None of us can afford a resilience that entrenches beliefs and ideals drawn from seventeenth-century dualism, eighteenth-century subjectivities, nineteenth-century masculine ideals, and twentieth-century capitalist values. Being resilient in revolutionary ways won't happen if we stay so attached to outdated and deeply corrupt ideals and beliefs.

Visionary hope and inventive futures are important because, at the most selfish, individual level, I don't want to lose my people, memories, home, or imagined future. I don't want to lose the person I am in relation to them. I want my loved ones, you, and others to have the same assurances. Isn't that how we should all feel?

Our hearts can be both aching and full. Life is fluid, change is constant, we adapt. We are built to know terrible pain and yet make memories of future pleasures. Our adapting has to, in the words of poet Georgina Herrera, be grounded in the belief in "the fleetingness of the terrible, and the permanence of the kind."

So, what will we do to change an entire worldview?

Thinking relationally and prioritizing mutual care have to direct our political lives and reshape our economies. We can educate children to cultivate a society that shares resources, meets basic needs, and embraces dignity as communal values. It is kindness to ensure that children are safe and fed; to treat all people with dignity, not in exchange for labor or suffering, but because they are alive, our neighbors, and deserving of care. It is kindness to be patient, to listen to people, and to allow others to bask in what and whom they love. It's also kindness to share what we have, to keep our water clean, to not poison the earth, and to recognize the impacts of our actions on the delicate balance of nature. It is kindness to ensure that the world of the future isn't an unmitigated hellscape.

Speaking for myself, when I encounter stress and hardship I become a magpie. In difficult and anxious moments, I use many of the resilience techniques and skills that we are taught might be effective, but with caution and moderation. I try to be optimistic and grateful for what I have. I work hard and persist in endeavors that are important to me. Whenever possible, I encourage my children to do the same. But none of these habits is what enables me to adapt, feel safe, find peace, and move forward each day.

What *does* is knowing that I am nurtured by my family and community. What matters is that there are people I trust and who trust me. What makes a difference are the many ways that I can rely on being the beneficiary of material privileges and psychological comforts conferred by my society. These relationships, connections, and political realities are essential to any individual strength I try to cultivate.

So, I try my best to love and accept others and help create a world where kindness is the rule instead of the exception. I often fail and grow weary; I make mistakes, feel ashamed, doubt myself, and fall back on habits of mind and comfort, feeling inept at the task. I take what I have for granted. I change my mind too slowly. Act politically with too much caution. But I persevere in my belief in care, connection, and mutual meaning-making, in respecting the vital materiality of life, in a shared future. I stand in grateful wonder at the world and its fierce beauties.

In closing, to answer our question as best as possible, I believe that resilience is the exercise of love, compassion, and care as our responsibility to one another. Resilience is what we make of it together.

ACKNOWLEDGMENTS

Writing this book has been a challenge and would have been impossible but for the many people who cheered me on. First and foremost, my unending thanks to Thomas, Isabelle, Noel, and Caroline. Over the truly endless process of my writing this book you were, in appropriate turns, excited, curious, mystified, patient, wry, and, always, encouraging. I truly could never persist without your love, trust, advice, intellectual insights, and, when I needed it most, sympathetic ire.

The same is true of friends who so generously and kindly entertained my ideas and my frustrations both. You lent an ear, made me laugh, fed me, and made it possible for me to write, rewrite, and write again. Beverly Frank, Jacqueline Bendy, Fanny Lim, Jaclyn Friedman, Catherine Buni, Kate McCarthy, Susan Crawford, Debra Eichenbaum, Cecile Fruman, Julia Coppinger, Tamara Belt, and Tara Jaye Frank. This book would not have been written without your immense good humor, care, insights, and companionship.

I also, always, owe a debt of gratitude and love to my mother, Norma, and my siblings, Edward, Korry, and Omar, for being my home.

Moreover, I want to extend my heartfelt thanks to my agent, Anna Sproul-Latimer, always patient, wise, and funny. Also to my very wonderful readers and editors Jane Fransson and Gail Winston. You contributed to my thinking in such important ways, challenged me to think in new directions, and improved my writing by sharing your expertise and opinions with patience and kindness. I am grateful to Julia Cheiffetz for taking on this project, to Abby Mohr and Annette Pagliaro Sweeney for shepherding it, to Nick Ciani and Libby McGuire for essential support, and to the entire team at One Signal and Simon & Schuster—Chelsea McGuckin, Alison Hinchcliffe, Morgan Pager, Maudee Genao, Karlyn Hixson, and Hannah Frankel.

In closing, as I was weighing the pros and cons of a land acknowledgment, I again found myself sitting outside in the summer heat. It was empty and quiet outside of the café, so it was impossible not to notice when a young man wearing an *actual* pith helmet appeared. He was a curious, random, walking, talking avatar of the past I was thinking about. On his arm, he carried a majestic Yellow and Blue Macaw. Even though these large parrots hail from South America, I've always thought of them as Bahamian birds because their primary colors—deep yellow, rich aqua, and black—are those of the flag. As the man walked into the café, he perched the parrot on the fence immediately next to me. We stared at one another for a long moment and then the bird very loudly said "hello" and I said "hello" back. An entire history brought us to our meeting and moved me, in the moment, to conclude by saying that I wrote large portions of this book in Nassau and in Washington, DC, the ancestral homelands of the Lucayan, Piscataway, and Anacostan peoples. I acknowledge these peoples as the traditional inhabitants of lands that were never ceded, and I pay my respect to and support elders, past and present. I also want to recognize the land itself and the life it sustains.

I stand in grateful wonder at the world and its fierce beauties.

Use this QR code to access and add to a Spotify playlist of the music I listened to on repeat while writing this book. Happy listening!

NOTES

PREFACE

1. Diane Coutu, "How Resilience Works," *Harvard Business Review*, May 2002, https://hbr.org/2002/05/how-resilience-works.
2. Andrew Zolli and Ann Marie Healy, *Resilience: Why Things Bounce Back* (New York: Simon & Schuster, 2013), 275–76.

1: THE MISGUIDED GOAL OF STRENGTH AND SELF-SUFFICIENCY

1. George A. Bonanno et al., "Psychological Resilience after Disaster: New York City in the Aftermath of the September 11th Terrorist Attack," *Psychological Science* 17, no. 3 (2006): 181–86, https://doi.org/10.1111/j.1467-9280.2006.01682.x.
2. Damian Hall, "A Love Affair: An Interview with Jasmin Paris," I Run Far, January 16, 2020, https://www.irunfar.com/a-love-affair-an-interview-with-jasmin-paris.
3. "Women May Have Advantage in the Long Run," University of Alaska News and Information, accessed August 17, 2023, https://www.uaf.edu/news/.
4. Marcus, Ezra, and Jonah Engel Bromwich. "A Short History of 'Simp,'" *New York Times*, July 7, 2020, https://www.nytimes.com/2020/07/07/style/simp-history-slang.html.
5. Sarah Lacy and Cara Ocobock, "The Theory That Men Evolved to Hunt and Women Evolved to Gather Is Wrong," *Scientific American*, n.d., accessed November 27, 2023, https://www.scientificamerican.com/article/the-theory-that-men-evolved-to-hunt-and-women-evolved-to-gather-is-wrong1/.
6. Cara Ocobock and Sarah Lacy, "Woman the Hunter: The Physiological

Evidence," *American Anthropologist*, 2023, https://doi.org/10.1111/aman.13915.

7. While today's research is becoming more nuanced in terms of how sex and gender are understood, historically 69 percent of research studies used male-only participants, while only 3 percent studied female-only subjects. Ocobock, "The Theory That Men Evolved to Hunt."

8. Virginia Zarulli et al., "Women Live Longer than Men Even during Severe Famines and Epidemics," PNAS 115, no. 4 (2018): e832–40.

9. Anticolonial psychotherapist Frantz Fanon described this state of nonbeing when he wrote about the category of "not-yet human" and the ways white supremacist thinking turns Black people into "photogenic" objects that "spark anxiety and fear in white people." Frantz Fanon, *Black Skin, White Masks* (New York: Grove Press, 1952).

10. An "English Rose" describes a girl or woman who possesses traditional feminine ideals of English womanhood: a fair complexion, beauty, and quiet elegance.

11. Kristy Eve Snow, "Colonial Hybridity and Irishness in Bram Stoker's *Dracula*," *Undergraduate Review* 11, no. 1 (2015): 114–19, https://vc.bridgew.edu/undergrad_rev/vol11/iss1/20.

12. A. F. Raza Kolb, *Epidemic Empire: Colonialism, Contagion, and Terror, 1817–2020* (Chicago: University of Chicago Press, 2021).

13. Fernando Durarte, "Coronavirus Face Masks: Why Men Are Less Likely to Wear Face Masks," BBC News, July 19, 2020, https://www.bbc.com/news/world-53446827.

14. Joshua A. Geltzer and Carrie Cordero, "We Learned Resilience after 9/11. But It's the Wrong Kind for Combatting a Virus," *Washington Post*, March 17, 2020, https://www.washingtonpost.com/outlook/2020/03/17/staying-home-is-resilience/.

15. Keith Churchwell et al., "Call to Action: Structural Racism as a Fundamental Driver of Health Disparities: A Presidential Advisory from the American Heart Association," *Circulation* 142, no. 24 (2020): e454–68.

16. Bill Chappell, "Republicans' Excess Death Rate Spiked after COVID-19 Vaccines Arrived, a Study Says," NPR, July 25, 2023, https://www.npr.org/2023/07/25/1189939229/COVID-deaths-democrats-republicans-gap-study.

17. Carolyn Crist, "CDC: Young White Men Least Likely to Wash Hands," WebMD, October 12, 2020, https://www.webmd.com/lung/news/20201011/cdc-says-young-white-men-least-likely-to-wash-hands.

18. "COVID Data Tracker," Center for Disease Control and Prevention, https://COVID.cdc.gov/COVID-data-tracker/#demographics.

19. L. M. Peterson et al., "Social–Contextual Factors Interact with Masculinity to Influence College Men's HPV Vaccination Intentions: The Role of Descriptive Norms, Prototypes, and Physician Gender," *Journal of Behavioral*

Medicine 45 (2022): 825–40, https://doi.org/10.1007/s10865-022-00350-1; and Angelica Puzio, "Why Is There Such a Gender Gap in COVID-19 Vaccination Rates?," *FiveThirtyEight*, July 21, 2021, https://fivethirtyeight .com/features/why-is-there-such-a-gender-gap-in-COVID-19-vaccination -rates/.

20. Leor Zmigrod et al., "The Psychological and Socio-Political Consequences of Infectious Diseases: Authoritarianism, Governance, and Nonzoonotic (Human-to-Human) Infection Transmission," *Journal of Social and Political Psychology* 9, no. 2 (2021): 456–74.

21. Mark Schaller, "The Behavioural Immune System and the Psychology of Human Sociality," *Philosophical Transactions of the Royal Society B* 366, no. 1583 (2011): 3406–17.

22. Gordon D. A. Brown, Corey L. Fincher, and Lukasz Walasek, "Personality, Parasites, Political Attitudes, and Cooperation: A Model of How Infection Prevalence Influences Openness and Social Group Formation," *Topics in Cognitive Science* 8, no. 1 (2016): 98–117.

23. Maria Lugones, "Toward a Decolonial Feminism." *Hypatia* 25, no. 4 (2010): 742–59.

24. Mychael Schnell, "Democrats Outraged after Manchin Opposes Biden Spending Bill," *The Hill*, December 19, 2021, https://thehill.com/home news/senate/586464-manchin-opposition-to-build-back-better-sends -shock-waves-through-political/.

25. Hilary Brueck, "A Yale Psychologist's Simple Thought Experiment Temporarily Turned Conservatives into Liberals," *Business Insider*, October 21, 2017, https://www.businessinsider.com/how-to-turn-conservatives-liberal -john-bargh-psychology-2017-10.

26. Veronica M. Lamarche, Ciara Atkinson, and Alyssa Croft, "A Cognitive Uncoupling: Masculinity Threats and the Rejection of Relationship Interdependence," *Social Psychological and Personality Science* 12, no. 6 (2021): 920–29.

27. Sean Coughlan, "Loneliness More Likely to Affect Young People," BBC News, April 10, 201, https://www.bbc.com/news/education-43711606.

28. Manuela Barreto et al., "Loneliness around the World: Age, Gender, and Cultural Differences in Loneliness," *Personality and Individual Differences* 169, no. 1 (2021): e110066.

29. Haley Weiss, "Losing a Spouse Makes Men 70% More Likely to Die within a Year," *Time*, March 22, 2023.

30. Soraya Chemaly, "Josh Hawley's Horrifically Misogynistic Book Signals a Much Bigger Problem," MSNBC, March 8, 2023, https://www.msnbc .com/opinion/msnbc-opinion/josh-hawley-conservative-white-christian -men-masculinity-rcna93104.

31. Brian Tome, *The Five Marks of a Man: Finding Your Path to Courageous Manhood* (Ada, MI: Baker Books, 2018).

32. Brendan Bures, "Guys Are Paying $10,000 to Become Real Men at Warrior Camps," *Vice*, January 24, 2022, https://www.vice.com/en/article/4awnqm/what-are-man-warrior-camps.

33. S. Ehrenhalt, "Green Line Theory Supports Misogynistic Notion That Women Are Less Dominant," *Yahoo Finance*, July 15, 2020, https://ca.finance.yahoo.com/news/green-line-theory-supports-misogynistic-095034265.html.

34. "State of American Men: From Crisis and Confusion to Hope," Equimundo, 2023, https://www.equimundo.org/resources/state-of-american-men/.

35. D. De Visé, "Most Young Men Are Single. Most Young Women Are Not," *The Hill*, February 22, 2023, https://thehill.com/blogs/blog-briefing-room/3868557-most-young-men-are-single-most-young-women-are-not/.

36. L. Plank, *For the Love of Men: A New Vision for Mindful Masculinity* (New York: St. Martin's Press, 2019).

37. T. DeAngelis, "Black Men's Mental Health Matters," *Monitor on Psychology* 50, no. 4 (2019): 38, https://www.apa.org/monitor/2019/04/black-men-mental-health.

38. E. W. Dolan, "Masculinity May Have a Protective Effect against the Development of Depression—Even for Women," *PsyPost*, August 22, 2021, https://www.psypost.org/2021/08/masculinity-may-have-a-protective-effect-against-the-development-of-depression-even-for-women-61730.

2: RESILIENCE AND THE BODY

1. Meaghan L. O'Donnell et al., "PTSD Symptom Trajectories: From Early to Chronic Response," *Behaviour Research Therapy* 45, no. 3 (2007): 601–6.

2. Emily A. Holmes et al., "Key Steps in Developing a Cognitive Vaccine against Traumatic Flashbacks: Visuospatial Tetris versus Verbal Pub Quiz," *PLoS ONE* 5, no. 11 (2010): e13706.

3. The technique was developed in 1987 by Francine Shapiro, a psychologist and cancer survivor studying the effects of memory and stress on immunity. She was walking in a park, recalling her distressing memories, when it occurred to her that her eye movements were reducing the intensity of her negative emotions. Exploring her hunch led her to develop EMDR, a therapy effectively used today to treat PTSD patients, grieving families, military veterans, people suffering from chronic anxiety, depression, and pain. Francine Shapiro, "EMDR, Adaptive Information Processing, and Case Conceptualization," *Journal of EMDR Practice and Research* 1, no. 2 (2007): 68–87; and Marco Pagani, "Neurobiological Foundations of EMDR Therapy," in *Eye Movement Desensitization and Reprocessing (EMDR) Therapy Scripted Protocols and Summary Sheets*, ed. Marilyn Luber (New York: Springer, 2018), xxiv–xxvi.

4. Danielle Gainer, Sara Alam, and Hannah Redding, "A Flash of Hope: Eye

Movement Desensitization and Reprocessing (EMDR) Therapy," *Innovations in Clinical Neuroscience* 17, no. 7–9 (2020): 12–20.

5. B. van der Kolk, *The Body Keeps the Score: Brain, Mind, and Body in the Healing of Trauma* (New York: Viking, 2014).

6. A. M. Allen et al., "Racial Discrimination, the Superwoman Schema, and Allostatic Load: Exploring an Integrative Stress-Coping Model among African American Women," *Annals of the New York Academy of Sciences* 1457, no. 1 (December 2019): 104–27, https://doi.org/10.1111/nyas.14188.

7. S. W. Porges, *The Polyvagal Theory: Neurophysiological Foundations of Emotions, Attachment, Communication, and Self-Regulation* (New York: W. W. Norton, 2011).

8. Thomas Pinna and Darren J. Edwards, "A Systematic Review of Associations between Interoception, Vagal Tone, and Emotional Regulation: Potential Applications for Mental Health, Wellbeing, Psychological Flexibility, and Chronic Conditions," Department of Public Health, Policy and Social Sciences, Swansea University, Swansea, UK, *Frontiers in Psychology*, August 5, 2020, https://doi.org/10.3389/fpsyg.2020.01792.

9. Antonio R. Damasio, *Descartes' Error: Emotion, Reason, and the Human Brain* (New York: Avon, 1995).

10. A. K. Seth, "Interoceptive Inference, Emotion, and the Embodied Self," *Trends in Cognitive Science* 17 (2013): 565–573.

11. L. Haase et al., "When the Brain Does Not Adequately Feel the Body: Links between Low Resilience and Interoception," *Biological Psychology* 113 (2016): 37–45.

12. Lourdes P. Dale et al., "Yoga Practice May Buffer the Deleterious Effects of Abuse on Women's Self-Concept and Dysfunctional Coping," *Journal of Aggression, Maltreatment & Trauma* 20, no. 1 (2011): 90–102.

13. Ann Gill Taylor et al., "Top-Down and Bottom-Up Mechanisms in Mind-Body Medicine: Development of an Integrative Framework for Psychophysiological Research," *Explore* 6, no. 1 (2010): 29–41; and David Muehsam et al., "The Embodied Mind: A Review on Functional Genomic and Neurological Correlates of Mind-Body Therapies," *Neuroscience & Biobehavioral Reviews* 73 (2017): 165–81.

14. Kaitlin Harding et al., "Mental and Physical Health Correlates of Pain Treatment Utilization among Veterans with Chronic Pain: A Cross-Sectional Study," *Military Medicine* 184, no. 3–4 (2019): e127–34; and Bruno Saconi et al., "The Influence of Sleep Disturbances and Sleep Disorders on Pain Outcomes among Veterans: A Systematic Scoping Review," *Sleep Medicine Reviews* 56 (2021): e101411.

15. David J. Linden, "Can a Neuroscientist Fight Cancer with Mere Thought?," *New York Times*, March 18, 2023.

16. M. M. Hanssen, "Optimism, the Natural Placebo: Cognitive, Behavioural

and Motivational Mechanisms of Resilience towards Pain" (PhD thesis, Maastricht University, 2014), https://doi.org/10.26481/dis.20141205mh.

17. Jutta Ernst et al., "Interoceptive Awareness Enhances Neural Activity during Empathy," *Human Brain Mapping* 34 (2013): 1615–24; and Poul L. Bak et al., "The Resilience Program: Preliminary Evaluation of a Monetization-Based Education Program," *Frontiers in Psychology* 6 (2015): e753.

18. Pavel Goldstein, Irit Weissman-Fogel, and Simone G. Shamay Tsoory, "The Role of Touch in Regulating Inter-Partner Physiological Coupling during Empathy for Pain," *Scientific Reports* 7 (2017): e3252; and Pavel Goldstein et al., "Brain-to-Brain Coupling during Handholding Is Associated with Pain Reduction," *PNAS* 115, no. 11 (2018): e2528–37.

19. Lawrence Williams and John Bargh, "Experiencing Physical Warmth Promotes Interpersonal Warmth," *Science* 322 (2008): 606–7, https://doi.org/10.1126/science.1162548.

20. Joel Salinas et al., "Association of Social Support with Brain Volume and Cognition," *JAMA Network Open* 4, no. 8 (2021): e2121122.

21. J. M. Kilner and R. N. Lemon, "What We Know Currently about Mirror Neurons," *Current Biology* 23, no. 23 (2013): R1057–62.

22. Drake Baer, "People Naturally Sync Their Bodies, Breathing—and Skin," *The Cut*, January 17, 2017, https://www.thecut.com/2017/01/how-interpersonal-synchrony-works.html.

23. E. Prochazkova et al., "Physiological Synchrony Is Associated with Attraction in a Blind Date Setting," *Nature Human Behaviour* 6, no. 2 (2022): 269–78, https://doi.org/10.1038/s41562-021-01197-3.

24. Leonie Koban, Anand Ramamoorthy, and Ivana Konvalinka, "Why Do We Fall into Sync with Others? Interpersonal Synchronization and the Brain's Optimization Principle," *Social Neuroscience* 14, no. 1 (2019): 1–9.

25. Scott S. Wiltermuth and Chip Heath, "Synchrony and Cooperation," *Psychological Science* 20, no. 1 (2020): 1–5.

26. Emily Butler, "Emotions Are Temporal Interpersonal Systems," *Current Opinion in Psychology* 17 (2017): 129–34, https://doi.org/10.1016/j.copsyc.2017.07.005.

27. Damasio, *Descartes' Error.*

28. Lydia Denworth, "Brain Waves Synchronize When People Interact," *Scientific American*, July 1, 2023, https://www.scientificamerican.com/article/brain-waves-synchronize-when-people-interact/.

29. Emily A. Butler, "Interpersonal Affect Dynamics: It Takes Two (and Time) to Tango," *Emotion Review* 7, no. 4 (2015): 336–41; and Emily A. Butler, "Temporal Interpersonal Emotional Systems: The 'TIES' That Form Relationships," *Personality and Social Psychology Review* 15, no. 4 (2011): 367–93.

30. "Fathers Stress Associated with Children's Emotional and Behavioral Problems at Age Two," *Neuroscience News*, October 22, 2022, https://

neurosciencenews.com/fathers-stress-child-emotion-21613/; Sara F. Waters, Tessa V. West, and Wendy Berry Mendes, "Stress Contagion: Physiological Covariation between Mothers and Infants," *Psychological Science* 25, no. 4 (2014): 934–42; and Isabelle Mueller et al., "Acute Maternal Stress Disrupts Infant Regulation and the Autonomic Nervous System and Behavior: A CASP Study," *Frontiers in Psychiatry* 12 (2021): e714664.

31. Shani Agron et al., "A Chemical Signal in Human Female Tears Lowers Aggression in Males," *PLoS Biology* 21, no. 12 (December 21, 2023): e3002442, https://doi.org/10.1371/journal.pbio.3002442.

32. S. J. Russo et al., "Neurobiology of Resilience," *Nature Neuroscience* 15, no. 11 (2012): 1475–84, https://doi,org/10.1038/nn.3234.

33. D. S. Dewi and H. Hamzah, "The Relationship between Spirituality, Quality of Life, and Resilience," *Proceedings of the 6th International Conference on Community Development*, 2019.

34. Junling Gao et al., "The Neurophysiological Correlates of Religious Chanting," *Scientific Reports* 9 (2019): e4262.

35. Ibid.; and L. Bernardi et al., "Effect of Rosary Prayer and Yoga Mantras on Autonomic Cardiovascular Rhythms: Comparative Study," *BMJ* 323, no. 7327 (2001): 1446–49, https://doi.org/10.1136/bmj.323.7327.1446.

36. A. C. Buck et al., "An Examination of the Relationship between Multiple Dimensions of Religiosity, Blood Pressure, and Hypertension," *Social Science Medicine* 68, no. 2 (January 2009): 314–22, https://doi,org/10.1016/j.socscimed.2008.10.010.

37. Caryle Murphy, "Q&A: Why Are Women Generally More Religious than Men?," Pew Research Center, March 23, 2016, https://www.pewresearch.org/short-reads/2016/03/23/qa-why-are-women-generally-more-religious-than-men.

38. M. Talal and M. Gruntman, "Visiting Nature in the City during the COVID-19 Pandemic. Front," *Young Minds* 11 (2023):1005823, https://doi.org/10.3389/frym.2023.1005823; and E. N. Spotswood et al., "Nature Inequity and Higher COVID-19 Case Rates in Less-Green Neighborhoods in the United States," *Nature Sustainability* 4 (2021): 1092–98, https://doi.org/10.1038/s41893-021-00781-9.

39. Alice G. Walton, "'Forest Bathing' Really May Be Good for Health, Study Finds," *Forbes*, June 10, 2018, https://www.forbes.com/sites/alicegwalton/2018/07/10/forest-bathing-really-may-be-good-for-health-study-finds/?sh=3569cbe8508e; and "Canada Doctors Are Prescribing Walking in Forests to Patients with Anxiety," News 18, February 10, 2022, https://www.news18.com/news/buzz/canada-doctors-are-prescribing-walking-in-forests-to-patients-with-anxiety-4755566.html.

40. "Tribes—Native Voices," NIH.gov, accessed August 17, 2023, https://www.nlm.nih.gov/nativevoices/timeline/296.html; and Elizabeth Nix, "At Least 3,000 Native Americans Died on the Trail of Tears," History.com, Novem-

ber 30, 2018, https://www.history.com/news/7-things-you-may-not-know -about-the-trail-of-tears.

41. Abby Carney, "Can Loneliness Be Cured with a Pill? Scientists Are Now Asking the Question," *Guardian*, August 6, 2020, https://www.theguard ian.com/lifeandstyle/2020/aug/06/loneliness-cure-pill-research-scien tists.

42. Crispin Sartwell, "Western White Supremacism and Non-Western Philosophy (A Reply to Manoharan)," *Philosophical Salon*, July 29, 2019, https:// thephilosophicalsalon.com/western-white-supremacism-and-non-western -philosophy-a-reply-to-manoharan/; and Avram Alpert, "Racism Is Baked into the Structure of Dialectical Philosophy," *Aeon*, September 24, 2020, https://aeon.co/essays/racism-is-baked-into-the-structure-of-dialectical -philosophy.

43. Orla T. Muldoon et al., "The Social Psychology of Responses to Trauma: Social Identity Pathways Associated with Divergent Traumatic Responses," *European Review of Social Psychology* 30, no. 1 (2019): 311–48, https://doi .org/10.1080/10463283.2020.1711628.

3: THE IMPORTANCE OF FORMATIVE EXPERIENCES

1. "Adverse Childhood Experiences (ACEs)," Centers for Disease Control and Prevention, CDC.gov, April 2, 2021, https://www.cdc.gov/violencepreven tion/aces/; Robert C. Whitaker et al., "The Interaction of Adverse Childhood Experiences and Gender as Risk Factors for Depression and Anxiety Disorders in U.S. Adults: A Cross-Sectional Study," *BMC Public Health* 21, no. 1 (2021): 2078; and Shelley Craig, "The Role of Adverse Childhood Events and Minority Stress on the Mental Health of Sexual and Gender Minority Youth" (presentation at the Society for Social Justice Work and Research 22nd Annual Conference, January 13, 2018), https://sswr.confex .com/sswr/2018/webprogram/Paper32209.html.

2. Michael A. Baxter et al., "Exploring the Relationship between Adverse Childhood Experiences and Hope," *Journal of Child Sexual Abuse* 26, no. 8 (2017): 948–56.

3. "Preventing Adverse Childhood Experiences," Centers for Disease Control and Prevention, CDC.gov, April 2, 2021, https://www.cdc.gov/violence prevention/aces/.

4. Jane Stevens, "What ACEs and PACEs Do You Have?," *PACEs Connection Blog*, January 1, 2017, https://www.pacesconnection.com/blog/got-your -ace-resilience-scores; and V. J. Felitti et al., "Relationship of Childhood Abuse and Household Dysfunction to Many of the Leading Causes of Death in Adults. The Adverse Childhood Experiences (ACE) Study," *American Journal of Preventative Medicine* 14, no. 4 (1998): 245–58, https:// doi.org/10.1016/s0749-3797(98)00017-8. The initial survey pool was

seventeen thousand, primarily white, college-educated, middle- and upper-middle-class people living in San Diego. They were employed, had health care, and were all affiliated with the Kaiser Permanente insurance company. The study was of people who weren't typically considered socially *at risk* or politically *vulnerable*, words that often encode gender, racial, ethnic, and cultural inequality.

5. Donte L Bernard et al., "Making the "C-ACE" for a Culturally-Informed Adverse Childhood Experiences Framework to Understand the Pervasive Mental Health Impact of Racism on Black Youth," *Journal of Child & Adolescent Trauma* 14, no. 2 (2020): 233–47, https://doi.org/ 10.1007/s40653 -020-00319-9; and Whitaker et al., "Interaction of Adverse Childhood Experiences," 2078.

6. R. F. Anda et al., "Inside the Adverse Childhood Experience Score: Strengths, Limitations, and Misapplications," *American Journal of Preventive Medicine* 58, no. 6 (2020): 707–14, https://www.ajpmonline.org/article /S0749-3797(20)30058-1/fulltext/.

7. L. Geller, "Two-Thirds of Mass Shootings Linked to Domestic Violence," Educational Fund to Stop Gun Violence, February 24, 2022, https://efsgv .org/press/study-two-thirds-of-mass-shootings-linked-to-domestic-violence/; and "Key Findings," Violence Project, accessed July 29, 2023, https://www .theviolenceproject.org/key-findings/.

8. S. Prokupecz, M. J. Friedman, and R. Clarke, "Uvalde Student Injured in Shooting Returns to School," CNN.com, September 6, 2022, https://www.cnn .com/2022/09/06/us/uvalde-injured-student-first-day-of-school/index.html.

9. Brian Lopez, "'I'm Scared That It Might Happen Again': Uvalde Parents Send Their Kids Back to School," *Texas Tribune*, September 7, 2022, www .texastribune.org/2022/09/07/uvalde-first-day-of-school/.

10. M. ElSherief et al., "Impacts of School Shooter Drills on the Psychological Well-Being of American K-12 School Communities: A Social Media Study," *Humanities and Social Science Communications* 8, no. 315 (2021), https:// doi.org/10.1057/s41599-021-00993-6.

11. Peter Wade, "Fox News Guest's Answer to Shootings: 'Plan to Kill Everyone You Meet,'" *Rolling Stone*, July 24, 2023, https://www.rollingstone.com /politics/politics-news/fox-news-guest-plan-to-kill-everyone-you-meet -1234731021/.

12. Ben Dawson, "The State of America's Children 2020—Child Hunger and Nutrition," Children's Defense Fund, February 2020, https://bit.ly/3YnKYqN.

13. K. N. Anderson et al., "Adverse Childhood Experiences during the COVID-19 Pandemic and Associations with Poor Mental Health and Suicidal Behaviors among High School Students—Adolescent Behaviors and Experiences Survey, United States, January–June 2021," *Morbidity and Mortality Weekly Report* 71, no. 41 (2022): 1301–5, http://dx.doi .org/10.15585/mmwr.mm7141a2.

14. "Children Exposed to Violence." Office of Justice Programs, accessed August 25, 2023, https://www.ojp.gov/program/programs/cev.

15. Samantha Schmidt and Hanna Natanson, "With Kids Stuck at Home, ER Doctors See More Severe Cases of Child Abuse," *Washington Post*, April 30, 2020, https://www.washingtonpost.com/education/2020/04/30/child-abuse-reports-coronavirus/.

16. S. D. Hillis et al., "COVID-19-Associated Orphanhood and Caregiver Death in the United States," *Pediatrics* 148, no. 4 (October 7, 2021), https://www.nih.gov/news-events/news-releases/more-140000-us-children-lost-primary-or-secondary-caregiver-due-COVID-19-pandemic.

17. "AAP-AACAP-CHA Declaration of a National Emergency in Child and Adolescent Mental Health," AAP.org, accessed August 17, 2023, https://www.aap.org/en/advocacy/child-and-adolescent-healthy-mental-development/aap-aacap-cha-declaration-of-a-national-emergency-in-child-and-adolescent-mental-health/.

18. Julia Hotz, "COVID Is Driving a Children's Mental Health Emergency," *Scientific American*, December 13, 2021, https://www.scientificamerican.com/article/COVID-is-driving-a-childrens-mental-health-emergency/.

19. I. H. Gotlib et al., "Effects of the COVID-19 Pandemic on Mental Health and Brain Maturation in Adolescents: Implications for Analyzing Longitudinal Data," *Biological Psychiatry: Global Open Science* 3, no. 4 (2023): 912–18, https://doi.org/10.1016/j.bpsgos.2022.11.002.

20. Dr. Russ Newman, "The Road to Resilience," American Psychological Association *Monitor on Psychology* 33, no. 9 (October 2002), https://www.apa.org/practice/programs/campaign/resilience.

21. "Positive Psychology in Schools and Education," PositivePsychology.com, July 20, 2023, https://positivepsychology.com/positive-psychology-schools-education/.

22. A 2018 analysis of school programs related to resilience found that lessons are integrated into social-competence, emotional-learning, and mental-health initiatives that aim to teach stress-management techniques, improve emotional intelligence, and teach goal- and achievement-focused habits. Most programs, the analysis showed, increase known protective factors such as strong connections and relationships with trustworthy adults and community building. Even though researchers identified these positive aspects of educational programming, they admitted that there are no shared definitions of resilience or even enough overlap to consistently compare programs across schools. There is also, they found, a strong element of resilience geared toward preparing children to meet future challenges, often at the expense of addressing enduring and current ones.

23. Angela Duckworth, *Grit: The Power of Passion and Perseverance* (New York: Scribner, 2016).

24. "DOD Annual Report on Sexual Harassment and Violence at MSAs APY21–22," Department of Defense, 2023, bit.ly/43Z8DPl.

25. B. N. Macnamara and A. P. Burgoyne, "Do Growth Mindset Interventions Impact Students' Academic Achievement? A Systematic Review and Meta-Analysis with Recommendations for Best Practices," *Psychological Bulletin* 149, no. 3–4 (2023): 133–73, https://doi.org/10.1037/bul0000352.

26. Valerie Strauss, "The Problem with Teaching 'Grit' to Poor Kids? They Already Have It. Here's What They Really Need," *Washington Post*, May 19, 2016, https://www.washingtonpost.com/news/answer-sheet/wp/2016/05/10/the-problem-with-teaching-grit-to-poor-kids-they-already-have-it-heres-what-they-really-need/.

27. Shadi Houshyar and Joan Kaufman, "Resiliency in Maltreated Children," in *Handbook of Resilience in Children*, ed. Sam Goldstein and Robert B. Brooks (Boston: Springer, 2005), 181–200.

28. Angela Duckworth, "Angela Duckworth Explains What Teachers Misunderstand about Grit," *Education Week*, September 20, 2023, https://www.edweek.org/leadership/opinion-angela-duckworth-explains-what-teachers-misunderstand-about-grit/2023/09.

29. Matt Wenzel, "Four Michigan State Football Players Charged with Assault Entering Diversionary Program," *Mlive*, January 27, 2023, https://www.mlive.com/spartans/2023/01/four-michigan-state-football-players-charged-with-assault-entering-diversionary-program.html.

30. "Rates of Injury from Sports, Recreation, and Leisure Activities among Children and Adolescents Aged 1–17 Years, by Age Group," National Health Interview Survey, United States, 2015–17, *Morbidity and Mortality Weekly Report* 68 (2019): 466, http://dx.doi.org/10.15585/mmwr.mm6820a6externalicon.

31. Thelma Gibson, *Forbearance: Thelma Gibson at TEDxCoconutGrove*, YouTube, February 16, 2019, https://www.youtube.com/watch?v=QzpriA8vAzs.

32. Thomas Curran and Andrew P. Hill, "Young People's Perceptions of Their Parents' Expectations and Criticism Are Increasing over Time: Implications for Perfectionism," *Psychological Bulletin* 148, no. 1–2 (2022): 107–28, https://doi.org/10.1037/bul0000347.

33. Jack Block and Adam M. Kremen, "IQ and Ego-Resiliency: Conceptual and Empirical Connections and Separateness," *Journal of Personality and Social Psychology* 70, no. 2 (1996): 349–61; and Jack Block, "The Role of Ego-Control and Ego-Resiliency in the Organization of Behavior," in *Development of Cognition, Affect, and Social Relations: The Minnesota Symposia on Child Psychology*, vol. 13, ed. W. A. Collins (Hillsdale, NJ: Erlbaum, 1980), 39–101.

34. Paul Hagan, "The Paradox of Resilience," Eastside Preparatory School, https://www.eastsideprep.org/insight-the-paradox-of-resilience/.

35. Alex Winninghoff, "Trauma by Numbers: Warnings against the Use of ACE

Scores in Trauma-Informed Schools," *Bank Street Occasional Paper Series* 43, no. 4 (2020).

36. Amanda Fenwick-Smith, Emma E. Dahlberg, and Sandra C. Thompson, "Systematic Review of Resilience-Enhancing, Universal, Primary School-Based Mental Health Promotion Programs," *BMC Psychology* 6 (2018): e30, https://doi.org/10.1186/s40359-018-0242-3.

37. Poul L. Bak et al., "The Resilience Program: Preliminary Evaluation of a Mentalization-Based Education Program," *Frontiers in Psychology* 16 (2015): e00753.

38. Susie O'Brien, "'Graceful Failure': The Privatization of Resilience," *Review of Education, Pedagogy, and Cultural Studies* 36, no. 4 (2014): 260–73, https://doi.org/10.1080/10714413.2014.938565.

39. Suniya S. Luthar and Samuel H. Barkin, "Are Affluent Youth Truly 'at Risk'? Vulnerability and Resilience across Three Diverse Samples," *Development and Psychopathology* 24, no. 2 (2012): 429–49, https://doi.org/10.1017/S0954579412000089; and Hiram E. Fitzgerald et al., "Fathers and Families: Risk and Resilience. An Introduction," *Adversity and Resilience Science* 2, no. 2 (2021): 63–69, https://doi.org/10.1007/s42844-021-00039-5.

40. O. Khazan, "These Teens Got Therapy. Then They Got Worse," *Atlantic*, November 6, 2023, https://www.theatlantic.com/ideas/archive/2023/11/teen-mental-health-dbt/675895/.

41. P. Sehgal, "The Profound Emptiness of 'Resilience,'" *New York Times*, December 1, 2015, https://www.nytimes.com/2015/12/06/magazine/the-profound-emptiness-of-resilience.html.

42. Fenwick-Smith, Dahlberg, and Thompson, "Systematic Review of Resilience-Enhancing," e30.

43. Emmy E. Werner and Ruth S. Smith, "A Report from the Kauai Longitudinal Study," *Journal of the American Academy of Child Psychiatry* 18, no. 2 (1979): 292–306, https://doi.org/10.1016/s0002-7138(09)61044-x.

44. National Scientific Council on the Developing Child, "Young Children Develop in an Environment of Relationships: Working Paper 1," Center on the Developing Child: Harvard University, updated and reprinted October 2009.

45. Ann S. Masten, Karin M. Best, and Norman Garmezy, "Resilience and Development: Contributions from the Study of Children Who Overcome Adversity," *Development and Psychopathology* 2, no. 4 (1990): 425–44; and Suniya S. Luthar, Dante Cicchetti, and Bronwyn Becker, "The Construct of Resilience: A Critical Evaluation and Guidelines for Future Work," *Child Development* 71, no. 1 (2000): 543–62.

46. A. L. van Harmelen et al., "Adolescent Friendships Predict Later Resilient Functioning across Psychosocial Domains in a Healthy Community Cohort," *Psychological Medicine* 47, no. 1 (2017): 2312–22.

47. Francesca Lionetti et al., "Dandelions, Tulips and Orchids: Evidence for the Existence of Low-Sensitive, Medium-Sensitive and High-Sensitive Individuals," *Translational Psychiatry* 8, no. 24 (2018).

48. Dave Davies, "Is Your Child an Orchid or a Dandelion? Unlocking the Science of Sensitive Kids," *NPR's Fresh Air*, March 4, 2019, https://www.npr.org/sections/health-shots/2019/03/04/699979387/is-your-child-an-orchid-or-a-dandelion-unlocking-the-science-of-sensitive-kids.

49. Jay Belski, "Opinion: The Downside of Resilience," *New York Times*, November 28, 2014, https://www.nytimes.com/2014/11/30/opinion/sunday/the-downside-of-resilience.html.

50. Lionetti et al., "Dandelions, Tulips and Orchids."

51. Hamidreza Zakeri, Bahram Jowkar, and Maryam Razmjoee, "Parenting Styles and Resilience," *Procedia—Social and Behavioral Sciences* 5 (2010): 1067–70, https://doi.org/10.1016/j.sbspro.2010.07.236.

52. Gwen Dewar, "Authoritarian Parenting Outcomes: What Happens to the Kids?," *Parenting Science*, 2022, https://parentingscience.com/authoritarian-parenting/.

53. Sofia Gimenez-Serrano, Fernando Garcia, and Oscar F. Garcia, "Parenting Styles and Its Relations with Personal and Social Adjustment beyond Adolescence: Is the Current Evidence Enough?," *European Journal of Developmental Psychology* 19, no. 5 (2022): 749–69, https://doi.org/10.1080/17405629.2021.1952863.

54. Christina Bethell, Narangerel Gombojav, and Robert C. Whitaker, "Family Resilience and Connection Promote Flourishing among US Children, Even amid Adversity," *Health Affairs* 38, no. 5 (2019): 729–37.

55. Kirsten Weir, "Maximizing Children's Resilience," *Monitor on Psychology* 48, no. 8 (2017): 40.

56. A. Advani, "Youth Disillusionment Is a Global Risk, but Teaching Resilience to Gen Z Could Mitigate It," World Economic Forum, June 21, 2021, https://www.weforum.org/agenda/2021/06/youth-disillusionment-global-risk-gen-z-resilience/.

57. Jamie Ducharme and Kara Milstein, "Suicide Bereavement Camps Help Kids Process Grief and Cope with Their Losses," *Time*, March 15, 2023, https://time.com/6286420/suicide-bereavement-camps-kids/.

58. Beverly Daniel Tatum, *Why Are All the Black Kids Sitting Together in the Cafeteria?* (New York: Basic, 2017).

59. "Insights Political Polarization, Gridlock, and COVID," *Los Angeles Times/Reality Check*, January 28, 2021, https://rci-production.s3.amazonaws.com/LAT_Polarization_final.pdf.

60. T. Patel, "Gen Z Voters Will Ensure the 2024 Election Won't Be a Replay of 2020," *Washington Post*, July 19, 2023, https://www.washingtonpost.com/opinions/2023/07/19/gen-z-voters-2024/.

4: THE NECESSITY OF NEGATIVITY

1. J. A. Shepperd et al., "Taking Stock of Unrealistic Optimism," *Perspectives on Psychological Science* 8, no. 4 (2013): 395–411, https://doi.org/10.1177/1745691613485247.

2. Jamie Ross, "Hurricane Dorian: Bahamas Government Denies Withholding True Death Toll," *Daily Beast*, September 9, 2019, https://www.thedailybeast.com/hurricane-dorian-bahamas-government-denies-withholding-true-death-toll.

3. Matthew Bristow and Ezra Fieser, "Island of 50,000 People Is 70% under Water as Dorian Moves Off," Bloomberg News, September 3, 2019, https://www.bloomberg.com/news/articles/2019-09-03/island-of-50-000-people-is-70-under-water-as-dorian-moves-off.

4. J. M. Shultz et al., "Double Environmental Injustice—Climate Change, Hurricane Dorian, and The Bahamas," *New England Journal of Medicine* 328 (2020): 1–3.

5. H. Leo Kim and Andrew West, "Bahamas Strong: After Hurricane Dorian, Hope Emerges" (video), *Tallahassee Democrat*, October 1, 2019, https://www.tallahassee.com/videos/news/2019/10/01/hurricane-dorian-one-month-later-pt-2/3822504002/.

6. M. Kruse, "The Power of Trump's Positive Thinking," *Politico*, October 13, 2017, https://www.politico.com/magazine/story/2017/10/13/donald-trump-positive-thinking-215704.

7. Todd Blodgett, "Trump, after Losing, Adheres to Norman Vincent Peale's Positive Thinking," *Des Moines Register*, November 19, 2020, https://bit.ly/3DOlh9h.

8. M. F. Scheier and C. S. Carver, "Optimism, Coping, and Health: Assessment and Implications of Generalized Outcome Expectancies," *Health Psychology* 4, no. 3 (1985): 219–47, https://doi.org/10.1037/0278-6133.4.3.219. PMID: 4029106.

9. Peter Gibbon, "Feature: Martin Seligman and the Rise of Positive Psychology," *Humanities: The Magazine of the National Endowment for the Humanities*, Summer 2020, https://www.neh.gov/article/martin-seligman-and-rise-positive-psychology.

10. M. E. P Seligman, *Flourish: A Visionary New Understanding of Happiness and Well-Being* (New York: Free Press, 2011).

11. "9/11: The Steel of American Resolve," George W. Bush Presidential Library and Museum, https://www.georgewbushlibrary.gov/explore/exhibits/911-steel-american-resolve.

12. Christopher Peterson and Martin E. P. Seligman, *Character Strengths and Virtues: A Handbook and Classification* (Washington, DC: American Psychological Association, 2004).

13. William J. Chopik et al., "Changes in Optimism and Pessimism in Re-

sponse to Life Events: Evidence from Three Large Panel Studies," *Journal of Research in Personality* 88 (2020), https://doi.org/10.1016/j.jrp.2020.103985.

14. "Capabilities," Templeton Foundation, March 8, 2004, http://capabilities.templeton.org/2004/joy03.html.

15. "Capabilities," Templeton Foundation.

16. S. Bains, "Questioning the Integrity of the John Templeton Foundation," *Evolutionary Psychology* 9, no. 1 (2011), https://doi.org/10.1177/147470491100900111.

17. John Weaver, "Big Questions about Templeton," Political Research Associates, 2015, https://politicalresearch.org/2015/08/12/big-questions-about-templeton-how-the-philanthropic-giant-legitimizes-faith-healing.

18. R. J. Brulle, "Institutionalizing Delay: Foundation Funding and the Creation of U.S. Climate Change Counter-Movement Organizations," *Climatic Change* 122 (2014): 681–94, https://doi.org/10.1007/s10584-013-1018-7.

19. Dorothy Bishop, "Should I Stay or Should I Go? When Debate with Opponents Should Be Avoided," *BishopBlog*, January 12, 2020, http://deevybee.blogspot.com/2020/01/should-i-stay-or-should-i-go-when.html.

20. Leonid Schneier, "Fixing Science: With Climate Denial, Misogyny and White Supremacism?," *For Better Science*, January 13, 2020, https://forbetterscience.com/2020/01/13/fixing-science-with-climate-denial-misogyny-and-white-supremacism/; and Michael Schulson, "A Remedy for Broken Science, or an Attempt to Undercut It?," *Undark*, April 18, 2018, https://undark.org/2018/04/18/national-association-of-scholars-reproducibility/.

21. Kim and West, "Bahamas Strong."

22. Maria Saccheti, "Haitians in The Bahamas Seek More Protection after Hurricane Dorian Aid Groups, News Cameras Leave," *Washington Post*, September 9, 2019.

23. Lynya Floyd, "This 'Optimism Training Plan' Will Improve Your Outlook in Just 5 Days," *Men's Health*, January 11, 2021, https://www.menshealth.com/health/a35179055/optimism-training-plan/.

24. E. H. Lee and S. Schnall, "The Influence of Social Power on Weight Perception," *Journal of Experimental Psychology: General* 143, no. 4 (2014): 1719–25.

25. J. K. Boehm et al., "Unequally Distributed Psychological Assets: Are There Social Disparities in Optimism, Life Satisfaction, and Positive Affect?," *PLoS ONE* 10, no. 2 (2015): e0118066., https://doi.org/10.1371/journal.pone.0118066.

26. Joshua Breslau et al., "Specifying Race-Ethnic Differences in Risk for Psychiatric Disorder in a USA National Sample," *Psychological Medicine* 36, no. 1 (January 26, 2006): 57–68, https://doi.org/10.1017/S0033291705006161.

27. "Youth Risk Behavior Survey Data Summary & Trends Report: 2011–2021," Centers for Disease Control and Prevention, 2023, https://www.cdc.gov/healthyyouth/data/yrbs/pdf/YRBS_Data-Summary-Trends_Report2023_508.pdf.

28. J. Guo, "Why Women Don't Use a Certain Rude Word," *Washington Post*, April 21, 2016, https://www.washingtonpost.com/news/wonk/wp/2016/04/21/why-women-dont-use-a-certain-rude-word/.

29. "State of American Men: From Crisis and Confusion to Hope," Equimundo, 2023, https://www.equimundo.org/resources/state-of-american-men/; and H. Fingerhut, "In Both Parties, Men and Women Differ over Whether Women Still Face Obstacles to Progress," Pew Research Center, August 6, 2016, https://www.pewresearch.org/fact-tank/2016/08/16/in-both-parties-men-and-women-differ-over-whether-women-still-face-obstacles-to-progress/.

30. Ellen Sinclair, Rona Hart, and Tim Lomas, "Can Positivity Be Counterproductive When Suffering Domestic Abuse?: A Narrative Review," *International Journal of Wellbeing* 10, no. 1 (January 2020): 26–53, https://doi.org/10.5502/ijw.v10i1.754.

31. Tessa Stuart, "The Next Front in the GOP's War on Women: No-Fault Divorce," *Rolling Stone*, May 2, 2023, https://www.rollingstone.com/politics/politics-features/stephen-crowder-divorce-1234727777/.

32. J. Polivy and C. P. Herman, "The False-Hope Syndrome: Unfulfilled Expectations of Self-Change," *Current Directions in Psychological Science* 9, no. 4 (2000): 128–31, http://www.jstor.org/stable/20182645.

33. G. A. Bonanno, C. Rennike, and S. Dekel, "Self-Enhancement among High Exposure Survivors of the September 11th Terrorist Attack: Resilience or Social Maladjustment," *Journal of Personality and Social Psychology* 88 (2005): 984–98.

34. Lisa Bortolotti and Magdalena Antrobus, "Costs and Benefits of Realism and Optimism," *Current Opinion in Psychiatry* 28, no. 2 (2015): 194–98.

35. D. Diamond, "Trump Pressured CDC to Downplay Coronavirus Severity, House Report Says," *Washington Post*, October 17, 2022, https://www.washingtonpost.com/health/2022/10/17/trump-cdc-pressure-COVID-pandemic-house-report/.

36. Bob Woodward, "The Trump Tapes: 20 Interviews That Show Why He Is an Unparalleled Danger," *Washington Post*, October 23, 2022, https://www.washingtonpost.com/opinions/interactive/2022/trump-tapes-bob-woodward-interviews-audiobook/.

37. Mark D. Seery et al., "The Effects of Negative Reflection for Defensive Pessimists: Dissipation or Harnessing of Threat?," *Personality and Individual Differences* 45, no. 6 (2008): 515–20, https://doi.org/10.1016/j.paid.2008.06.004; https://www.sciencedirect.com/science/article/abs/pii/S0191886908002109.

5: RESISTING THE LURE OF PRODUCTIVITY

1. J. Marcuson, *Leaders Who Last: Sustaining Yourself and Your Ministry* (New York: Seabury Books, 2009).
2. Caroline Alexander, *The* Endurance*: Shackleton's Legendary Antarctic Expedition* (New York: Alfred A. Knopf, 1998).
3. Kathryn M. Connor and Jonathan R. T. Davidson, "Development of a New Resilience Scale: The Connor-Davidson Resilience Scale (CD-RISC)," *Depression and Anxiety* 18 (2003): 76–82.
4. E. Riska, "From Type A Man to the Hardy Man: Masculinity and Health," *Sociology of Health & Illness* 24 (2002): 347–58, https://doi .org/10.1111/1467-9566.00298.
5. T. Parker-Pope, "How to Build Resilience in Midlife," *New York Times*, July 26, 2017, https://www.nytimes.com/2017/07/25/well/mind/how -to-boost-resilience-in-midlife.html.
6. Judith Butler, Zeynep Gambetti, and Leticia Sabsay, eds., *Vulnerability in Resistance* (Durham, NC: Duke University Press, 2016).
7. Claire Cane Miller, "Nearly Half of Men Say They Do Most of the Home Schooling. 3 Percent of Women Agree," *New York Times*, May 8, 2020.
8. Josh Taylor, "South Dakota Teachers Scramble for Dollar Bills in 'Demeaning' Game," *Guardian*, December 14, 2021.
9. Graham Colton, "'The Five': Teachers Unions Have Redefined Teaching 'as Selfish and Lazy,'" Fox News, January 2022, https://www.foxnews.com /media/the-five-teachers-unions-redefined-teaching-selfish-lazy.
10. With permission for publication from Tracy Edwards (@tracyrenee70), "Sat through a webinar on teacher resilience & was asked to share my thoughts." Twitter, March 1, 2022, www.twitter.com/tracyrenee70/status /1498812420239675392.
11. Angela McRobbie, *Feminism and the Politics of Resilience: Essays on Gender, Media and the End of Welfare* (Oxford, England: Polity Press, 2020).
12. D. J. Paoni, "The Rise of the Resilient Workforce," *Washington Post*, October 7, 2020, https://www.washingtonpost.com/brand-studio/wp/2020 /10/07/the-rise-of-the-resilient-workforce/.
13. Heather Landi, "Third of Nurses Plan to Leave Their Jobs in 2022, Survey Finds," *Fierce Healthcare*, February 14, 2022, https://www.fiercehealthcare .com/providers/third-nurses-plan-leave-their-jobs-2022-survey-finds.
14. *The Innovation Handbook: A Nurse Leader's Guide to Transforming Healthcare*, American College of Healthcare Executives, 2022, https://health careexecutive.org/-/media/ache/healthcare-executives/mj22/he_mj22 _downloadedition.pdf.
15. "Workplace Wellness and Resilience Training Program," Academy of Brain-Based Leadership, July 22, 2021, https://brainleadership.com/solution /wellness-resilience/.

16. "Kroger's COVID-19 Response," Kroger.com, accessed August 28, 2023, http://sustainability.kroger.com/Kroger-COVID-19-Response-Overview.pdf.

17. Jason Lalljee, "Kroger Workers Experienced Hunger, Homelessness, and Couldn't Pay Their Rent in 2021. Its CEO Made $22 Million the Previous Year," *Business Insider*, January 14, 2022, https://www.businessinsider.com/1-in-7-kroger-workers-homeless-many-food-insecure-rent-2022-1.

18. *Kroger Corporate ESG Report 2021*, Kroger Company, 2021, https://www.thekrogerco.com/wp-content/uploads/2021/07/Kroger-2021-ESG-Report.pdf.

19. Errol Schweizer, "Why Is Food Insecurity So Widespread in the Grocery Industry?," *Forbes*, January 19, 2022, https://www.forbes.com/sites/errolschweizer/2022/01/19/why-is-food-insecurity-so-widespread-in-the-grocery-industry/?sh=303234297cc8.

20. Carmen Reinicke, "20% of Americans Couldn't Pay Their Energy Bill in the Last Year. How to Keep Costs Down," CNBC, December 21, 2021, https://www.cnbc.com/2021/12/23/20percent-of-americans-couldnt-pay-their-energy-bill-in-the-last-year.html.

21. Joan Williams, "Why Many Women of Color Don't Want to Return to the Office," *Harvard Business Review*, May 9, 2022, https://hbr.org/2022/05/why-many-women-of-color-dont-want-to-return-to-the-office.

22. N. Bloom, "Don't Let Employees Pick Their WFH Days," *Harvard Business Review*, May 17, 2022, https://hbr.org/2021/05/dont-let-employees-pick-their-wfh-days.

23. *Gallup Global Emotions Report 2022*, Gallup, June 29, 2022, https://www.gallup.com/analytics/349280/gallup-global-emotions-report.aspx.

24. Megan Brenan, "Approval of Labor Unions at Highest Point since 1965," Gallup. September 2, 2021, https://news.gallup.com/poll/354455/approval-labor-unions-highest-point-1965.aspx.

25. Alex Seitz-Wald, "Multipronged $50 Million Campaign Backed by Labor Aims to Prioritize Child and Senior Care," NBC News, August 4, 2023, https://www.nbcnews.com/politics/politics-news/multipronged-50-million-campaign-backed-labor-aims-prioritize-child-se-rcna98012.

26. Jonathan Mahler, "'The Most Dangerous Person in the World Is Randi Weingarten,'" *New York Times*, April 28, 2023, https://www.nytimes.com/2023/04/28/magazine/randi-weingarten-teachers-unions.html.

27. Sara G. Miller, "Funny Guy Gets the Girl? How Humor Makes You More Attractive," *Live Science*, August 7, 2017, https://www.livescience.com/60060-humor-increases-attractiveness.html.

28. Kayla Sergent and Alexander D. Stajkovic, "Women's Leadership Is Associated with Fewer Deaths during the COVID-19 Crisis: Quantitative and Qualitative Analyses of United States Governors," *Journal of Applied Psychology* 105, no. 8 (2020): 771–83.

29. "Ernest Shackleton May Have Had a Hole in His Heart, Say Researchers," *BBC News*, January 14, 2016, https://www.bbc.com/news/uk-england -cambridgeshire-35303072; and *The Shackleton Expedition*, American Natural History Museum, January 1, 1999, https://www.amnh.org/exhibitions /shackleton/the-expedition.

30. Rebecca Farley, "'By Endurance We Conquer': Ernest Shackleton and Performances of White Male Hegemony," *International Journal of Cultural Studies* 8, no. 2 (2005): 231–54.

31. Tom Butler, "Tom Hardy Sets Next Big Movie as Ernest Shackleton Biopic," Yahoo!, February 7, 2020, https://uk.movies.yahoo.com/tom-hardy -shackleton-biopic-125650544.html.

32. "AI Generated Images Are Biased, Showing the World through Stereotypes," *Washington Post*, November 1, 2023, https://www.washingtonpost .com/technology/interactive/2023/ai-generated-images-bias-racism-sexism -stereotypes/.

33. "The Behavioral Risk Factor Surveillance System (BRFSS)," Centers for Disease Control and Prevention, accessed July 25, 2023, https://www.cdc .gov/brfss/index.html.

34. Samantha Kenny et al., "Mothers' and Fathers' Sleep: Is There a Difference between First-Time and Experienced Parents of 6-Month-Olds?," *Journal of Sleep Research*, 2020, https://doi.org/10.1111/jsr.13238.

35. Tricia Hersey, *Rest Is Resistance: A Manifesto* (New York: Hachette, 2020).

36. Victoria Uwumarogie, "The Nap Ministry Founder Tricia Hersey on Rest as Protest against White Supremacy and Capitalism," *Essence*, February 16, 2022, https://www.essence.com/lifestyle/tricia-hersey-the-nap-ministry/.

37. Jeremy Rifkin, *The Age of Resilience: Reimagining Existence on a Rewilding Earth* (New York: St. Martin's Press, 2022).

6: THE PARADOXES OF SOLDIERING ON

1. Larry Brown, "Naomi Osaka Shows Ultimate Privilege, Elitism by Refusing to Do Media Events," *Larry Brown Sports*, May 26, 2021, https://larrybrown sports.com/tennis/naomi-osaka-privilege-media-events/579514.

2. Sally Jones, "If You Can't Handle the Pressure, Don't Play the Game, Says Sally Jones; as Naomi Osaka Quits the French Open Citing the Stress of Press Interviews, One Former Tennis Writer Serves Up a Provocative View," *Daily Mail*, June 2, 2021, https://www.dailymail.co.uk/femail/article -9645637/If-handle-pressure-dont-play-game-Naomi-Osaka-quits-French -Open.html.

3. João Mauricio Castaldelli-Maia et al., "Mental Health Symptoms and Disorders in Elite Athletes: A Systematic Review on Cultural Influencers and Barriers to Athletes Seeking Treatment," *British Journal of Sports Medicine* 53, no. 11 (2019): 707–21, https://doi.org/10.1136/bjsports-2019-100710.

4. Elisha Fieldstadt, "Texas Deputy Attorney General Apologizes after Calling Simone Biles a 'National Embarrassment,'" NBC News, July 28, 2021, https://www.nbcnews.com/news/olympics/texas-deputy-attorney-general -apologizes-after-calling-simone-biles-national-n1275375.

5. S. H. Schmidt et al., "An Analysis of Colin Kaepernick, Megan Rapinoe, and the National Anthem Protests," *Communication & Sport* 7, no. 5 (2019): 653–77, https://doi.org/10.1177/2167479518793625.

6. Friedrich Nietzsche, *Twilight of the Idols*, ed. Duncan Large (London: Oxford University Press, 2008).

7. Maya Yang, "People in Counties That Voted Trump More Likely to Die from COVID—Study," *Guardian*, December 7, 2021, https://www.theguardian .com/us-news/2021/dec/07/trump-voters-counties-more-likely-die-COVID -study.

8. Shan-Estelle Brown and Zoe Pearson, "Human Sacrifices, Not Heroes: U.S. Essential Workers and the COVID-19 Pandemic," *Exertions*, 2020, https:// doi.org/10/21428/1d6be30e.53617da1.

9. Z. Khan, Y. Iwai, and S. DasGupta, "Military Metaphors and Pandemic Propaganda: Unmasking the Betrayal of 'Healthcare Heroes,'" *Journal of Medical Ethics* 47 (2021): 643–44.

10. Sophia E. Kakarala and Holly G. Prigerson, "COVID-19 and Increased Risk of Physician Suicide: A Call to Detoxify the U.S. Medical System," *Frontiers in Psychiatry* 13 (2022), https://doi.org/10.3389/fpsyt .2022.791752.

11. C. Fernandez et al., "Assessing the Relationship between Psychosocial Stressors and Psychiatric Resilience among Chilean Disaster Survivors," *British Journal of Psychiatry* 217, no. 5 (2020): 630–37, https://doi.org/10.1192 /bjp.2020.88; and U. A. Mitchell et al., "'What Doesn't Kill You, Makes You Stronger': Psychosocial Resources and the Mental Health of Black Older Adults," *Annual Review of Gerontology and Geriatrics* 41, no. 1 (2021): 269–302, PMID: 36311274.

12. Dylan Matthews, "The Horrifying Sexual Misconduct Allegations against Missouri Gov. Eric Greitens, Explained," *Vox*, April 11, 2018, https://www .vox.com/2018/4/11/17227132/eric-greitens-missouri-governor-rape -sexual-assault-nonconsensual-force-revenge-porn-blackmail.

13. Associated Press, "Republican Senate Hopeful Eric Greitens Accused of Abuse by Ex-Wife," *Guardian*, March 21, 2022, https://www.theguardian .com/us-news/2022/mar/21/eric-greitens-accused-physical-abuse-ex-wife -missouri-republican.

14. Judith Herman, *Trauma and Recovery: The Aftermath of Violence—from Domestic Abuse to Political Terror* (London: Basic, 2022).

15. Dani Blum, "PTSD: Symptoms, Diagnosis, and Treatment," *New York Times*, April 4, 2022, https://www.nytimes.com/2022/04/04/well/mind /ptsd-trauma-symptoms.html.

16. Barbara Ehrenreich, *Bright-Sided: How the Relentless Promotion of Positive Thinking Has Undermined America* (New York: Metropolitan Books, 2009).

17. Steven Weitzman, "Strategic Spirituality: Positive Psychology, the Army, and the Ambiguities of 'Spirituality Fitness,'" *Journal of the American Academy of Religion* 89, no. 1 (March 2021): 240–71, https://doi.org/10.1093/jaarel /lfab010.

18. R. Cornum, M. D. Matthews, and M. E. Seligman, "Comprehensive Soldier Fitness: Building Resilience in a Challenging Institutional Context," *American Psychologist* 66, no. 1 (January 2011): 4–9, https://doi.org/10 .1037/a0021420.

19. Barbara Bradley Hagerty, "Army's 'Spiritual Fitness' Test Angers Some Soldiers," NPR, January 13, 2011, https://www.npr.org/2011/01/13/132 904866/armys-spiritual-fitness-test-angers-some-soldiers.

20. Maria M. Steenkamp, William P. Nash, and Brett T. Litz, "Post-Traumatic Stress Disorder," *American Journal of Preventive Medicine* 44, no. 5 (2013): 507–12, https://doi.org/10.1016/j.amepre.2013.01.013.

21. D. Defraia, "The Unknown Legacy of Military Mental Health Programs," *Task & Purpose*, January 5, 2020, https://taskandpurpose.com/military -life/the-unknown-legacy-of-military-mental-health-programs/.

22. Gregg Zoroya, "Army Morale Low despite 6-Year, $287M Optimism Program," *USA Today*, April 16, 2015, https://www.usatoday.com/story/news /nation/2015/04/16/army-survey-morale/24897455/.

23. Benjamin R. Bryce, "Sexual Assault Is a Huge Threat to Women in US Military. We Have a Duty to Do Better," *USA Today*, April 27, 2023, https:// www.usatoday.com/story/opinion/2023/04/27/military-sexual-as sault-harassment-problem-us-national-security/11081662002/.

24. Amy Amidon, "Moral Injury and Moral Repair," DeploymentPsych.org, accessed August 28, 2023, https://deploymentpsych.org/blog/guest-perspective -moral-injury-and-moral-repair.

25. Charles A. Ogunbode et al., "The Resilience Paradox: Flooding Experience, Coping and Climate Change Mitigation Intentions," *Climate Policy* 19, no. 6 (2019): 703–15, https://doi.org/10.1080/14693062.2018.1560242.

26. S. Sidner, A.-M. Rappard, and M. Cohen, "Capitol Riot Arrests: Active-Duty Military Veterans Charged," CNN, Februarly 4, 2021, https://www .cnn.com/2021/01/31/us/capitol-riot-arrests-active-military-veterans -soh/index.html.

27. R. Pape, "The Capitol Insurrection Arrests: A CPOST Analysis," *Washington Post*, April 6, 2021, https://www.washingtonpost.com/opinions /2021/04/06/capitol-insurrection-arrests-cpost-analysis/.

28. Jennifer Steinhauer, "Veterans Fortify the Ranks of Militias Aligned with Trump's Views," *New York Times*, September 11, 2020, https://www.ny times.com/2020/09/11/us/politics/veterans-trump-protests-militias .html.

29. Roland Martin and Leah Lakins, *White Fear: How the Browning of America Is Making White Folks Lose Their Minds* (Dallas, TX: BenBella Books, 2022).

30. Garen J. Wintemute et al., "Views of American Democracy and Society and Support for Political Violence: First Report from a Nationwide Population-Representative Survey," BioRxiv, 2022, https://doi.org/10.1101/2022.07.15.22277693.

31. Tara Suter, "42 Percent of GOP Iowa Caucusgoers Say 'Poisoning the Blood' Remarks Make Them More Likely to Support Trump: Poll," *The Hill*, December 20, 2023, https://thehill.com/homenews/campaign/4370059-42-percent-of-gop-iowa-caucus-goers-say-poisoning-the-blood-remarks-make-them-more-likely-to-support-trump-poll/; and Rebecca Shabad, "Trump on 'Poisoning the Blood' Remarks: 'I Never Knew That Hitler Said It,'" NBC News, updated December 22, 2023, https://www.nbcnews.com/politics/donald-trump/trump-poisoning-blood-remarks-never-knew-hitler-said-rcna130958.

32. Gerald V. O'Brien, *Contagion and the National Body: The Organism Metaphor in American Thought* (London: Routledge, 2018).

33. Jeff Sharlet, *The Undertow: Scenes from a Slow Civil War* (New York: W. W. Norton, 2023).

34. Nicholas Michelsen and Pablo De Orellana, "Discourses of Resilience in the US Alt-Right," *Resilience* 7, no. 3 (2019): 271–87, https://doi.org/10.1080/21693293.2019.1609199.

35. Alan Page Fiske and Tage Shakti Rai, *Virtuous Violence: Hurting and Killing to Create, Sustain, End, and Honor Social Relationships* (Cambridge, England: Cambridge University Press, 2014).

36. Wolfgang Merkel and Anna Lührmann, "Resilience of Democracies: Responses to Illiberal and Authoritarian Challenges," *Democratization* 28, no. 5 (2021): 869–84, https://doi.org/10.1080/13510347.2021.1928081.

7: THE FANTASY OF BOUNCING BACK

1. Christopher Columbus, "The Letter to the Nurse," trans. John Boyd Thatcher, in *Christopher Columbus: His Life, His Work, His Remains as Revealed by Original Printed and Manuscript Records*, ed. John Boyd Thatcher (New York: Knickerbocker Press, 1903), 434–44.

2. Mark Charles and Soong-Chan Rah, *Unsettling Truths: The Ongoing, Dehumanizing Legacy of the Doctrine of Discovery* (Westmont, IL: InterVarsity Press, 2019).

3. Newton Creede, "SCOTUS Expands Indigenous Claims, but Ancient Law Limits Freedoms," Al Jazeera, July 14, 2020 https://www.aljazeera.com/news/2020/7/14/scotus-expands-indigenous-claims-but-ancient-law-limits-freedoms.

4. 251 Nicole Winfield, "Responding to Indigenous, Vatican Rejects Discovery

Doctrine," Religion News Service, March 30, 2022, https://religionnews
.com/2023/03/30/responding-to-indigenous-vatican-rejects-discovery
-doctrine/https://religionnews.com/2023/03/30/responding-to-indigenous
-vatican-rejects-discovery-doctrine/.

5. S. R. Lowe, K. Lustig, and H. B. Marrow, "African American Women's Reports of Racism during Hurricane Katrina: Variation by Interviewer Race,"
New School Psychology Bulletin 8, no. 2 (2011): 46–57, PMID: 23459229;
and "White New Orleans Has Recovered from Hurricane Katrina. Black
New Orleans Has Not," Talk Poverty, August 29, 2016, https://talkpoverty
.org/2016/08/29/white-new-orleans-recovered-hurricane-katrina-black
-new-orleans-not/index.html.

6. Steve Benen, "Trump: Puerto Rico Is 'an Island Surrounded by . . . Big
Water,'" MSNBC, September 29, 2017; and Emily Cochrane and Mark
Walker, "House Approves Puerto Rico Aid Package, but a Path Forward
Is Murky," *New York Times*, February 7, 2020, https://www.nytimes
.com/2020/02/07/us/politics/house-puerto-rico-aid-package.html.

7. Megan Pagaduan, "The Modern American Colony: Puerto Rico," *Berkeley
Political Review*, January 21, 2020, https://bpr.berkeley.edu/2020/01/21
/the-modern-american-colony-puerto-rico/.

8. Juan Giusti-Cordero, "In Puerto Rico, We Invented Resilience," *New York
Times*, October 24, 2017, https://www.nytimes.com/2017/10/24/opinion
/puerto-rico-hurricane-resilience.html.

9. John Harfouch, *Another Mind-Body Problem: A History of Racial Non-Being*
(New York: SUNY Press, 2018).

10. In 2017, in a speech celebrating the election of Donald Trump, white na-
tionalist alt-right leader Richard Spencer declared: "To be white is to be a
striver, a crusader, an explorer, and a conqueror. We build, we produce, we
go upward. And we recognize the central lie of American race relations:
we don't exploit other groups. We don't gain anything from their presence.
They need us, not the other way around. Within the very blood in our
veins, as children of the sun, lies the potential for greatness. That is the
great struggle we are called to." *The Atlantic* (2016), *"Hail Trump!": Richard
Spencer Speech Excerpts*, YouTube, accessed: January 15, 2024, https://www
.youtube.com/watch?v=1o6-bi3jlxk.

11. Pauline Boss, *Ambiguous Loss: Learning to Live with Unresolved Grief* (Boston:
Harvard University Press, 1999).

12. "About Ambiguous Loss," Ambiguous Loss: Pioneered by Pauline Boss,
https://www.ambiguousloss.com/about/.

13. Sheryl Sandberg and Adam Grant, *Option B: Facing Adversity, Building Resilience, and Finding Joy* (London: W. H. Allen, 2019).

14. G. Albrecht et al., "Solastalgia: The Distress Caused by Environmental
Change," *Australas Psychiatry* 15, suppl. 1:S (2007): 95–98, https://doi.org
/10.1080/10398560701701288.

15. Paul Crutzen and Eugene Stoermer, "The 'Anthropocene,'" *Global Change Newsletter* 41 (May 2000).

16. L. Rist et al., "Applying Resilience Thinking to Production Ecosystems," *Ecosphere* 5, no. 6 (2014): 1–11.

17. Zoe Todd, "Indigenizing the Anthropocene," in *Art in the Anthropocene: Encounters among Aesthetics, Politics, Environment and Epistemology*, ed. Heather Davis and Etienne Turpin (London: Open Humanities Press, 2015), 241.

18. Jocelyn Timperley, "Who Is Really to Blame for Climate Change?," BBC Future, June 18, 2020, https://www.bbc.com/future/article/20200618 -climate-change-who-is-to-blame-and-why-does-it-matter.

19. Niall McCarthy, "Report: The U.S. Military Emits More CO_2 Than Many Industrialized Nations," *Forbes*, June 13, 2019, https://www.forbes.com /sites/niallmccarthy/2019/06/13/report-the-u-s-military-emits-more-co2 -than-many-industrialized-nations-infographic/?sh=63d33e6a4372.

20. Kristin Toussaint, "If 100 Companies Are Responsible for 70% of Emissions, What Can You Do?," Fast Company, October 13, 2021, https:// www.fastcompany.com/90680284/heres-how-to-push-for-action-on-the -climate-crisis.

21. Erle C. Ellis et al., "Dating the Anthropocene: Towards an Empirical Global History of Human Transformation of the Terrestrial Biosphere," *Elementa: Science of the Anthropocene*, January 1, 2013, 1: 000018, https:// doi.org/10.12952/journal.elementa.000018.

22. Alexander Koch et al., "Earth System Impacts of the European Arrival and Great Dying in the Americas after 1492," *Quaternary Science Reviews* 207 (2019), https://doi.org/10.1016/j.quascirev.2018.12.004.

23. Theodore Grudin, "Hope in the Time of the Petrolocene," *Earth Island Journal*, May 15, 2020, https://www.earthisland.org/journal/index.php /articles/entry/hope-in-the-time-of-the-petrolocene.

24. Donna Haraway, "Anthropocene, Capitalocene, Plantationocene, Chthulucene: Making Kin," *Environmental Humanities* 6, no. 1 (2015): 159–65.

25. Salar Mameni, *Terracene: A Crude Aesthetics* (Durham, NC: Duke University Press, 2023).

26. Jason W. Moore, "The Capitalocene, Part I: On the Nature and Origins of Our Ecological Crisis," *Journal of Peasant Studies* 44, no. 3 (2017): 594–630.

27. Emerging Technology from the arXiv, "The Trillion Internet Observations Showing How Global Sleep Patterns Are Changing," *MIT Technology Review*, January 13, 2017, https://www.technologyreview.com/2017/01 /31/154273/the-trillion-internet-observations-showing-how-global-sleep -patterns-are-changing/.

28. In 1931, for example, Joseph Stalin justified his brutal regime by arguing that the Soviet Union was "fifty or a hundred years behind the advanced countries. We must make good this distance within the next ten years." In 1955, Brazilian president Juscelino Kubitschek envisioned "fifty years of progress in five years

of government." Three years later, China's Chairman Mao Zedong announced the Great Leap Forward, a Communist Party campaign that ended, after the deaths of anywhere from 15 to 55 million people, in 1962 as the result of the largest known famine in history. "Such calls [for time-gap-closing progress above] were the stuff of dromopolitics," writes cultural anthropologist David Rojas, "the politics of speed whereby cities, highways, and industrial parks were built to spur the movement of masses that would drive kinetic empires forward. Speed was a means of creating dreamworlds—utopian futures that would justify the industrial catastrophes that made them possible."

29. Sarah Kaplan and Wanda J. Orlikowski, "Temporal Work in Strategy Making," *Organization Science* 24, no. 4 (2013): 965–95.

30. Trenton Alma Williams and Dean A. Shepherd, "Bounding and Binding: Trajectories of Community-Organization Emergence following a Major Disruption," *Organization Science* 32, no. 3 (2021): 824–55.

31. Hans Berends, Elco van Burg, and Raghu Garud, "Pivoting or Persevering with Venture Ideas: Recalibrating Temporal Commitments," *Journal of Business Venturing* 36, no. 4 (2021): e106126; and Oana Branzei and Ramzi Fathallah, "The End of Resilience? Managing Vulnerability through Temporal Resourcing and Resisting," *Entrepreneurship Theory and Practice*, December 2021.

32. Hartmut Rosa, *Social Acceleration: A New Theory of Modernity*, trans. Jonathan Trejo-Mathys (New York: Columbia University Press, 2013).

8: RISK AND THE BURDEN OF RESILIENCE

1. According to the founders of YouTube, the desire to see videos of the tsunami was one of the events that provoked the launch of YouTube. The second was the tearing of Janet Jackson's costume at the 2004 Super Bowl.

2. Leslie Kern, *Feminist City: Claiming Space in a Man-Made World* (London: Verso, 2021).

3. Tom Temin, "East Palestine Shows Need for Community Resilience," Federal News Network, February 27, 2023, https://federalnewsnetwork .com/tom-temin-commentary/2023/02/east-palestine-shows-need-for -community-resilience/.

4. "Hazardous Materials," U.S. Department of Transportation, Federal Railroad Administration, accessed August 8, 2023, https://railroads.dot.gov /railroad-safety/divisions/hazardous-materials/hazardous-materials.

5. Nadja Popovich, Livia Albecki-Ripka, and Kendra Pierre-Louise, "The Trump Administration Rolled Back More Than 100 Environmental Rules. Here's the Full List," *New York Times*, January 20, 2021, https://www.nytimes .com/interactive/2020/climate/trump-environment-rollbacks-list.html.

6. "HHS Provides SAMHSA Emergency Response Grants to Support Community Wellness, Resilience following Recent East Palestine Train

Derailment, Chemical Spill," U.S. Department of Health and Human Services, March 27, 2023, https://www.hhs.gov/about/news/2023/03/27/hhs-provides-samhsa-emergency-response-grants-support-community-wellness-resilience-following-recent-east-palestine-train-derailment-chemical-spill.html.

7. Naomi Klein, *The Shock Doctrine: The Rise of Disaster Capitalism* (New York: Picador, 2007).

8. Mark Fisher, "The Privatisation of Stress," *Soundings* 48 (Summer 2011): 123–33, https://doi.org/10.3898/136266211797146882.

9. I am indebted to my longtime collaborator and writing partner, Catherine Buni, for her contributions to my thinking on this topic, which she and I have explored for many years.

10. James Flynn, Paul Slovic, and C. K. Mertz, "Gender, Race, and Perception of Environmental Health Risks," *Risk Analysis* 14, no. 6 (1994): 1101–8, https://doi.org/10.1111/j.1539-6924.1994.tb00082.x.

11. Ibid., 1101–8.

12. A. Olofsson and S. Rashid, "The White (Male) Effect and Risk Perception: Can Equality Make a Difference?," *Risk Analysis* 31, no. 6 (June 2011): 1016–32, https://doi.org/10.1111/j.1539-6924.2010.01566.x.

13. Dan M. Kahan, "Cultural Cognition as a Conception of the Cultural Theory of Risk," in *Handbook of Risk Theory*, ed. S. Roeser (Amsterdam: Springer, 2008).

14. Subir Bhaumik, "Tsunami Folklore Saved Lives," BBC News Online, January 20, 2005, http://news.bbc.co.uk/1/hi/world/south_asia/4181855.stm.

15. Anthony Oliver-Smith and Susanna M. Hoffman, eds., *The Angry Earth: Disaster in Anthropological Perspective* (New York: Routledge, 1999).

16. Susie Cagle, "'Fire Is Medicine': The Tribes Burning California Forests to Save Them," *Guardian*, November 21, 2019, https://www.theguardian.com/us-news/2019/nov/21/wildfire-prescribed-burns-california-native-americans.

17. Cristina Eisenberg et al., "Out of the Ashes: Ecological Resilience to Extreme Wildfire, Prescribed Burns, and Indigenous Burning in Ecosystems," *Frontiers in Ecology and Evolution* 7 (2019), https://doi.org/10.3389/fevo.2019.00436.

18. Nicholas Bogel-Burroughs and Serge F. Kovaleski, "Warning Sirens Never Sounded on Maui, State Official Says," *New York Times*, August 12, 2023, https://www.nytimes.com/2023/08/12/us/warning-sirens-never-sounded-maui.html.

19. Barbara Rodriguez, "Women Lawmakers in Minnesota Are in the Vanguard of the Democracy Movement," *The 19th*, February 3, 2023, https:/19thnews.org/2023/02/women-minnesota-democracy-caucus/.

20. Sara Atske, "6. Journalists Give Industry Mixed Reviews on Newsroom Diversity, Lowest Marks in Racial and Ethnic Diversity," Pew Research

Center's Journalism Project, June 14, 2022, https://www.pewresearch
.org/journalism/2022/06/14/journalists-give-industry-mixed-reviews
-on-newsroom-diversity-lowest-marks-in-racial-and-ethnic-diversity/;
and "US Journalists' Beats Vary Widely by Gender and Other Factors,"
Pew Research Center, April 4, 2023, https://www.pewresearch.org/short
-reads/2023/04/04/us-journalists-beats-vary-widely-by-gender-and-other
-factors/.

21. K. Gray, "The Racial Divide on News Coverage, and Why Representation
Matters," Knight Foundation, accessed November 28, 2023, https://knight-
foundation.org/articles/the-racial-divide-on-news-coverage-and-why-rep-
resentation-matters/; and "Issue 23: Shaping Stigma: An Analysis of
Mainstream Print and Online News Coverage of Abortion, 2014-2015,"
Berkeley Media Studies Group, January 31, 2017.

22. Today, in the United States, white men, almost all Christian, heterosexual, and conservative, are disproportionately represented as risk decision-
makers. As a demographic group, the same cohort comprises the majority
of CEOs, political leaders, technologists, engineers, bankers, and tenured
professors. For instance, 82 percent of venture capitalists making decisions
about new technologies in the United States are white, and 78 percent are
men. Among the engineers, 75 percent are men, and 71 percent are white.

23. "How Resilient Are You by Jordan Peterson: Big Ideas," Instawise, YouTube,
December 10, 2018, https://www.youtube.com/watch?v=h3jQKd6GCQI.

24. M. Andreessen, *The Techno-Optimist Manifesto*, Andreessen Horowitz, October 16, 2023, https://a16z.com/the-techno-optimist-manifesto/; and
Émile P. Torres and Dr. Timnit Gebru use the acronym TESCREAL (trans-
humanism, Extropianism, Singularitarianism, Cosmism, Rationalism, Effective Altruism, and Longtermism) to debunk techno-utopianism and explain
it, effectively, as a new necropolitics. Émile P. Torres, "The Acronym behind
Our Wildest AI Dreams and Nightmares," Truthdig, June 15, 2023, https://
www.truthdig.com/articles/the-acronym-behind-our-wildest-ai-dreams
-and-nightmares/.

25. Samuel Bazzi, Martin Fiszbein, and Mesay Gebresilass, "Frontier Culture:
The Roots and Persistence of 'Rugged Individualism' in the United States,"
Econometrica: Journal of the Econometric Society 88, no. 6 (2020): 2329–68,
https://doi.org/10.3982/ecta16484.

26. "The Demographics of Gun Ownership," Pew Research Center, June 22, 2017,
https://www.pewresearch.org/social-trends/2017/06/22/the-demographics
-of-gun-ownership/.

27. Ari Shapiro, "Loaded Words: How Language Shapes the Gun Debate,"
National Public Radio, February 15, 2013, https://www.npr.org/sections
/itsallpolitics/2013/02/26/172882077/loaded-words-how-language
-shapes-the-gun-debate.

28. Jeanine Santucci, "Trump to Women at Michigan Rally: 'We're Getting Your

Husbands Back to Work,'" *USA Today*, October 27, 2020, https://www
.usatoday.com/story/news/politics/2020/10/27/president-trump-rally
-women-were-getting-your-husbands-back-work/3755175001/.

29. I. Katznelson, *When Affirmative Action Was White: An Untold History of Racial Inequality in Twentieth-Century America* (New York: W. W. Norton, 2006).

30. Cara Daggett, "Petro-masculinity: Fossil Fuels and Authoritarian Desire," *Millennium: Journal of International Studies* 47, no. 1 (2018): 25–44.

31. Amanda McGowan, "What Rachel Carson Can Teach Us about 2018," GBH, April 27, 2018, https://www.wgbh.org/news/local/2018-04-27 /what-rachel-carson-can-teach-us-about-2018.

32. Damian Carrington, "Microplastics Revealed in the Placentas of Unborn Babies," *Guardian*, December 22, 2020, https://www.theguardian.com/environ ment/2020/dec/22/microplastics-revealed-in-placentas-unborn-babies.

33. Mark Hamilton Lytle, *The Gentle Subversive: Rachel Carson, Silent Spring, and the Rise of the Environmental Movement* (Oxford: Oxford University Press, 2007).

34. P. Slovic et al. "Approaches to Acceptable Risk: A Critical Guide," Work Performed for U.S. Nuclear Regulatory Commission, 1982, https://www .nrc.gov/docs/ML0716/ML071650351.pdf.

35. C. Cohn. "Sex and Death in the Rational World of Defense Intellectuals," *Signs* 12, no. 4 (1987): 687–718.

36. Daryll Fears and Dino Grandoni, "EPA Just Detailed All the Ways Climate Change Will Hit U.S. Racial Minorities the Hardest. It's a Long List," *Washington Post*, September 1, 2012, https://www.washingtonpost.com/climate -environment/2021/09/02/ida-climate-change/; and Phil McKenna, "EPA Finds Black Americans Face More Health-Threatening Air Pollution," *Inside Climate News*, March 2, 2018, https://insideclimatenews.org/news /02032018/air-pollution-data-african-american-race-health-epa-research/.

37. Emily Chang, "The Consequences for Tech Whistleblowers: 'People Come After You,'" Bloomberg News, July 23, 2023.

38. Chenyang Xiao and Aaron M. McCright, "Explaining Gender Differences in Concern about Environmental Problems in the United States," *Society & Natural Resources* 25, no. 11 (2012): 1067–84, https://doi.org/10.1080 /08941920.2011.651191.

39. Astghik Mavisakalyan and Yashar Tarvedi, "Gender and Climate Change: Do Female Parliamentarians Make a Difference?," *European Journal of Political Economy* 56 (2019): 151–64, https://doi.org/10.1016/j.ejpoleco .2018.08.001.

40. S. E. Soares and N. M. Sidun, "Women Leaders during a Global Crisis: Challenges, Characteristics, and Strengths," *International Perspectives in Psychology: Research, Practice, Consultation* 10, no. 3 (2021): 130–37, https:// doi.org/10.1027/2157-3891/a000020.

41. Caitlyn Moran, "Being Greta Thunberg, the World's Most Extraordinary

Teenager," London *Times*, October 14, 2022, https://www.thetimes.co.uk
/article/being-greta-thunberg-the-world-s-most-extraordinary-teenager-cait
lin-moran-l6fhqqpl6.

42. Armenak Antinyan et al., "Political Narratives and the US Partisan Gender
Gap," *Frontiers in Psychology* 12 (2021): https://doi.org/10.3389/fpsyg
.2021.675684.

43. Lisa Lerer, "That Word," *New York Times*, July 23, 2020, https://www
.nytimes.com/2020/07/23/us/politics/aoc-women-ted-yoho.html.

44. Dharna Noor, "'Project 2025': Plan to Dismantle US Climate Policy for Next
Republican President," *Guardian*, July 27, 2023, https://www.theguardian
.com/environment/2023/jul/27/project-2025-dismantle-us-climate-policy
-next-republican-president.

9: MEANING, BELONGING, AND THE STORIES WE TELL

1. Neel Burton, "The Meaning of Nostalgia," *Psychology Today*, November 27,
2014, https://www.psychologytoday.com/us/blog/hide-and-seek/201411
/the-meaning-nostalgia.

2. Jaimee Bell, "Nostalgia Triggers a Reward Pathway in Our Brains, according
to Science," *Big Think*, April 1, 2020, https://bigthink.com/neuropsych
/nostalgia-reward-system/.

3. D. M. Sloan et al., "Written Exposure Therapy vs Prolonged Exposure
Therapy in the Treatment of Posttraumatic Stress Disorder: A Randomized
Clinical Trial," *JAMA Psychiatry* 80, no.11 (November 2023):1093–1100,
doi:10.1001/jamapsychiatry.2023.2810.

4. Joel Salinas et al., "Association of Social Support with Brain Volume and
Cognition," *JAMA Network Open* 4, no. 8 (2021): e2121122.

5. P. M. Bal and M. Veltkamp, "How Does Fiction Reading Influence Empathy?
An Experimental Investigation on the Role of Emotional Transportation," *PLoS
One* 8, no. 1 (2013): e55341, https://doi.org/10.1371/journal.pone.0055341.

6. Among the family's many investments was a company named Plasmaferesis,
which harvested blood plasma from Nicaragua's poorest citizens for sale in
the United States. "Company of US-Backed Somoza Dictatorship Sucked
Nicaraguan Blood—Literally," teleSUR, July 19, 2016, https://www.tele
surenglish.net/news/Company-of-US-backed-Somoza-Sucked-Nicaraguan
-Blood--Literally-20160719-0022.html.

7. "How Does Storytelling Help Build Resilience in Children?," *Brain Language & Intersenory Perception*, https://blogs.ntu.edu.sg/blip/how-does
-storytelling-help-build-resilience-in-children/.

8. Richard Pérez-Peña, "Woman Linked to 1955 Emmett Till Murder Tells
Historian Her Claims Were False," *New York Times*, January 28, 2017,
https://www.nytimes.com/2017/01/27/us/emmett-till-lynching-carolyn
-bryant-donham.html.

9. Viviane Saleh-Hanna, "Black Feminist Hauntology: Rememory of the Ghosts of Abolition?," *Champ pénal/Penal field* 12 (2015): e9168.

10. Elizabeth Alexander, "'Can You Be Black and Look at This?': Reading the Rodney King Video(s)," *Public Culture* 7 (1994): 77–94.

11. Elizabeth Alexander, "The Trayvon Generation," *New Yorker*, June 15, 2020, https://www.newyorker.com/magazine/2020/06/22/the-trayvon-generation.

12. Juliette Kayyem, "The Jacksonville Killer Wanted Everyone to Know His Message of Hate." *Atlantic Monthly*, August 27, 2023, https://www.theatlantic.com/ideas/archive/2023/08/jacksonville-killer-wanted-everyone-know-his-message-hate/675155/.

13. Jasmine Liu, "Nine-Foot Bronze of Emmett Till Is Unveiled in Mississippi," *Hyperallergic*, October 27, 2022, https://hyperallergic.com/774264/bronze-statue-of-emmett-till-is-unveiled-in-mississippi/.

14. Patricia San José Rico, *Creating Memory and Cultural Identity in African American Trauma Fiction* (Leiden, Netherlands: Brill, 2019).

15. Caroline Randall Williams, "Opinion: You Want a Confederate Monument? My Body Is a Confederate Monument," *New York Times*, June 26, 2020, https://www.nytimes.com/2020/06/26/opinion/confederate-monuments-racism.html.

16. Ryan Best, "Confederate Statues Were Never Really about Preserving History," *FiveThirtyEight*, June 8, 2020, https://projects.fivethirtyeight.com/confederate-statues/.

17. Nathaniel Vincent Mohatt et al., "Historical Trauma as Public Narrative: A Conceptual Review of How History Impacts Present-Day Health," *Social Science & Medicine* 106 (2014): 128–36; and Stephanie A. Fryberg et al., "Of Warrior Chiefs and Indian Princesses: The Psychological Consequences of American Indian Mascots," *Basic and Applied Social Psychology* 30 (2008): 208–18.

18. "National Monument Audit, 2023," Monument Lab.

19. Justin Gamble, "Race Left out of Rosa Parks Story in Revised Weekly Lesson Text for Florida Schools Highlights Confusion with New Law," CNN, March 23, 2023, https://www.cnn.com/2023/03/22/us/florida-textbook-race-rosa-parks-reaj/index.html.

20. Maria Wiering, "Troubling Past: The Church's Role in America's Indian Boarding School Era," *Catholic Spirit*, April 26, 2022, https://thecatholicspirit.com/news/local-news/troubling-past-the-churchs-role-in-americas-indian-boarding-school-era/.

21. Suzanne Cross, "Indian Boarding Schools: Reverberation of Generational Trauma Resulting from a Historical U.S. Child Welfare Policy," *Native News Online*, July 17, 2021, https://nativenewsonline.net/opinion/indian-boarding-schools-reverberation-of-generational-trauma-resulting-from-a-historical-u-s-child-welfare-policy; and Sarah Klotz, *Writing Their Bodies: Restoring Rhetor-*

ical Relations at the Carlisle Indian School (Logan: Utah State University Press, 2021).

22. Les B. Whitbeck et al., "Conceptualizing and Measuring Historical Trauma among American Indian People," *American Journal of Community Psychology* 33, no. 3–4 (2004): 119–30; Les B. Whitbeck et al., "Discrimination, Historical Loss and Enculturation: Culturally Specific Risk and Resiliency Factors for Alcohol Abuse among American Indians," *Journal of Studies on Alcohol and Drugs* 65, no. 4 (2004): 409–18; and Melissa L. Walls and Les B. Whitbeck, "Maturation, Peer Context, and Indigenous Girls' Early-Onset Substance Use," *Journal of Early Adolescence* 31, no. 3 (2011): 415–42.

23. Maria Yellow Horse Brave Heart, "The Return to the Sacred Path: Healing the Historical Trauma and Historical Unresolved Grief Response among the Lakota through a Psychoeducational Group Intervention," *Smith College Studies in Social Work* 68, no. 3 (1998): 287–305.

24. Maria Yellow Horse Braveheart, "Integrating Trauma Informed and Historical Trauma Informed Care in Behavioral Health Interventions with American Indians and Alaska Natives: Part 3," slides for presentation given August 8, 2017, https://www.ihs.gov/sites/telebehavioral/themes /responsive2017/display_objects/documents/slides/traumainformedcare /ticintegratingthree080817.pdf.

25. Brave Heart, "Return to the Sacred Path," 287–305.

26. Resmaa Menakem, *My Grandmother's Hands: Racialized Trauma and the Pathway to Mending Our Hearts and Bodies* (Las Vegas: Central Recovery Press, 2017).

27. Sarah Souli, "Does America Need a Truth and Reconciliation Commission?," *Politico*, August 16, 2020, https://www.politico.com/news/magazine /2020/08/16/does-america-need-a-truth-and-reconciliation-commission -395332.

28. M. Li, B. Leidner, G. Hirschberger, & J. Park, "From Threat to Challenge: Understanding the Impact of Historical Collective Trauma on Contemporary Intergroup Conflict," *Perspectives on Psychological Science* 18, no.1 (2023): 190–209, https://doi.org/10.1177/17456916221094540.

AFTERWORD

1. Jonathan Pugh and David Chandler, *Anthropocene Islands: Entangled Worlds* (London: University of Westminster Press, 2021).

BIBLIOGRAPHY

I have had the great fortune to learn from, and think about and with, others through their brilliant words and deeds. To write here, I returned to and discovered books that challenged my thinking, helped shape my ideas, clarified my thinking, and, in their depth and compassion, gave me hope for the future.

Agathangelou, Anna M., and Kyle D. Killian, eds. 2017. *Time, Temporality and Violence in International Relations: (De)Fatalizing the Present, Forging Radical Alternatives.* London, England: Routledge.

Ajari, Norman. 2023. *Darkening Blackness: Race, Gender, Class, and Pessimism in 21st-Century Black Thought.* Translated by Matthew B. Smith. Oxford, England: Polity Press.

Alexander, Elizabeth. 1994. "'Can You Be Black and Look at This?': Reading the Rodney King Video(s)." *Public Culture* 7 (1): 77–94. https://doi.org/10.1215/08992363-7-1-77.

Appiah, Kwame Anthony. 2021. *The Lies That Bind: Rethinking Identity.* New York, NY: Liveright Publishing Corporation.

Balkin, Jack M. 2020. *The Cycles of Constitutional Time.* New York, NY: Oxford University Press.

Bavel, Bas van, Daniel R. Curtis, Jessica Dijkman, Matthew Hannaford, Maika de Keyzer, Eline van Onacker, and Tim Soens. 2020. *Disasters and History: The Vulnerability and Resilience of Past Societies.* Cambridge, England: Cambridge University Press.

Bazzi, Samuel, Martin Fiszbein, and Mesay Gebresilasse. 2020. "Frontier Culture: The Roots and Persistence of 'Rugged Individualism' in the United

States." *Econometrica: Journal of the Econometric Society* 88 (6): 2329–68. https://doi.org/10.3982/ecta16484.

Benjamin, Ruha, ed. 2019. *Captivating Technology: Race, Carceral Technoscience, and Liberatory Imagination in Everyday Life*. Durham, NC: Duke University Press.

Bennett, Jane. 2020. *Vibrant Matter: A Political Ecology of Things*. Duke University Press.

Bennett, Jill. 2005. *Empathic Vision: Affect, Trauma, and Contemporary Art*. Palo Alto, CA: Stanford University Press.

Birdsong, Mia. 2020. *How We Show up: Reclaiming Family, Friendship, and Community*. USA: Hachette Go.

Blackhawk, Ned. 2023. *The Rediscovery of America: Native Peoples and the Unmaking of U.S. History*. New Haven, CT: Yale University Press.

Boss, Pauline. 2006. *Loss, Trauma, and Resilience: Therapeutic Work with Ambiguous Loss*. New York, NY: W. W. Norton.

Braidotti, Rosi. 2012. *Nomadic Theory: The Portable Rosi Braidotti*. New York, NY: Columbia University Press.

———. 2022. *Posthuman Feminism*. Oxford, England: Polity Press.

Brison, Susan J. 2023. *Aftermath: Violence and the Remaking of a Self*. Princeton, NJ: Princeton University Press.

Brock, Rita Nakashima, and Gabriella Lettini. 2012. *Soul Repair: Recovering from Moral Injury after War*. Boston, MA: Beacon Press.

Brooks, Lisa. 2019. *Our Beloved Kin: A New History of King Philip's War*. New Haven, CT: Yale University Press.

Brown, Adrienne. 2017. *Emergent Strategy: Shaping Change, Changing Worlds*. Edinburgh, Scotland: AK Press.

Brown, Wendy. 2017. *Walled States, Waning Sovereignty*. New York, NY: Zone Books.

———. 2020. *States of Injury: Power and Freedom in Late Modernity*. Princeton, NJ: Princeton University Press. https://doi.org/10.2307/j.ctvzgb898.

Bryson, Valerie. 2007. *Gender and the Politics of Time: Feminist Theory and Contemporary Debates*. Bristol, England: Policy Press.

Butler, Judith. 2020. *Precarious Life: The Powers of Mourning and Violence*. London, England: Verso Books.

Butler, Judith, Zeynep Gambetti, and Leticia Sabsay, eds. 2016. *Vulnerability in Resistance*. Durham, NC: Duke University Press.

Calvo, Paco. 2023. *Planta Sapiens: The New Science of Plant Intelligence*. New York, NY: W. W. Norton.

Campbell, Sue. 2003. *Relational Remembering: Rethinking the Memory Wars*. Lanham, MD: Rowman & Littlefield.

Canales, Jimena. 2016. *The Physicist and the Philosopher: Einstein, Bergson, and the Debate That Changed Our Understanding of Time*. Princeton, NJ: Princeton University Press.

Caruth, Cathy. 1995. *Trauma: Explorations in Memory*. Baltimore, MD: Johns Hopkins University Press.

———. 2013. *Literature in the Ashes of History*. Baltimore, MD: Johns Hopkins University Press.

Casper, Monica J., and Eric Wertheimer, eds. 2016. *Critical Trauma Studies: Understanding Violence, Conflict and Memory in Everyday Life*. New York, NY: New York University Press. https://doi.org/10.18574/nyu/9781479896561.001.0001.

Cerulo, Karen A. 2006. *Never Saw It Coming: Cultural Challenges to Envisioning the Worst*. Chicago, IL: University of Chicago Press.

Charles, Mark, and Soong-Chan Rah. 2019. *Unsettling Truths: The Ongoing, Dehumanizing Legacy of the Doctrine of Discovery*. Downers Grove, IL: Inter-Varsity Press.

Cherepanov, Elena. 2020. *Understanding the Transgenerational Legacy of Totalitarian Regimes: Paradoxes of Cultural Learning*. London, England: Routledge.

Cooper, Rachel. 2014. *Psychiatry and Philosophy of Science*. London, England: Routledge. https://doi.org/10.4324/9781315711843.

Curran, Thomas, and Andrew P. Hill. 2022. "Young People's Perceptions of Their Parents' Expectations and Criticism Are Increasing over Time: Implications for Perfectionism." *Psychological Bulletin* 148 (1–2): 107–28. https://doi.org/10.1037/bul0000347.

Dahl, Adam. 2018. *Empire of the People: Settler Colonialism and the Foundations of Modern Democratic Thought*. Lawrence, KS: University Press of Kansas.

Damasio, Antonio R. 1995. *Descartes' Error: Emotion, Reason, and the Human Brain*. New York, NY: Avon Books.

Damasio, Antonio. 2019. *The Strange Order of Things: Life, Feeling, and the Making of Cultures*. New York, NY: Random House.

Darby, Seyward. 2020. *Sisters in Hate: American Women on the Front Lines of White Nationalism*. New York, NY: Little Brown and Company.

Deer, Sarah. 2015. *The Beginning and End of Rape: Confronting Sexual Violence in Native America*. Minneapolis: University of Minnesota Press.

Degroot, Dagomar. 2018. *The Frigid Golden Age: Climate Change, the Little Ice Age, and the Dutch Republic, 1560–1720*. Cambridge, England: Cambridge University Press.

Degruy, Joy Angela. 2005. *Post Traumatic Slave Syndrome: America's Legacy of Enduring Injury and Healing*. Joy Degruy Publications.

Deleuze, Gilles, and Felix Guattari. 2003. *Anti-Oedipus: Capitalism and Schizophrenia*. London, England: Mansell Publishing.

Deleuze, Gilles, Felix Guattari, and Brian Massumi. n.d. *A Thousand Plateaus: Capitalism and Schizophrenia*. Minneapolis, MN: University of Minnesota Press.

Diehl, Emily. n.d. "Is Perfectionism Growth-Minded?" Mindsetworks.com. Accessed August 25, 2023. https://blog.mindsetworks.com/entry/is-perfectionism-growth-minded.

Dossey, Larry. 1982. *Space, Time & Medicine*. Boston, MA: Shambhala Publications.

Dossey, Larry. 1982. *Space, Time & Medicine*. London, England: Routledge.

Doward, Jamie. 2016. "Men Much Less Likely to Seek Mental Health Help than Women." *The Guardian*, November 5, 2016. https://www.theguardian.com/society/2016/nov/05/men-less-likely-to-get-help--mental-health.

Draaisma, Douwe. 2001. *Metaphors of Memory: A History of Ideas about the Mind*. Translated by Paul Vincent. Cambridge, England: Cambridge University Press.

Du Mez, Kristin Kobes. 2021. *Jesus and John Wayne: How White Evangelicals Corrupted a Faith and Fractured a Nation*. New York, NY: Liveright Publishing Corporation.

Duffy, Mignon. 2020. *Making Care Count: A Century of Gender, Race, and Paid Care Work*. New Brunswick, NJ: Rutgers University Press. https://doi.org/10.36019/9780813550770.

Dunbar-Ortiz, Roxanne. 2023. *Indigenous Peoples' History of the United States (10th Anniversary Edition), An*. Boston, MA: Beacon Press.

Dutton, Kevin. 2020. *Black and White Thinking: The Burden of a Binary Brain in a Complex World*. London, England: Bantam Press.

Ehrenreich, Barbara. 2009. *Bright-Sided: How the Relentless Promotion of Positive Thinking Has Undermined America*. Metropolitan Books.

Eisenberg, Cristina, Christopher L. Anderson, Adam Collingwood, Robert Sissons, Christopher J. Dunn, Garrett W. Meigs, Dave E. Hibbs, et al. 2019. "Out of the Ashes: Ecological Resilience to Extreme Wildfire, Prescribed Burns, and Indigenous Burning in Ecosystems." *Frontiers in Ecology and Evolution* 7. https://doi.org/10.3389/fevo.2019.00436.

Eisenstein, Zillah R., ed. 1979. *Capitalist Patriarchy and the Case for Socialist Feminism*. New York, NY: Monthly Review Press.

Escobar, Arturo. 2018. *Designs for the Pluriverse: Radical Interdependence, Autonomy, and the Making of Worlds*. Durham, NC: Duke University Press.

Estes, Nick. 2023. *Our History Is the Future: Standing Rock versus the Dakota Access Pipeline, and the Long Tradition of Indigenous Resistance*. London, England: Verso Books.

Federici, Silvia. 2018. *Re-Enchanting the World: Feminism and the Politics of the Commons*. Oakland, CA: PM Press.

Finchelstein, Federico. 2019. *From Fascism to Populism in History*. Berkeley, CA: University of California Press.

Fineman, Martha Albertson. 2005. *The Autonomy Myth: A Theory of Dependency*. New York, NY: New Press.

Fiske, Alan Page, and Tage Shakti Rai. 2014. *Virtuous Violence: Hurting and Killing to Create, Sustain, End, and Honor Social Relationships*. Cambridge, England: Cambridge University Press.

Flanagan, Kylie. 2023. *Climate Resilience: How We Keep Each Other Safe, Care for Our Communities, and Fight Back against Climate Change*. Berkeley, CA: North Atlantic Books.

Flynn, J., P. Slovic, and C. K. Mertz. 1994. "Gender, Race, and Perception of Environmental Health Risks." *Risk Analysis: An Official Publication of the Society for Risk Analysis* 14 (6): 1101–8. https://doi.org/10.1111/j.1539-6924.1994 .tb00082.x.

Fregoso, Rosa Linda, ed. 2003. *MeXicana Encounters: The Making of Social Identities on the Borderlands (American Crossroads)*.

Galison, Peter. n.d. *Einstein's Clocks, Poincare's Maps: Empires of Time*. New York, NY: W. W. Norton.

Garbes, Angela. 2022. *Essential Labor: Mothering as Social Change*. New York, NY: Harper.

Ghosh, Amitav. 2021. *The Nutmeg's Curse: Parables for a Planet in Crisis*. New Delhi, India: Penguin.

Gilroy, Paul. 1995. *The Black Atlantic: Modernity and Double-Consciousness*. London, England: Harvard University Press.

Golden, Kristen Brown, and Bettina G. Bergo, eds. 2009. *The Trauma Controversy: Philosophical and Interdisciplinary Dialogues*. Albany, NY: State University of New York Press.

Graeber, David, and David Wengrow. 2023. *The Dawn of Everything: A New History of Humanity*. New York, NY: Picador.

Grusin, Richard, ed. 2017. *Anthropocene Feminism*. Minneapolis, MN: University of Minnesota Press.

Hacker, Jacob S. n.d. *The Great Risk Shift: The New Economic Insecurity and the Decline of the American Dream, Second Edition*. New York, NY: Oxford University Press.

Hager, Shirley, and Mawopiyane. 2022. *The Gatherings: Reimagining Indigenous-Settler Relations*. Toronto, ON, Canada: University of Toronto Press.

Hagerty, Barbara Bradley. 2011. "Army's 'Spiritual Fitness' Test Angers Some Soldiers." *NPR*, January 13, 2011. https://www.npr.org/2011/01/13/132904866 /armys-spiritual-fitness-test-angers-some-soldiers.

Hall, Stuart, and Bill Schwarz. 2023. *Familiar Stranger: A Life between Two Islands*. Edited by Bill Schwarz. Durham, NC: Duke University Press.

Haraway, Donna J. 2016. *Staying with the Trouble: Making Kin in the Chthulucene*. Durham, NC: Duke University Press.

Harris, Nadine Burke. 2018. *The Deepest Well: Healing the Long-Term Effects of Childhood Trauma and Adversity*. New York, NY: HarperCollins.

Herman, Judith. 2022. *Trauma and Recovery: The Aftermath of Violence—from Domestic Abuse to Political Terror*. London, England: Basic Books.

Hübl, Thomas, and Julie Jordan Avritt. 2023. *Healing Collective Trauma: A Process for Integrating Our Intergenerational and Cultural Wounds*. Louisville, CO: Sounds True.

James, Robin. 2015. *Resilience & Melancholy: Pop Music, Feminism, Neoliberalism*. Alresford, England: Zero Books.

Joseph-Gabriel, Annette K. 2020. *Reimagining Liberation: How Black Women Transformed Citizenship in the French Empire*. Baltimore, MD: University of Illinois Press.

Kaba, Mariame, and Tamara K. Nopper. n.d. *We Do This 'Til We Free Us: Abolitionist Organizing and Transforming Justice*. Chicago, IL: Haymarket Books.

Kahan, Dan M. 2012. "Cultural Cognition as a Conception of the Cultural Theory of Risk." In *Handbook of Risk Theory*, 725–59. Dordrecht: Springer Netherlands.

Kahan, Dan M., Paul Slovic, Donald Braman, and John Gastil. 2005. "Fear of Democracy: A Cultural Evaluation of Sunstein on Risk." https://papers.ssrn.com/abstract=801964.

Kaplan, E. n.d. *Climate Trauma: Foreseeing the Future in Dystopian Film and Fiction*. New Brunswick, NJ: Rutgers University Press.

Kayyem, Juliette. 2023. "The Jacksonville Killer Wanted Everyone to Know His Message of Hate." *Atlantic Monthly (Boston, Mass.: 1993)*, August 27, 2023. https://www.theatlantic.com/ideas/archive/2023/08/jacksonville-killer-wanted-everyone-know-his-message-hate/675155/.

Kern, Leslie. 2021. *Feminist City: Claiming Space in a Man-Made World*. London, England: Verso Books.

King, Debra Walker. 2008. *African Americans and the Culture of Pain*. Charlottesville, VA: University of Virginia Press.

Klotz, Sarah. 2021. *Writing Their Bodies: Restoring Rhetorical Relations at the Carlisle Indian School*. Utah State University Press.

Knowles, Caroline. 1997. *Family Boundaries: The Invention of Normality and Dangerousness*. Toronto, ON, Canada: University of Toronto Press.

Lakoff, George. 1987. *Women, Fire and Dangerous Things: What Categories Reveal about the Mind*. Chicago, IL: University of Chicago Press.

———. 1999. *Philosophy in the Flesh: The Embodied Mind and Its Challenge to Western Thought*. London, England: Basic Books.

Lalami, Laila. 2020. *Conditional Citizens: On Belonging in America*. New York, NY: Pantheon.

LaLonde, Julie S. 2020. *Resilience Is Futile: The Life and Death and Life of Julie S. LaLonde*. Toronto, ON, Canada: Between the Lines.

Landa, Manuel de. 2000. *A Thousand Years of Nonlinear History*. New York, NY: Zone Books.

Leese, Peter, Jason Crouthamel, and Julia Barbara Köhne, eds. 2021. *Languages of Trauma: History, Memory, and Media*. Toronto, ON, Canada: University of Toronto Press.

Lefebvre, Alexandre. 2008. *The Image of Law: Deleuze, Bergson, Spinoza*. Palo Alto, CA: Stanford University Press.

Leger, Krystal R., Rosemary A. Cowell, and Angela Gutchess. 2023. "Do Cultural Differences Emerge at Different Levels of Representational Hierarchy?" *Memory & Cognition*. https://doi.org/10.3758/s13421-023-01459-7.

Levine, Peter A. 2012. *In an Unspoken Voice: How the Body Releases Trauma and Restores Goodness*. Berkeley, CA: North Atlantic Books.

———. 2015. *Trauma And Memory*. Berkeley, CA: North Atlantic Books.

Leys, Ruth. 2000. *Trauma: A Genealogy*. Chicago, IL: University of Chicago Press.

Liboiron, Max. 2021. *Pollution Is Colonialism*. Durham, NC: Duke University Press.

Liebermann, Oren, Ellie Kaufman, and Barbara Starr. 2022. "Reports of Sexual Assault in the US Military Increased by 13%." *CNN*, September 1, 2022. https://www.cnn.com/2022/09/01/politics/sexual-assault-military-report/index.html.

Lister, Ruth. 2021. *Poverty*. 2nd ed. Oxford, England: Polity Press.

Lloyd, Genevieve. 1993. *The Man of Reason: "Male" and "Female" in Western Philosophy*. 2nd ed. London, England: Routledge.

Luckhurst, Roger. 2013. *The Trauma Question*. London, England: Routledge.

Mahler, Jonathan. 2023. "'The Most Dangerous Person in the World Is Randi Weingarten.'" *New York Times*, April 28, 2023. https://www.nytimes.com/2023/04/28/magazine/randi-weingarten-teachers-unions.html.

Mallett, Robyn K., and Margo J. Monteith, eds. 2019. *Confronting Prejudice and Discrimination: The Science of Changing Minds and Behaviors*. San Diego, CA: Academic Press.

Malm, Andreas, and The Zetkin Collective. 2021. *White Skin, Black Fuel: On the Danger of Fossil Fascism*. London, England: Verso Books.

Martin, Roland, and Leah Lakins. 2022. *White Fear: How the Browning of America Is Making White Folks Lose Their Minds*. Dallas, TX: BenBella Books.

Masten, Ann S. 2015. *Ordinary Magic: Resilience in Development*. New York, NY: Guilford Publications.

Maté, Gabor, and Daniel Maté. 2022. *The Myth of Normal: Trauma, Illness & Healing in a Toxic Culture*. London, England: Vermilion.

Mazzucato, Mariana. 2015. *The Entrepreneurial State: Debunking Public vs. Private Sector Myths*. London, England: Anthem Press.

McGowan, Amanda. 2018. "What Rachel Carson Can Teach Us about 2018." GBH. April 27, 2018. https://www.wgbh.org/news/local/2018-04-27/what-rachel-carson-can-teach-us-about-2018.

McKittrick, Katherine, ed. 2015. *Sylvia Wynter: On Being Human as Praxis*. Durham, NC: Duke University Press.

McRobbie, Angela. 2020. *Feminism and the Politics of Resilience: Essays on Gender, Media and the End of Welfare*. Oxford, England: Polity Press.

Menakem, Resmaa. 2017. *My Grandmother's Hands: Racialized Trauma and the Pathways to Mending Our Hearts and Bodies*. Las Vegas, NV: Central Recovery Press.

Merchant, Carolyn. 1982. *The Death of Nature: Women, Ecology, and the Scientific Revolution*. San Francisco, CA: HarperOne.

Michelsen, Nicholas, and Pablo De Orellana. 2019. "Discourses of Resilience in the US Alt-Right." *Resilience* 7 (3): 271–87. https://doi.org/10.1080/21693293.2019.1609199.

Mignolo, Walter D. 2011. *The Darker Side of Western Modernity: Global Futures, Decolonial Options*. Durham, NC: Duke University Press.

Miller-Karas, Elaine. 2023. *Building Resilience to Trauma: The Trauma and Community Resiliency Models*. 2nd ed. London, England: Routledge.

Milstein, Cindy, ed. 2017. *Rebellious Mourning: The Collected Works of Grief*. Edinburgh, Scotland: AK Press.

Mitchell, Timothy. 2023. *Carbon Democracy: Political Power in the Age of Oil*. 3rd ed. London, England: Verso Books.

Moore, Jason W. 2015. *Capitalism in the Web of Life: Ecology and the Accumulation of Capital*. London, England: Verso Books.

Morrison, Aaron, and Ayanna Alexander. 2023. "Thousands Converge on National Mall to Mark the March on Washington's 60th Anniversary." AP News. August 26, 2023. https://apnews.com/article/march-on-washington-mlk-dream -speech-anniversary-washington-7639b60f26948fe614978dc6a763cc84.

Moyn, Samuel. 2021. *Humane: How the United States Abandoned Peace and Reinvented War*. New York, NY: Farrar, Straus and Giroux.

Murphy Paul, Annie. 2021. *The Extended Mind: The Power of Thinking Outside the Brain*. New York, NY: Harper.

Nanni, Giordano. 2020. *The Colonisation of Time: Ritual, Routine and Resistance in the British Empire*. Manchester, England: Manchester University Press.

Neal, Arthur G. 2018. *National Trauma and Collective Memory: Extraordinary Events in the American Experience*. London, England: Routledge.

Nestor, James. 2021. *Breath: The New Science of a Lost Art*. London, England: Penguin Life.

Nicholas, Kimberly. 2021. *Under the Sky We Make: How to Be Human in a Warming World*. New York, NY: Penguin Putnam.

Nietzsche, Friedrich. 2008. *Twilight of the Idols*. Edited by Duncan Large. London, England: Oxford University Press.

Nixon, Rob. 2013. *Slow Violence and the Environmentalism of the Poor*. London, England: Harvard University Press.

Noys, Benjamin. 2014. *Malign Velocities: Accelerationism and Capitalism*. Alresford, England: Zero Books.

O'Brien, M. E. 2023. *Family Abolition: Capitalism and the Communizing of Care*. London, England: Pluto Press.

Page, Cara. 2023. *Healing Justice Lineages: Dreaming at the Crossroads of Liberation, Collective Care, and Safety*. Berkeley, CA: North Atlantic Books.

Patel, Raj, and Jason W. Moore. 2020. *A History of the World in Seven Cheap Things A History of the World in Seven Cheap Things: A Guide to Capitalism, Nature, and the Future of the Planet*. London, England: Verso Books.

Piepznia-Samarasinha, Leah Lakshmi. 2018. *Care Work: Dreaming Disability Justice*. Vancouver, BC, Canada: Arsenal Pulp Press.

Plank, Liz. 2019. *For the Love of Men: A New Vision for Mindful Masculinity*. St. Martin's Press.

Poovey, Mary. 1998. *A History of the Modern Fact: Problems of Knowledge in the Sciences of Wealth and Society*. Chicago, IL: University of Chicago Press.

Porges, Stephen W. 2011. *The Polyvagal Theory: Neurophysiological Foundations of Emotions, Attachment, Communication, and Self-Regulation*. New York, NY: W. W. Norton.

Puig de la Bellacasa, Maria. 2017. *Matters of Care: Speculative Ethics in More than Human Worlds*. Minneapolis, MN: University of Minnesota Press.

Raza Kolb, Anjuli Fatima. 2021. *Epidemic Empire: Colonialism, Contagion, and Terror, 1817-2020*. Chicago, IL: University of Chicago Press.

Re-Enchanting the World: Feminism and the Politics of the Commons (Kairos) Kairos Feminism and the Politics of the Commons (Books) Federici. n.d. Silvia, Linebaugh, Peter: PM Press.

Richards, David A. J. n.d. *Fundamentalism in American Religion and Law: Obama's Challenge to Patriarchy's Threat to Democracy*. Cambridge, England: Cambridge University Press.

Rifkin, Jeremy. 2022. *The Age of Resilience: Reimagining Existence on a Rewilding Earth*. New York, NY: St. Martin's Press.

Riley Snorton, C. 2017. *Black on Both Sides: A Racial History of Trans Identity*. Minneapolis, MN: University of Minnesota Press.

Rodriguez, Barbara. 2023. "Women Lawmakers in Minnesota Are in the Vanguard of the Democracy Movement." 19th News. February 3, 2023. https://19thnews.org/2023/02/women-minnesota-democracy-caucus/.

Rosa, Hartmut. 2021. *Resonance: A Sociology of Our Relationship to the World*. Translated by James Wagner. Oxford, England: Polity Press.

Ross, Jamie. 2019. "Hurricane Dorian: Bahamas Government Denies Withholding True Death Toll." The Daily Beast. September 9, 2019. https://www.thedailybeast.com/hurricane-dorian-bahamas-government-denies-withholding-true-death-toll.

Roth, Michael. 2011. *Memory, Trauma, and History: Essays on Living with the Past*. New York, NY: Columbia University Press.

Rothberg, Michael. 2020a. *Multidirectional Memory: Remembering the Holocaust in the Age of Decolonization*. Stanford University Press. https://doi.org/10.1515/9780804783330.

———.2020b. *The Implicated Subject: Beyond Victims and Perpetrators*. Palo Alto, CA: Stanford University Press. https://doi.org/10.1515/9781503609600.

Rothe, Anne. 2011. *Popular Trauma Culture: Selling the Pain of Others in the Mass Media*. New Brunswick, NJ: Rutgers University Press.

Sandberg, Sheryl, and Adam Grant. 2019. *Option B: Facing Adversity, Building Resilience, and Finding Joy*. London, England: W. H. Allen.

Sandel, Michael J. 2021. *The Tyranny of Merit: What's Become of the Common Good?* Harlow, England: Penguin Books.

Saul, Jack. 2022. *Collective Trauma, Collective Healing: Promoting Community Resilience in the Aftermath of Disaster*. London, England: Routledge.

Savoy, Lauret. 2016. *Trace: Memory, History, Race, and the American Landscape*. Berkeley, CA: Counterpoint.

Scarry, Elaine. 1988. *The Body in Pain: The Making and Unmaking of the World.* New York, NY: Oxford University Press.

Scheuerman, William E. n.d. *Liberal Democracy and the Social Acceleration of Time (Books) Scheuerman.* Johns Hopkins University Press.

Schuller, Kyla. 2018. *The Biopolitics of Feeling: Race, Sex, and Science in the Nineteenth Century.* Durham, NC: Duke University Press.

Scott, James C. 1999. *Seeing like a State: How Certain Schemes to Improve the Human Condition Have Failed.* New Haven, CT: Yale University Press.

Soboroff, Jacob. 2023. *Separated: Inside an American Tragedy.* New York, NY: HarperCollins.

Solnit, Rebecca. 2009. *A Paradise Built in Hell.* New York, NY: Viking Books.

Speed, Shannon. 2019. *Incarcerated Stories: Indigenous Women Migrants and Violence in the Settler-Capitalist State.* Chapel Hill, NC: University of North Carolina Press.

Spinney, Laura. 2018. *Pale Rider: The Spanish Flu of 1918 and How It Changed the World.* PublicAffairs.

Stengers, Isabelle. 2015. *In Catastrophic Times: Resisting the Coming Barbarism.* London, England: Open Humanities Press.

Strings, Sabrina. 2019. *Fearing the Black Body: The Racial Origins of Fat Phobia.* New York, NY: New York University Press.

Taussig, Rebekah. 2021. *Sitting Pretty: The View from My Ordinary Resilient Disabled Body.* New York, NY: HarperOne.

Taylor, Astra. 2023. *The Age of Insecurity: Coming Together as Things Fall Apart.* Toronto, ON, Canada: House of Anansi Press.

Tervsy, Barbara. *2019. Mind in Motion: How Action Shapes Thought How Action Shapes Thought.* New York, NY: Basic Books.

Thrasher, S. W. 2024. *The Viral Underclass: The Human Toll When Inequality and Disease Collide.* New York, NY: St. Martin's Press.

Topa, Wahinkpe, and Darcia Narvaez. 2023. *Restoring the Kinship Worldview: Indigenous Voices Introduce 28 Precepts for Rebalancing Life on Planet Earth.* Richmond, BC, Canada: ReadHowYouWant.com.

Tsing, Anna Lowenhaupt. 2021. *The Mushroom at the End of the World: On the Possibility of Life in Capitalist Ruins.* Princeton, NJ: Princeton University Press.

van Dernoot Lipsky, Laura, and Connie Burk. 2009. *Trauma Stewardship: An Everyday Guide to Caring for Self While Caring for Others.* Oakland, CA: Berrett-Koehler Publishers.

Varela, Francisco J., Evan Thompson, and Eleanor Rosch. 2017. *The Embodied Mind: Cognitive Science and Human Experience.* London, England: MIT Press.

Vince, Gaia. 2023. *Nomad Century: How to Survive the Climate Upheaval.* Harlow, England: Penguin Books.

Washington, Harriet A. 2020. *A Terrible Thing to Waste: Environmental Racism and Its Assault on the American Mind*. New York, NY: Little, Brown & Company.

Washington Post (Washington, D.C.: 1974). 2019. "Haitians in The Bahamas Seek More Protection after Hurricane Dorian Aid Groups, News Cameras Leave," September 12, 2019. https://www.washingtonpost.com/world/the_americas/haitians-in-the-bahamas-seek-more-protection-after-hurricane-dorian-aid-groups-news-cameras-leave/2019/09/12/138d6428-d4c7-11e9-8924-1db7dac797fb_story.html.

Wendell, Susan. 2013. *The Rejected Body: Feminist Philosophical Reflections on Disability*. Routledge.

Wilderson, Frank B. 2021. *Afropessimism*. New York, NY: W. W. Norton.

Wintemute, Garen J., Sonia Robinson, Andrew Crawford, Julia P. Schleimer, Amy Barnhorst, Vicka Chaplin, Daniel Tancredi, Elizabeth A. Tomsich, and Veronica A. Pear. 2022. "Views of American Democracy and Society and Support for Political Violence: First Report from a Nationwide Population-Representative Survey." *BioRxiv*. https://doi.org/10.1101/2022.07.15.22277693.

Winter, Alison. 2013. *Memory: Fragments of a Modern History*. Chicago, IL: University of Chicago Press.

Wittmann, Marc. 2018. *Altered States of Consciousness: Experiences out of Time and Self*. Translated by Philippa Hurd. London, England: MIT Press.

Wong, Alice. 2020. *Disability Visibility*. New York, NY: Random House.

Wynter, Sylvia. 2013. *We Must Learn to Sit Together and Talk about a Little Culture: Decolonizing Essays 1967-1984*. Leeds, England: Peepal Tree Press.

Yusin, Jennifer, ed. 2018. *The Future Life of Trauma: Partitions, Borders, Repetition*. 1st ed. Fordham University Press.

Yusoff, Kathryn. 2018. *A Billion Black Anthropocenes or None*. Minneapolis, MN: University of Minnesota Press.

Zolli, Andrew, and Ann Marie Healy. 2013. *Resilience: Why Things Bounce Back*. London, England: Business Plus.

INDEX

ABOUT THE AUTHOR

Soraya Chemaly is an award-winning writer and activist whose work focuses on the role of gender in culture, politics, religion, and media. She is the director of the Women's Media Center Speech Project and an advocate for women's freedom of expression and expanded civic and political engagement. A prolific writer and speaker, her articles appear in *Time*, the Verge, the *Guardian*, the *Nation*, *HuffPost*, and the *Atlantic*. Follow her work and learn more at www.SorayaChemaly.com.